RELIGION
AND THE
POLITICAL ORDER

RELIGION AND THE POLITICAL ORDER
edited by
Jacob Neusner

RELIGION AND THE POLITICAL ORDER

POLITICS IN CLASSICAL AND CONTEMPORARY CHRISTIANITY, ISLAM, AND JUDAISM

edited by
Jacob Neusner

Scholars Press
Atlanta, Georgia

RELIGION AND THE POLITICAL ORDER
POLITICS IN CLASSICAL AND
CONTEMPORARY CHRISTIANITY,
ISLAM, AND JUDAISM

edited by
Jacob Neusner

Published by Scholars Press
for the University of South Florida, University of Rochester,
and Saint Louis University

© 1996
University of South Florida

Funds for the publication of this volume were provided by

The Tyson and Naomi Midkiff Fund for Exellence
of the Department of Religious Studies at the University of South Florida

The Max Richter Foundation of Rhode Island

and

The Tisch Family Foundation of New York City

Library of Congress Cataloging in Publication Data
Religion and the political order : politics in classical and
    contemporary Christianity, Islam, and Judaism / edited by Jacob
    Neusner.
            p.   cm. — (South Florida-Rochester-Saint Louis studies on
    religion and the social order ; 15)
        Includes bibliographical references and index.
        ISBN 0-7885-0310-3 (cloth : alk. paper)
        1. Religion and politics. 2. Religion and politics—Biblical
    teaching, 3. Bible. O.T.—Criticism, interpretation, etc.
    4. Judaism and politics. 5. Christianity and politics. 6. Islam
    and politics. I. Neusner, Jacob, 1932-   . II. Series: South
    Florida-Rochester-Saint Louis studies on religion and the social
    order ; v. 15.
    BL65.P74336 1996
    291.1'77—dc20   96-30129

Printed in the United States of America
on acid-free paper

CONTENTS

Part III
Christianity

Part IV
Islam

Part V
Contemporary USA

Preface

Some of the world's great religions turn to political institutions and public policy not only to achieve their goals but to make part of their systemic statement. Others do not. Building on the heritage of ancient Israel, the three monotheist religions, Judaism, Christianity, and Islam, concur that politics provides a medium for making part of their respective systemic statements. All of them through history have accumulated experience in accomplishing their goals through public policy. After considering the case of ancient Israel, we here focus on the classical, or formative, and on the contemporary periods of each.

We seek generalizations on the character of the public order envisioned – and sometimes actually realized – by Islam, Judaism, and Christianity. For these three formative religions, in both their formative periods and in the world today, propose to speak through politics as much as through theology or rite or liturgy. These religions invest politics with sacrality, assign sacred tasks to political action, and, above all, deem political action a perfectly natural arena for religious expression. Teaching ourselves how to understand these statements that religions make through politics, in theory and practice alike, presents difficulty. For the radical secularization of politics that in theory and in law has taken place in the twentieth century makes it difficult to deal with religious theories of political institutions and activities.

The prevailing theory of political legitimacy – politics is the science of legitimate violence – presents to contemporary society difficulties in making sense of the political aspirations and actions of important elements of contemporary Islam, Christianity, and Judaism. Sudan, Libya, Iran, India and Pakistan, the USA, Poland, and the State of Israel – these diverse nation-states find themselves conflicted in the confrontation with religious theories of the political order. Islam, Christianity, and Judaism define politics in quite other terms than those involving (merely) secular, legitimate violence (who does what to whom). For them politics forms a medium of sanctification.

Practical realities, moreover, challenge us to make sense of that for which our prevailing theory of matters does not prepare us. The religious divisions of secular nation-states, such as Germany, Netherlands, Belgium, Ireland (Northern and the Republic), and the former-Yugoslavia, with its Muslim, Catholic, and Eastern Orthodox Christian segments – these divisions bear not only theological but political consequences. When religion and politics unite and populations divide in accord with theological, not only political, conviction, religion makes all the more difficult the formulation of a coherent consensus in the public interest. We take for granted, then, that religion forms part of the problem but no part of the solution of social disintegration. The fault lines of the contemporary social order run along the walls of churches, mosques, and synagogues, so much so that assigning to religion, rather than nationalism, responsibility for civic war and social upheaval proves plausible. No one now denies the enormous impact of religious tradition upon the political crises awaiting resolution throughout the world.

The radical secularization of politics that in theory has taken place in the twentieth century makes it difficult to deal with religious theories of political institutions and activities. These invest politics with sacrality, assign sacred tasks to political action, and, above all, deem political action a perfectly natural arena for religious expression. The prevailing theory of political legitimacy – politics is the science of legitimate violence – presents to contemporary society difficulties in making sense of the political aspirations and actions of important elements of contemporary Islam, Christianity, and Judaism. Sudan, Libya, Iran, India and Pakistan, the USA, Poland, and the State of Israel – these diverse nation-states find themselves conflicted in the confrontation with religious theories of the political order. Not only so, but the religious divisions of secular nation-states, such as Germany, Netherlands, Belgium, Ireland (Northern and the Republic), and the former-Yugoslavia, with its Muslim, Catholic, and Eastern Orthodox Christian segments – these divisions bear not only theological but political consequences.

The Abode of Islam, the City on the Hill and the Holy Roman Empire, the Kingdom of Priests and the Holy People – these political metaphors of Islam, Christianity, and Judaism, respectively, bear in common testimony to the political dimensions of theological conviction. The three world religions deem politics contingent, not autonomous, and find wanting the secular theory of politics as the theory of legitimate violence. All focus on the issue of legitimacy, finding the source and guarantor in divine revelation. We are not used to thinking in those terms, and it is clear we must learn how to do so. The secular theory of politics, deeming legitimate violence utterly disconnected from religious theories of the social order, and regarding political coercion through power as disembedded from religious conviction about God's will, simply does not prepare us to understand the world we now confront. Indeed, some would persuasively maintain that the world of the militantly secular state, whether in France or the USA, treated as marginal and expendable convictions that in fact motivated masses of its own population even in their political activities, as Prohibition in the USA and Christian Fascism in France suggest.

Our own country, with its explicit constitutional prohibition against the establishment of any religion, or of religion in general, even now struggles to sort out the confused lines of order and structure that validate, in political activity, one sort of relationship with religions and that invalidate others. The State of Israel, with an established religion, has yet to formulate a theory of religious freedom to accommodate the convictions of the majority of its population, which does not practice Orthodox Judaism in any form. Islam in Britain and other parts of Western Europe has yet to frame a theory of politics congruent to the situation of a minority, and the explicit rejection of the politics of democracy and individual rights put forth by some Muslim theologians in Britain only underscores the problems that have yet to be worked out. And the political crisis of Algeria represents yet another kind of dilemma confronting Islamic theology.

In the Western democratic nation-states that opt for a theory of secularized politics we find ourselves no better equipped to deal with the interplay of religion and the political order than are the nation-states characterized by a politically established religion, whether Muslim or Judaic or Christian. Some maintain that the First Amendment not only forbids political establishment of a religion or of religion but also prohibits the entry of religious convictions into the political arena. But that position takes slight account of the aspirations of vast numbers of American citizens, Catholic, Protestant, Buddhist, Muslim, and Judaic alike, who bring to politics the religious teachings concerning truth, right, and morality that originate in their respective faiths. Public policy for them cannot contradict religious conviction, and legitimacy cannot in the end derive only from the will of the governed. And, more generally, the prevailing theory of modernity, which not only deems religion a relic of a fading past but an unwanted wraith in the political order, finds itself unable to make sense of the activity and power of those faiths. What proves self-evident to the secular theory of religion presents an incomprehensible picture to religious theories of politics, and what assumes the power of common sense and mere rationality to religious groups enormously threatens the foundations of a politics of reason and persuasion that secularism posits.

Here the academy makes its contribution, that of learning and reasoned inquiry, and this conference is meant to bring to the debate accurate knowledge and clear perspective. When faced with two irreconcilable theories of the public order, fiercely espoused by two (or more) large and powerful components of that order, as is the situation of world civilization today, we of the academy are used to turning to learning to seek understanding and find a path to conciliation. For, it is clear, if the social order of a nation facing civil conflict is to endure, all parties to the conflict must find the rationality of the position of the other, make sense of what each perceives to be the other's nonsense. Without understanding not only what the other proposes for public policy, but the whys and wherefores of the other's theory of the political order, each party to the political conflict will see the other as irrational, to be dealt with through naked force, if possible, or through deceit, if not. That is to say, we of the academy think learning matters, and we take for granted that the rationality that we share with all parties bears the power to impart sense and order to the points of conflict that divide us from one another. The first step toward reasoned debate, resting upon shared principles of aspiration and argument, requires learning.

What we need to know at this early stage in public discourse is simple. What theory of politics as a medium for religious activity governs the political order of Islam, Christianity, and Judaism, viewed both in their classical theological formulations and in their contemporary political activities? How may we understand the interplay of theological and political theory in the influential religions of monotheism? In the situation of Judaic, Muslim, and Christian theologians of various kinds, what problems await attention in sorting out the legitimacy and limits of religious engagement with public policy? What validates the state and legitimates its use of violence for those vast bodies of believers that reject the desacralization of politics to begin with, and propose to replace secular with theological theories of political right today? Indeed, for the monotheist religions, all of them political to the core, what conception of legitimacy of violence laid the foundation for a theory of politics in the classical canon? And what efforts at realizing that theory in the setting of contemporary politics have come to the fore? Until we formulate answers to questions of knowledge and reasoned analysis, we shall have no means for understanding the political aspirations and actions of entire nations, on the one side, and large sectors of the social order at home and overseas, on the other.

The following papers form the record of a conference, Religion and the Political Order, held at the University of South Florida, Tampa, on February 24-26, 1996. The conference was held to set forth religious theories of politics as a medium for the sacred ordering of legitimate power in the monotheist religions, Islam, Judaism, and Christianity. These religious traditions from their beginnings to the present have wrestled with the problem of how to attain religious goals through political activity, each religious tradition maintaining that the state bears responsibility, in one way or another, for the accomplishment of God's purposes set forth in revelation (the Torah, the Bible, and the Qur'an and associated traditions, for Judaism, Christianity, and Islam, respectively). Each of the religions therefore sets forth for itself an account of the ideal political order, for example, the Kingdom of Priests and the Holy People, the Heavenly City, and the Abode of Islam, and associated constructs, for the three religious traditions. The conference examined these theories side by side, in two dimensions, the classical and the contemporary. The papers allow us to compare and contrast the classical constructs, and also try to sort out some of the issues – areas of comprehension and incomprehension – in contemporary politics in Christian, Judaic, and Muslim states, respectively.

The scholars who have joined in this project conceive that an understanding of both the ideal statements of the three traditions and the articulation of those statements in the here and now will gain from a systematic and coherent account of matters. In our view, a systematic presentation of the political theory of the three kindred religious traditions, together with an overview of contemporary issues affecting the USA and overseas societies as well, will help us to understand events of acute contemporary concern. The fact that the University of South Florida has a significant number of scholarly specialists in the several areas, as well as practicing Christians, Muslims, and Judaists taking courses in the field of religious studies, makes our university a natural, in many ways ideal, setting for such a sharing of learning and conviction as took place here. The benefit to learning is complemented by the practical benefit we seek, which is, attaining mutual understanding through disciplined and accurate, dispassionate learning. So far as we know, at this time, informed accounts, produced by specialists in the three traditions, of religious theories of the political order, treating the several traditions side by side, are not many, and such accounts with special interest in the US scene are still fewer.

The conference was supported by the Earhart Foundation, Ann Arbor, Michigan, the Office of the Provost, University of South Florida, the Dean of the College of Arts and Science, University of South Florida, the Dean of the University of South Florida at St. Petersburg, the Max Richter Foundation, and the Tisch Family Foundation, New York City. To all of these partners in the project, I express thanks from all who will derive intellectual benefit from it.

The principal papers are the chapters by Professors Cox, Mandell, Gruenwald, Green and Porton, Chilton, Greeley, Sonn, and Capps, and by this writer. The other chapters record the responses by other colleagues. Having read and discussed all the papers in advance, students in the seminar attached to the conference also prepared questions for further discussion at the conference. USF colleagues who presented papers or responses also taught seminar sessions and discussed their papers with the students, revising them in response to student comment. The conference-seminar therefore aimed at the union of scholarship and teaching in what we hope represents a model of academic education. In my view, all supererogatory activities on an academic campus should encompass a concrete educational goal, an opportunity for students in a systematic way to advance their learning.

As organizer of the conference and editor of the volume, I express my personal gratitude to both my academic home and home-away-from-home. As Professor of Religious Studies at Bard College, I express my thanks to the President and the Dean of the Faculty of Bard College, Dr. Leon Botstein and Dr. Stuart Levine, respectively, for their cordial interest in my research. I find my colleagues at Bard remarkably stimulating and welcoming, and I always look forward to my visits. Our shared projects, in both writing and teaching, provide me much intellectual pleasure. That two colleagues from Bard participated in the conference yet further attests to the advantages of association with so vigorous a department. We at Bard are now working on joint conference-seminar projects with our Department of Religious Studies at the University of South Florida, one part at Bard with an October conference, the other part at USF with a late February conference. That each conference coincides with the nicest part of the year in the Hudson Valley and in West Central Florida is a mere serendipity.

Besides organizing the entire project, I wrote my chapter of this book at the University of South Florida, which has afforded me an ideal situation in which to conduct a scholarly life. No work of mine can omit reference to the exceptionally favorable circumstances in which I conduct my research. I express my thanks for not only the advantage of a Distinguished Research Professorship, which must be the best job in the world for a scholar, but also of a substantial research expense fund, ample research time, and some stimulating and cordial colleagues. In the prior chapters of my career, I never knew a university that prized professors' scholarship and publication and treated with respect those professors who actively and methodically pursue research.

The University of South Florida, and all ten universities that comprise the Florida State University system as a whole, exemplify the high standards of professionalism that prevail in publicly sponsored higher education in the USA and provide the model that privately sponsored universities would do well to emulate. Here there are rules, achievement counts, and presidents, provosts, and deans honor and respect the university's principal mission: scholarship, scholarship alone – both in the classroom and in publication. Here at last I find integrity, governing in the lives of people true to their vocation and their mission. The presence at the conference of all of my colleagues and a great many of our students, and the participation in the program of most of them, show what collegiality means.

JACOB NEUSNER

Distinguished Research Professor of Religious Studies
UNIVERSITY OF SOUTH FLORIDA, TAMPA
AND
Professor of Religious Studies
BARD COLLEGE, ANNANDALE-ON-HUDSON, NEW YORK

1

Religion and Politics
after *The Secular City*

Harvey Cox
University of South Florida

Much has happened since my book *The Secular City* first appeared in 1965 to remind us how urgent and important is the topic we confront this week. What is the meaning of the present, unanticipated global resurgence of religion? Is it good news or bad news? What is the proper relationship of religion to politics?

I can remember five years ago when I saw an account on TV of the first bar mitzvah to be held in Warsaw for forty-nine years. A young man was being called to the Torah, and I could hardly control my emotions. This, in a country which had come perilously close to becoming purged of all Jews, *Judenfrei*, by the Nazis. Here, this ancient faith was reasserting itself. That was good news. Then, Igal Amin, the twenty-seven-year-old Israeli settler and student of Torah who assassinated Prime Minster Yitzak Rabin, was reported today to have said, "I acted alone on God's orders, and I have no regrets." That was *bad* news.

I can remember five years ago, on a visit to the former Soviet Union, being present in a small city in Russia when an Orthodox church which had been closed for seventy years was reopened. People wept and embraced before they went in to pray. This was obviously good news, but when I read about the slaughter of one thousand Muslims by Hindu extremists three years ago in Bombay, that was bad news. When I saw the television pictures of those gasping victims of the release of the poisonous gas in the subway of Tokyo by a religious group called Aum

Shinnikyo, that was bad news. The relation of politics to religion is no light matter.

Still, it's hard to imagine a conference here at the University of South Florida or at Harvard or anywhere else on religion and politics – let's say forty years ago. No one would have considered religion a significant factor in political life then. And forty years is not that long in the history of religions and the history of cultures. Forty years ago, before Vatican II, Pius XII was still the pope of the Roman Catholic Church. Protestants were considered heretics. Orthodox were considered schismatics. The mass was said in Latin everywhere, and the world was conveniently divided between the good believers on the one side and the bad nonbelievers on the other. The Union of Soviet Socialist Republics was still under the boot of Communism although Stalin had died in 1953. Religion was stifled or controlled in Russia and Eastern Europe. Now there is freedom of religion in all of those areas. We watch with apprehensiveness, however, wondering if the rebirth of Russian Orthodoxy might stimulate a wave of xenophobia or cultural nationalism or even anti-Semitism in the old terrain of Russia. The scene is a little more complex.

Forty years ago in the Islamic countries, the only counterideology to Western dominance was a mixture of socialism and nationalism, perhaps epitomized by President Nasser of Egypt. Forty years ago the Islamic renaissance was a dream in the minds of scholars and a few mullahs. Now many Middle Eastern regimes, often corrupt and authoritarian ones, are threatened by a region-wide Islamic renaissance which is challenging the oppressive rule of many postcolonial governments.

In the US forty years ago President Eisenhower said, the only way for our form of government to survive is if it is based on a firm religious belief and, " I don't care what that belief is." In the meantime even some theologians began to wonder what was going to happen to religion. Martin Buber, the great Jewish philosopher, wrote a book called *The Eclipse of God*. There was a blip on national television called the "Death of God" theology back in the 1960s. Most so-called informed observers said that religion would wither away; or it would survive, but as a matter of personal faith, perhaps familial practice, or as something which ethnic groups might indulge in on quaint ceremonial occasions. However, religion would surely have no further impact on public policy, on politics, or on international relations. This was confidently predicted by many observers, and not all that long ago.

Now, however, something else has happened. It is 1996, and for students of domestic and international politics, without saying whether religion is good news or bad news, from the strictly scholarly point of view, how can you explain the following:

- the fragile civil peace in places like Algeria or Egypt or indeed the role of the Middle East as its importance in international affairs increases without understanding the Islamic renaissance and all that it means in our common cultural and political history;

- the turmoil in Israel so dramatically represented by the murder of Yitzak Rabin and the role of Jewish fundamentalism and Islamic radicalism in that small confined area;

- the peaceful transition of South Africa from a land of apartheid into a multiracial democracy without mentioning the name of Bishop Desmond Tutu and the role played by the churches in South Africa;

- the continuing turmoil and bloodshed in India without understanding the tensions between Muslim and Hindu communities there;

- closer to home, is it possible really to understand the Republican victories in 1994 and the congressional election without weighing in, in some way, the 1.7 million-member Christian Coalition and its contribution?

We could add the Million Man March, led by a prominent leader of the Nation of Islam, or the firm opposition the Roman Catholic bishops have voiced against dismantling the welfare system. I think the point is clear. To try to understand either domestic politics or international relations without the factor of religion in 1996 is a fool's errand. However you may feel about religion – committed to it, against it, or indifferent – it simply has to be taken seriously or you don't understand the picture. In fact, my colleague at Harvard, Prof. Samuel Huntington, has recently published a controversial article in which he claims that the global fault lines in the next decades will run along the old lines of religious rivalry. We are in for, as he calls it, "a clash of civilizations," generated by religious visions clashing with each other. I think he's wrong; nevertheless, this is an idea now prominently displayed and prominently discussed.

Is this good news or bad news? Of course, it's both. It is the nature of human life and it's the nature of human religiousness that it's both. You can't study religions and the history of their development as long as I have without realizing that religion is the nuclear energy of the human enterprise. It can be used for wonderfully constructive purposes; it can be used for immensely destructive purposes. Religion generates compassion, vision, love, solidarity; but it also generates xenophobia, hatred, bigotry, zealotry. I'm not comfortable reporting this, but I simply have to remind you of the facts of religious history.

We are in the midst of a religious resurgence all around the world, and without realizing, measuring, and weighing in the importance of this resurgence, we don't understand the world we are living in. We don't understand it unless we realize that there are millions of people who are willing to die for their faith, and – unfortunately – there are numbers of people who are willing to kill for their faith. So here we are at the end of the twentieth century which was supposed to see the withering away or the marginalization of religion, but something quite different is happening. We will be thinking about this, analyzing it, weighing it, wondering what it means.

Now I want to say three things about this religious resurgence:

• First, that it was *unanticipated* by most of the scholars, observers, critics only forty years ago.

• Second, it is a *global* resurgence.

• And third is that it is *complex.* It is ambiguous and multifaceted. This all means that it will take some hard, clear thinking to try to understand it.

Why was it *unanticipated?* I think it was unanticipated because the scholars who were thinking about religion forty years ago were still steeped in the myth of modernity, in the idea of progress, of the gradual overcoming of superstition by science and technology and rationality. They were *so* sure that religion could be explained away on the basis of sociological, psychological, or neurological theories that they really didn't appreciate how profound – and I would say ineradicable – the religious dimension of human life is. It is not going to go away. As blessing or as bane it will continue to assert itself. So, this is an unanticipated development, and a lot of the people writing those things twenty to thirty years ago are surprised and maybe a bit embarrassed.

When I say the religious resurgence is *global,* this is important because many people believe that what we were seeing here is mainly a Muslim revival, or a surge of something called the "Christian Right." But this is not the case. All over Latin America, for example, there is both among Roman Catholics and among Pentecostal Christians a remarkable reclaiming of aspects of the Christian faith, in a continent which had been wrongly dismissed as a boneyard of superstition and obscurantism.

I was in Japan a few years ago, and we shouldn't think of Japan only as the home of one fanatic sect, this Aum Shinnikyo sect. Japan has generated a variety of new religious movements, most of them based on Buddhism, and many of them constructive, global, international in their vision. We see this happening everywhere. It's a global resurgence, and not just in the turf most familiar to us.

But I want to emphasize a bit more the third characteristic of this development – the sheer *complexity* of it. Resurgent religions, whether Christian or Islamic or Buddhistic or Hindu or Shinto or Jewish, *are not the same as the traditional religions that they hark back to* – parts of which they reclaim. This may be the most important thing I want to say from a strictly scholarly point of view. These newly resurgent religions are expressions *of* and to some extent in continuity *with* their classical expressions; but they are *different in important respects.* I want to register some of those important respects in which the religious resurgences are different from their classical expressions because these differences shape their very different kinds of political structures.

All these descriptions will start with a "de-." I do this because, of course, words starting with the prefix *de* (and beginning, of course, with "deconstruction") are very fashionable today.

The first I call *deregionalization.* There was a time in which it was more or less correct to think of the major world religions as occupying "spheres of influence" in particular areas of the world. There was Christianity in Europe, North America, and in the places in the world in which European culture had penetrated largely: "Christendom" people called it. And there were a few exceptions, like Ethiopia, which has one of the oldest Christian churches in the world.

The Muslims were more or less "over there" in the Middle East – from Morocco through the Middle East and out to Indonesia. That was kind of "Muslim territory." The Hindus were safely confined "over there" on the subcontinent of India. The Buddhists were largely in Southeast Asia.

But now it is completely different, because everyone is everywhere. The largest mosque in the world outside of the old Islamic homeland is now in Rome. It was dedicated two years ago and high officials of the Roman Catholic Church attended the ceremony. I visited that mosque last summer. It is amazing to see it standing there in Rome: a mosque in the capital of world Catholicism. There is also a mosque towering over New York City now. There are hundreds of mosques in the US. There are forty-seven Buddhist temples in the city of Los Angeles. We in the US are quickly becoming a religiously pluralistic country unlike anything our forefathers could possibly have imagined. Religion has been "deregionalized." There are Buddhists in almost every place in the world. The fastest growing religion in South Korea is Christianity. There's a Christian movement now in China albeit still underground.

Deregionalization means religious pluralism. Anyone who lives in an American city of any size knows that the religious complexion of New

York, Los Angeles, San Francisco, Boston, has been radically altered in the last years in the direction of religious pluralism. We no longer have "spheres of influence" – the distribution of religious groups that was once the case. It's not there. This is why, by the way, I disagree with my colleague Professor Huntington, who talks about "fissures" and "tension points" between the civilizations motivated by religion. What he doesn't realize is the "marbling" of religions around the world. There are American Buddhists, and there are Chinese Christians, and there are British Muslims. Time was when only the Jews were everywhere. But, now *everybody* is everywhere. It is misleading to think of this as civilizations in conflict generated by religious vision.

The second quality is what I call *deprivatization*. Somewhere around the end of the nineteenth century both Christianity and the other religions settled temporarily for an expression of religion only in the private realm. The idea was to allow the public sector, with its public decision making and political discourse, to be handed over to an allegedly "neutral," or secular, idiom and keep religion only in the private realm.

Now as Professor Luise Casanova says in his new book on public religion: "We are witnessing a massive de-privatization of religion." Religious persons are also citizens. They understandably want to express themselves not just in the private but in the public realm, to be part of the discourse, to enter into the conversation about how public policy is formed. Now our question here in the US is how can this happen? How can we encourage this in a religiously *pluralistic* democracy? I am not a supporter of the so-called religious Right, but I welcome conservative Christians into the political discussion. How can we in America possibly ban religious discourse from the public arena when 94% of Americans in a Gallup poll claim they believe in God, and that God is the basis of their understanding of what is right and wrong? If all religious discourse is to be banned from the public realm, doesn't this exclude something very important from our common discussion? The question is *how* do we relate our faith to public policy in a religiously pluralistic democracy where no one particular religious view can be legitimately legalized for everyone else? That is the "deprivatization" challenge we face.

The next is the religious equivalent of what is called *deregulation* in the economic sphere. This simply means that we are now in an era in which religious institutions – churches, denominations, hierarchies – don't have any monopoly on distributing the religious "product." It's "out there" in the movies, in music, in poetry, and in the theater. We have Madonna's MTV's, Gregorian chant, and the hit play *Racing Demon*. Religious ideas are floating around without their traditional grounding in the religious institutions and churches which once sought – although always with limited success – to control them. You might say that from a marketing point of view they tried to control the distribution. People now want to pick and choose – to say, well I like this particular aspect of that religion, but not that aspect – to put disparate pieces together, to make a kind of collage, to take what is useful, believable, credible, and leave the rest. I think this is going to continue to happen even though many ministers, priests, and rabbis are infuriated by the tendency. But deregulation is a fact of life. It is part of our market culture. People are going to make their own choices, or more correctly, choices they are led to think are their own.

I watched the historic visit of John Paul II to America on television last October, and I welcome many of the things he said: his warning that we should not slam the door on immigrants; that we should not dismantle the welfare system; that we should not support the UN. But I was also somewhat amused when I saw some interviews of young people who had come to the masses in Central Park. Many of them were really not Catholics, but came, had a wonderful time ("great music," "wonderful costumes," "nice day in Central Park"). The pope, it seems, represents *something*. It's hard to put your finger on *what* he represents. Many of the young people interviewed indicated in the interviews that they really didn't know very much about what he was teaching. When one young man wearing a T-shirt with the pope's picture on it was being interviewed, he said he thought it was all "just wonderful." He wasn't Catholic. This was the first mass he'd ever come to, but he really liked it ("awesome"). He thought it was very colorful, wonderful; it reminded him that there is another way of life, something other than "the daily rat race." Then the interviewer said, "Well, you know that he teaches rather pointedly that one should not use any contraceptive devices – even in marriage. What do you think about that?" This young man thought for a moment, and said, "Well, he's entitled to his point of view."

Now I think that Pope John Paul II thinks he's entitled to a little bit more than just "his point of view" on what he is saying. But this is a very good example of what I call deregulation – a kind of market mentality, the collage-building, pragmatic approach which characterizes this religious renaissance.

The fourth characterization of the present religious resurgence is what I call the *dedogmatization*. People now are less and less interested in the intellectual doctrinal structure, or even the institutional packaging of a religion. They are simply interested in will it help me, will it touch me, will it bring some sense of meaning to my life, give me some sense of direction, purpose, significance? They are asking an existential and pragmatic question.

It is also a search for a special kind of *experience*. The last couple of years I've been closely studying the Pentecostal movement – the fastest growing Christian movement in the world, perhaps the fastest growing religious movement in the world. What is most characteristic of most Pentecostals in most places in the world is that they do not emphasize institutions or belief, but *experience* – the direct experience of God, of the Spirit – unstrained through what they dismiss as "man-made creeds and dead institutions." But there are comparable movements in other religions as well: getting back to the experience, cutting through the institutional packaging, the dogmatic structure, to the central core – the encounter with the transcendent. This is "dedogmatization." It may be a tough time for theologians in the next years. (Maybe it's good I am close to retirement. Theology may not be the central aspect of religion.) What is central is becoming what was there at the start – a bo tree, a cross, a burning bush – an experience of God.

Finally, I use one other "de-": *depatriarchalization*. I am referring to the unprecedented new leadership that women are giving to most of the religious traditions of the world. Most of us today do not understand the depth of this change in religiousness around the world and in virtually every tradition. Think about the fact that in your lifetime, even if you are a young person, for the first time in five thousand years there are women rabbis interpreting Torah in synagogues. That's a tidal change. Or think about that in the Anglican communion around the world, a Catholic communion, there are women priests presiding over the eucharist, and becoming bishops. It is hard to grasp how momentous that change is. And it is also happening in the other traditions. Six years ago there was the first gathering in history in Southeast Asia of Buddhist nuns, to talk about what it means to be a woman in the tradition of Buddhism. Muslim women are beginning to write commentaries on the Qur'an.

In some ways this is the most profound of all the changes because what it does is not just make religion an "equal opportunity profession" but changes our deepest understanding of God. Especially, if you belong to a liturgical church, where the priest represents God, to have a woman presiding over the eucharist is indeed shattering to the narrow notions that have restricted the huge, fathomless expanse of the mystery of God. This is a movement of the Spirit of the first order of importance, and I personally believe that even though the Vatican has recently announced that its teaching against the ordination of women is infallible, the Roman Catholic Church will eventually change as well. The new role of women is changing every religion in the world. They will never be the same.

These are the five major changes. It will be evident immediately that each has evoked a countermovement – a backlash – wherever it has appeared. Thus in every tradition now there are tendencies – sometimes called "fundamentalist" – to identify religion with nationalism; to have nothing to do with public life; to regain monopoly control of its distribution; to shore up dogmas, institutions, and hierarchies; to keep women from assuming any real leadership.

But our question today is what implications do these five changes carry for the relationship of religion to politics? For a clear answer to that question we will have to wait a long time. But here are a few of my personal hunches.

1.   The *deregionalization* of religion means that it will be increasingly harder for religion to combine in the dangerous way it sometimes has in the past with extreme nationalism.

2.   The *deprivatization* of religion suggests that our common distinction between carefully segregated private and public realms may itself no longer obtain. It was always a distinction without a significant difference anyway. For many women, the home *is* the place of work. At the same time issues of identity, family, cultural values, and moral norms are becoming themes of debate in the public square.

3.   The *deregulation* of religion means that in the future religion will influence politics not so much through the actions and pronouncements of religious bodies, but through "seepage," the suffusion of religious values throughout the culture.

4.   The *dedogmatization* of religion suggests that the local, congregational, and familial units of religious practice – settings where people can sort through and evaluate experiences and ideas – will become more important. This in turn could mean that religious influences on community life (and vice versa) could take a quite localistic turn.

5.   And what will the *depatriarchalization* of religion mean? This is the hardest one to predict. If the feminist scholars who contend that women's experience is *essentially* less hierarchical and linear than men's are right, this could be significant. If however women, as they assume responsibility and power in religion and politics, simply replicate the same paradigms men have created, then the impact of this particular change would be minimal.

Why have these changes in religion begun to appear? There are a lot of theories about why this all happened which I won't try to register. I do not accept theories of the resurgence of religion which are based solely on sociological and psychological analyses. Our present religious resurgence is something much more profound than that. It marks a tidal change in human spirituality. It is a recognition that modernity has in some measure failed, and that for many people, the bright promise of what science was supposed to do for us has now turned to ashes. The scientists themselves, perhaps more than anyone else, now recognize that we should count on science for a much more limited role. We are thankful for what science can do, but we don't count on it as the Messiah. The age of scientific and technological messianism is over, and now the door is open for something else. I think that religions are going to play an important role in whatever that "something else" is. But it is going to be good news *and* bad news.

I hope however that the various religions of the world can agree on at least one thing, and that is that modern commodity capitalism, as it now spreads all around the world, does not have the last word to say about human life, about what our values should be, what our future will be like. There is a danger that the marketization of the world will turn human beings into customers rather than full human beings. Last year Vaclav Havel, the president of the Czech Republic, spoke to us at the Harvard commencement. Remember that Havel went from being a prisoner of the Communists in Czechoslovakia to being the president of his country within six months. He asked us the question: "Did we escape from the gulag, the prison of Communism, just in order to live out our lives in a shopping mall? I hope not. There's got to be a better way." And I think there is.

When I was a visiting scholar in Japan a few years ago I lived near a Buddhist temple in Kyoto. Once I noticed a statue of the founder just in front of the temple, and I asked a Japanese colleague what the legend around the bottom of the statue said. He peered at it, then looked up: "It says: I only know one thing: how much is enough." That was worth a trip to Japan. We live in a society in which every media message tries to persuade, "You never have enough. You need more, more, more." The great question – a profound *religious* question – is, *can we have an infinitely expanding economic system on a finite planet?* The answer is no, we cannot. In the twenty-first century this will become the most important political, moral and religious question of them all. Until now, no economic or political system has honestly faced it. But it is a question that Islam, Judaism, Buddhism, Christianity all have some agreement about. *How much is enough* is going to become a very important thing to learn in the years ahead.

2

The Risks of Religious Resurgence

Laurie Patton
Bard College

In his elegant overview of the global resurgence of religion, Professor Cox emphasizes a particular characteristic – that of its sheer complexity. Resurgent religions, whether Christian or Muslim or Buddhist or Hindu or Shinto or Jewish, are not the same as the traditional religions to which they hearken back – parts of which they reclaim. This hearkening back is, for Professor Cox, the most important aspect of resurgence for scholars of religion. As he puts it, "These newly resurgent traditions are expressions of, and to some extent in continuity with, their classical expressions, but they are different in important respects."

Professor Cox's terms for this resurgence are deregionalization, deprivatization, deregulation, dedogmatization, and depatriarchalization. All start with "de-," Professor Cox adds, in a slightly tongue-in-cheek bow to the fashionable rhetoric of the day. For each of his five developments (forgive the pun), he mentions the inevitable "backlash" to each of them, thus creating in his paper a kind of movement/countermovement framework. Yet the backlashes are not really addressed as such, and it is here that I would like to focus a bit more. I do so first because many of the backlashes claim to be closer to their classical traditions than their contemporary counterparts. I do so also because the countermovements may well have legitimate reasons for responding as they do to the resurgences. In this light I would like to address briefly the risks contained in these aspects of religious resurgence outlined by Professor Cox, and thereby identify some of the tensions that might exist between these movements and countermovements. I want to focus on the "de-" words one by one, and, in a quite unfashionable way, raise some relevant questions which take the "de-" out.

I should note here that I raise these questions from the perspective of my own expertise. I am a scholar neither of Judaism, nor Christianity, nor Islam, but of Hinduism and Hinduism's early commentarial traditions. My examples will therefore refer frequently to India. By virtue of this seemingly arcane scholarship I am deeply implicated in the project of Hindu nationalism which has so inflamed Hindu-Muslim relations in India over the past ten years. I am implicated because Hindus are returning to and recreating their ancient Vedic tradition with political as well as spiritual vigor. Because I visit India frequently in a kind of public capacity as a research scholar, I have no choice but to take a stand on the profoundly conservative, anti-Muslim resurgent tradition that is part of this return to ancient Indian ways of thought. There are very few scholars of Vedic Sanskrit who are sympathetic to Muslims in India, although there should indeed be more.

So, to begin with the "de-" words: Professor Cox writes of deregionalization, using the wonderful term *marbling* of religions around the world – American Buddhists, British Muslims, Chinese Christians, and so forth. He is descriptively correct in this assessment; and he is right, I think, to argue with Samuel Huntington's predictions of fissures between civilizations motivated by religion. However, the marbled presence of religious traditions risks superficiality. It can often mean no more than the tourist's delight at the irony of a Muslim mosque next to a Starbucks coffee shop, or of an old Jewish neighborhood near a Barnes and Noble bookstore with a heftier-than-usual religion and philosophy section.

And this, I think, is part of what motivates a countermovement of de-regionalization – the question of place becomes important precisely because it has been so richly forgotten. Because the regional boundaries in which Muslims practice Islam or Christians Christianity might be shifting and exploding, the imaginative ties to a place of origin may become all the stronger. Might we not speak, then, of the possibility not only of an aesthetically pleasing marbling, but also of a global diaspora of all religious traditions? And is it not therefore incumbent upon the scholar to understand the possibility of reaction to this diaspora – specifically the resacralizing of particular places (mountains, shrines, mosques, temple walls) with renewed political and exegetical vigor?

In a marbled religious world, sacred sites become remembered as the point from which these religions extended themselves. To put it another way, all religions might develop a response to deregionalization – a Jerusalem with the attendant potential for violence. Certainly this has happened in the Indian state of Uttar Pradesh, where the attempt to recreate Ayodhya, the sacred birthplace of the Hindu god Rama, has led to sustained bloodshed. This attempt is, I might add, largely funded by expatriate Hindus making their money abroad. This has also occurred in the Indian state of Bihar, where the situation remains tense as Buddhists have disputed Hindu rule over the temple at Bodh Gaya, the place where the Buddha attained enlightenment.

Hence, we might pose a scholarly question to ourselves about deregionalization: How might we examine attempts to recreate, and remember, sacred place within classical traditions – not from some warmed-over perspective of symbolic analysis, but more from the perspective of how and why the ideal place was represented? What were the political motivations of creating such an ideal city or state, and was it ever intended to be a physical reality? What are the dynamics of translation from classical to contemporary understandings of place as the basis of a religious theory of politics?

Professor Cox also speaks of deprivatization. Here too I would like to point out some of the risks that the deprivatization of religion, in its present form, has for contemporary public life. As Professor Cox tells us, "Religious persons are also citizens, and indeed we must relate our faith to public policy in a religiously pluralistic democracy where no particular religious view can be legitimately legalized for everyone else." Yet at the same time I doubt very much that Robert Bellah's most famous of private religions – "Sheila-ism" – is dead. Sheila-ism is, just to remind ourselves, simply Sheila's own private religion. Sheila-ism represented in Bellah's work the capacity to create a kind of self-sustaining world of spirituality which had no particular accountability to any institution, group, or individual besides Sheila herself. Part of Bellah's critique of Sheila-ism was its inability to talk about itself persuasively. What I found most troubling about Sheila-ism is that it existed in a protected haze of inarticulacy.

While Sheila herself might have gone more public and joined the local church choir in the 1990s, she has not yet developed a language in which to talk about her beliefs to others. Deprivatization does not exist yet in a world where religious persons are trained to argue for their convictions in a public forum. Religion cannot be effectively deprivatized if it cannot explain itself to others. And, in present public language, religion frequently exists as the assertion of a "right" or "special interest." Thus the deprivatization of religion – not a backlash, exactly, but a persistent refusal to make itself articulate. In a secular state religious persons must still speak in a kind of cunning and covert way. They must speak in code about their activities, not formulate them according to explicit standards of argument. One thinks, for example, of the Christian Right's own version of the men's movement, "The Promise-

Keepers," where men discover their own lost Christian manhood by the thousands in weekend retreats. This movement has all the language of the liberal Left, but in fact it reinforces the Christian Right's ideology of the nuclear family. So, too, the secular Left appropriates the Christian Right's language of "family values," without really expounding what it could mean in a liberal agenda. The Left blames the Right and the Right blames the Left for co-opting its own language, coding terms which "really mean something religious" or "really mean something secular," because there is not legitimate language in which religious debate can take place. The Hindu Right's plea for a common civil code is another example: while on the face of it, a common civil code seems appropriate and reasonably compatible with a secular state, for many Muslims it is in fact veiled language for the denial of a way of life already granted them by the existing Indian constitution.

Professor Neusner has commented on the ways in which a secular theory of politics does not prepare us to deal with the world we now confront; I would add to that important insight that a secular theory of politics coerces the linguistic style of the religiously committed who would like to participate in public life. At present, even if deprivatized, the debate about religion must be veiled, translated, and therefore potentially twisted and unproductive.

Thus a second question for us to pose to ourselves: Might we not re-examine the possibilities for public language found in classical traditions' debates about religion? If the worlds of public and private don't exist in the same configuration, what were the fora in which such debates took place, and what gave the advocates and detractors their authority of voice?

Professor Cox also speaks of the deregulation of religion – its infusion within market-consumer culture, a collage-building pragmatic approach and laissez-faire attitude that allowed the young man in Central Park magnanimously to grant the pope his point of view on birth control. Yet those concerned with the risks of such deregulation would argue that it is not deregulation at all, but in fact, the reregulation of religion according to the whims of capitalist forces. The images that come immediately to mind are those of Star TV in India – the mass-marketed cable-TV network which, for the past five years, has beamed Madonna and MTV into the more affluent homes of Bombay, and now into the slums of Delhi as well. On one Star TV channel which has gone more "native" than MTV, an advertisement features a family arguing about which station to watch when suddenly, out of the blue, the god Śiva appears to settle their despite and bring harmony – the final choice of station, of course, being Star TV, whose origins are in fact in Hong King. Something has radically changed about Śiva – not because media such as TV and radio are used for religious purposes, for that has been common Hindu practice for decades. It is because Śiva has become a trademark used by the Star-TV conglomerate to represent Hindus to themselves. This indeed is regulation of a very powerful kind.

There is nothing new in the fact that religion is part of a profitable medium. And it is straightforward enough that market forces have, in fact, been part of the religious picture all along. What is new is the kind of "pseudoalliance" between deregulation and religious symbols, which masks a very grave danger. People may pay more attention to the media representation of religion than the practice of religion itself. It is no accident that most young Indians now know the term *Nirvana* as the name of a grunge rock band from the United States and are surprised to learn of the word's origins in the mind of a religious leader who lived in a northeast kingdom of their own country. At best, such an alliance between deregulation and religious symbols results in the trivialization of such symbols, and at worst, it results in replacing the religious teaching that the classical traditions have long held are best handed down person to person, physical body to physical body.

A third question for us to ponder then: What happens to the classical tradition when it is represented and promulgated by market forces, specifically media-market forces? What is the effect on classical understandings of religious education? What claims are being made by the new forms of transmission to augment, or even to replace, the old form?

The fourth "de-" word that Professor Cox considers is that of dedogmatization: the claim to religious experience has become paramount and the move away from church doctrine is palpable. This term in fact gave me the most trouble from the start. Although I could understand the other forms of resurgence as descriptively accurate, I'm not sure what kind of distinction Professor Cox is trying to make here. The claim that religious experience is divorced from institutional formation seems descriptively inaccurate. If scholars of religious experience as divergent as Yandell, Proudfoot, Katz, Forman, and many others have had any say in the matter over the past decade, it is that religious institutions and religious experiences mutually implicate each other in important and ineradicable ways. Such experiences might be attested to or practiced outside of institutional contexts, and they might in fact challenge those contexts explicitly. But their language of resistance will inevitably be formed by dogmatic teachings of some kind.

There are numerous historical examples which challenge distinctions between dogma and experience. One thinks, for example, of traditions where experience *is* dogma – not to be separated by semantic distinctions of any kind. The 500 B.C.E. Upanishads are best viewed, I think, as a set of collated mental notebooks about experience – notebooks that have formed the basis of Hindu dogma for three millennia. One might also point to the medieval Chishti movement of Maharasthra and Rajasthan, where the media of Hindu Sanskrit epic (a very dogmatic form) and royal court narrative were in fact the only forms in which Sufi experience could safely grow.

It seems to me, then, that we might ask our questions about religious experience and dogma in a different way: How do institution and experience balance and inform each other? What are the historical conditions in which experience challenges institution, and in which institution challenges experience?

Turning finally to the question of depatriarchalization – what Professor Cox calls the profoundest change of all: depatriarchalization, too, implies several risks – one of which is disrespect for the traditions many women wish to preserve. Thus it is understandable that what began as a feminist assertion of the strength of women in their freedom has been answered, in part, with a conservative assertion of the strength of women in their traditional roles. Even if we promote wholeheartedly the language of depatriarchalization, we still lack the language to differentiate between the various claims that are now being made about and on behalf of the bodies, minds, and livelihoods of women. Do the women in Turkey who refused to uncover their heads in court, shouting for their right to do so against the will of the secular state and defended at gunpoint against their prosecutors, have the same status as the local female temple priest in the small town near Delhi, who has taken up where her male teacher left off, simply because nobody seemed to mind, her rates were cheaper, and there was nobody else to do it? Self-evidently not. Yet these are both examples of depatriarchalization; they are simply not the kind that the liberal West has imagined. The Hindu and Muslim women are both still bound up with patriarchy, and as such, as far from the Western feminist perspective as could possibly be.

Yet they are also more "liberal-minded" than what I have come to call the profoundly conservative aspects of the contemporary goddess movement in America – the attempt to reconstruct a historical matriarchy where none can definitively be said to exist. In this, contemporary liberal feminists are no different from those who want to rebuild Ayodhya, and we need to take account of this aspect of Western feminism in all its political implications.

A fifth and final question, then, concerns depatriarchalization: What about the profound ambivalence of depatriarchalizers toward traditional symbols of the female? How might they take better account of the various catch-22's of Western feminism – its refusal, for instance, to essentialize in the political realm and its eagerness to do so in the religious one? Or its refusal of historical accuracy in its construction of the past and its eagerness to claim it when those outside its boundaries tell the narrative? And, after considering this ambivalence, how might we take better historical and theological account of the reassertion of tradition for the sake of women all the world?

To review, then, the five questions that Professor Cox's paper has inspired me to think about further: First, what are the dynamics of translation from classical to contemporary understandings of place as the basics of a religious theory of politics? Second, what are the possibilities for public language found in classical traditions' debates about religion, and how might we learn from them? Third, what happens to classical traditions when they are represented and promulgated by market forces, specifically media-market forces, and how are their forms of religious educational and transmission affected? Fourth, how do the historical conditions of the late twentieth-century religious resurgence affect the ways in which experience challenges institution, and institution challenges experience? Fifth, how can we take better historical and theological account of the reassertion of tradition for the sake of women?

If these questions are answered we might well be on a better path to understanding what theories of politics have acted as a medium for the sacred ordering of legitimate power. We might understand resurgent religions not only from a scholarly perspective, but also from a critical knowledge of the threat those very resurgences can pose to those who would disagree. Countermovements are not just fundamentalisms, they are not just the denial of public life, nor unthinking nationalism, nor monopoly control of resources, nor the straight denial of the religious authority of women. Countermovements have profound and reasonable reasons, a kind of legitimate sense. When we understand this our political systems will have a chance of being the morally persuasive powers that we hope them to be.

3

Religion and Modernization: Secularization or Sacralization

Danny Jorgensen
University of South Florida

Thirty years ago many scholars anticipated the increased secularization of culture and society as a consequence of modernization and the eventual demise of religion, at least in the West.[1] In 1965, for instance, Harvey Cox's immensely popular *The Secular City* announced the collapse of traditional religion and the secularization of modern cultures and societies.[2] While Cox, like other intellectuals, saw these secularizing tendencies as humanizing and liberating, still other observers – especially traditional religionists – found them apocalyptic.[3] Yet almost no one expected that modernity would result in anything other than greater secularization.

Today, however, the secularization thesis is almost as unpopular as it was fashionable thirty years ago. Reflecting a new scholarly consensus, Harvey Cox's contribution to this volume, "Religion and Politics after *The Secular City*," points to indications of a "global resurgence of religion." This signifies what Cox describes as "a tidal change in human

---

[1] See, for example, Bryan Wilson, *Religion in Secular* Society (London: C. A. Watts, 1966); Peter L. Berger, *The Sacred Canopy: Elements of a Sociological Theory of Religion* (Garden City, NY: Doubleday, 1967); Thomas Luckmann, *The Invisible* Religion (New York: Macmillan, 1967); and Anthony F. C. Wallace, *Religion: An Anthropological View* (New York: Random House, 1966).
[2] Harvey Cox, *The Secular City* (New York: Macmillan, 1965).
[3] See Darrell J. Fasching, *The Ethical Challenge of Auschwitz and Hiroshima: Apocalypse or Utopia?* (Albany: State University of New York Press, 1993), especially chapter 2, for an outstanding summary of different scholarly evaluations of secularization.

spirituality," and his essay ponders the meaning of this unanticipated, revolutionary turn of events. While there is considerable agreement that religion is being revived and revitalized throughout the world, very few scholars have formulated an alternative theory of sacralization or re-sacralization.

The work of Rodney Stark and his associates provides a modest exception.[4] They theorize that secularization is self-limiting. There is a constant, ongoing human need for the rewards that religion provides and the functions it serves, they believe. Viewed in this way, religion does not decline but instead changes to meet these needs. The theory of religion advanced by Stark and his colleagues is demonstrably mistaken on a variety of accounts, although some of its contentions point to issues in need of further scholarly discussion.[5]

Whether one accepts or rejects the secularization thesis or judges the consequences to be good or bad, the fundamental issues this matter raises still are of the utmost importance for the scholarly study of religion.[6] How significant is religion for people today? What roles does – and should – it play in contemporary public life? These questions impel us to the essence of this book's concern for "religion and the political order."

The purpose of this chapter is to reflect, briefly and critically, on the matter of secularization. I take Harvey Cox's work on this subject as a primary frame of reference since his views have been and are exceptionally prominent. Many people, like Harvey Cox, think that religion somehow has changed over the last thirty years; yet few of them offer much explanation for this seemingly unexpected occurrence or why they now see things differently. I wonder: Were the proponents of the secularization thesis, including Harvey Cox, simply mistaken thirty years ago? Why or why not? Are Cox and many other observers correct

---

[4] Rodney Stark and William Sims Bainbridge, *The Future of Religion: Secularization, Revival, and Cult Formation* (Berkeley: University of California Press, 1985); also see Roger Finke and Rodney Stark, "Religious Economies and Sacred Canopies: Religious Mobilization in American Cities," *American Sociological Review* 53 (February 1988): 41-49; Roger Finke and Rodney Stark, "How the Upstart Sects Won America: 1776-1850," *Journal for the Scientific Study of Religion* 28 (1): 27-44. Also see Robert Wuthnow, *Rediscovering the Sacred: Perspectives on Religion in Contemporary Society* (Grand Rapids, MI: William B. Eerdmans, 1992).
[5] See Roy Wallis and Steven Bruce, *Sociological Theory, Religion, and Collective Action* (Belfast: Queen's University, 1986), for a thorough critique of the Stark-Bainbridge thesis.
[6] See Steven Bruce, ed., *Religion and Modernization: Sociologists and Historians Debate the Secularization Thesis* (New York: Oxford University Press, 1992), for a valuable, recent discussion of this issue.

in proclaiming a worldwide religious resurgence today? And, either way, what sense are we to make of this complex and confusing situation?

Secularization?

Contrary to what many observers anticipated thirty years ago, religion remains an important fact of life throughout most of the world, including many Western societies, today. Yet I am not at all certain that Professor Cox and the other advocates of the secularization thesis were entirely wrong. There are at least three reasons, other than just being contrary, for thinking that contemporary societies have become more secular.

A first reason involves the forms that religion takes under distinct social and cultural conditions. Modern societies are substantially different from traditional societies (or communities): They are more differentiated in terms of specialized social roles and institutions; more industrial, urban, and universalistic; as well as much more rationalistic.[7] Daily life in modern societies generally is dominated by economic roles, relationships, and organizations which compete with more traditional, primary groups such as the family and religion. Industrial technology is everywhere, and very few modern people live without automobiles, televisions, telephones, computers, other work-saving appliances, or the vast assortment of consumer goods this technology produces. Social life has been divorced from local communities and replaced by the more abstract, anonymous, secondary relationships characteristic of urbanism. Where they still exist, villages and towns have been invaded by urban culture and linked directly with it, particularly by industrial technologies and mass communications. Most areas of modern life have been rationalized. Mechanisms of rational efficiency, as vividly demonstrated by the pervasiveness of bureaucracy, dictate the manner in which people currently relate to one another and organize their activities socially almost everywhere.

Religion in modern, as opposed to traditional, societies also is distinctive. It generally is: diverse and pluralistic; voluntary and otherwise contingent upon individualism; as well as separate from and in competition with other exceptionally influential, nonreligious beliefs

---

[7] My use of "modernity" and related concepts is informed by Anthony Giddens's *The Consequences of Modernity* (Stanford, CA: Stanford University Press, 1990). Although highly abstract, Giddens' comparison and contrast among different forms of social life, traditional, modern, radically modern, and postmodern, is exceptionally informative.

and organizations.[8] In modern societies there are more varieties of religion. The individual is free to choose a religion, sometimes more than one religion, or no religion at all. Religion in modern societies commonly is regulated by government, and forbidden from particular expression in certain areas of public life, such as schools and government. It competes, in almost all areas of traditional concern (family, psychological and physical well-being, education, values, morality, ethics, and so on) with secular bodies of knowledge and belief, particularly science, as well as their representative social organizations and institutions. Religion simply is not as institutionally prominent in modern societies as in traditional ones. Modern society is more secular – no matter how it is defined and measured – than traditional society.

A second reason for thinking that previous predictions of secularization may have been partly correct pertains to the matter of evidence. Consequential changes in culture and society are difficult to discern and interpret. None of the indicators of religious change or the patterns of resurgence noted by Professor Cox and other observers are beyond dispute or reinterpretation.

What, for example, does it mean to say that 94 percent of Americans believe in God or a universal spirit? Is this the God of a traditional religion or a deity of some new, generic, common, or civil religion? It is notable that only 58 percent of this same population regards religion as "very important."[9] Even fewer Western Europeans say that they believe in God or a universal spirit – from 88 to 65 percent – or that religion is "very important" – from 36 percent to 17 percent. How do we reconcile these data with the claimed renaissance of religion and its greater influence in the world today?

Contemporary religion is more globally diffuse and pluralistic. Yet whether or not some of the trends Harvey Cox and others observe – deregionalization, deregulation, or dedogmatization – mean that religion is more, rather than less, powerful is not at all clear. Having more religious options less securely bound by ethnicity, nationality, or authoritative religious organizations may signify religion's greater cultural pervasiveness and, perhaps, influence; but probably at the expense of its power to affect secular institutions.

More varieties of religion, as implied by the pluralism Professor Cox and others observe, raise critical questions about the character of these

---

[8] See, for example, Elizabeth K. Nottingham, *Religion: A Sociological View* (New York: Random House, 1971), for a still useful typology of religion in different kinds of societies.
[9] George Gallup, "Religion at Home and Abroad," *Public Opinion*, March-May 1979: 38-99.

religions. Simply observing that there are more religions, without reflecting on their spirit, does not refute the secularization thesis.

Some religions – such as Catholicism and Pentecostalism – oppose modernity. They, in other words, generally seek to preserve a more traditional way of life. Other religions, like mainline Protestantism, are comfortable with modernity and frequently promote it. Protestantism is a highly rationalistic form of religion, a reflection of modernity itself, and it sustains the basic economic, political, and other cultural values of modernity. Still other religions, such as Judaism, Islam, Buddhism, and Hinduism, selectively embrace and oppose particular characteristics of modernism. They manifest different forms, some of which seek to preserve traditional communities, some of which support modern economic and political values, and some of which anticipate promoting transformations and creating new social and cultural worlds.

Similarly, the depatriarchalization of religion that Harvey Cox and many other scholars envision clearly reflects change, but not necessarily opposition to secularization. Traditionally, all of the biblical religions, at least, promote status hierarchies based on gender. None of them traditionally accord women principal leadership roles or authority for matters of general concern to their entire religious communities, except in the less public sphere of the home and family. De-patriarchalization derives instead from the radically individualistic and egalitarian values inherent in modernity. The appropriation of these values by religion reflects change, but this transformation breaks with, rather than supports, tradition.

Religion, like culture and society generally, always is undergoing change to some extent. Because of its unique appeal to the ultimate conditions of human existence, religion contains tremendous potential for resisting change and legitimating the established social order as well as seeking small and large transformations of existing cultures and societies. Change, then, as it involves religion may be aimed in highly divergent directions and at many different goals. Furthermore, whether a religion promotes social preservation or reform, reactionary or revolutionary change, it must either achieve social dominance or accommodate the larger, typically secular, society.[10]

Throughout much of the world today, religion remains very closely related to nationality, ethnicity, social stratification (caste and class), as well as conventional religious organizations. In most cases, including highly pluralistic ones, the predominant form or forms of a nation's

---

[10] See Max Weber, *The Sociology of Religion*, trans. Ephraim Fischoff (Boston: Beacon Press), for a classic discussion of the interrelationship of religion and society, and the role of religion in social change.

religion are easily identifiable, even when there are several or more significant minority religions. Protestantism, for example, remains socially dominant in the United States, although Catholicism is the single largest denomination, and in spite of other consequential religious minorities, such as Jews and Mormons. Similarly, many other nations are identifiable as predominantly Christian, Islamic, Buddhist, and so on, or divided between prominent religions, such as Protestants and Catholics, Muslims and Hindus, and the like.

It is impossible to talk about ethnicity in many, perhaps most, cases without also discussing religion. This is especially so in societies sharply divided by ethnic cleavages, such as in the Middle East, much of Asia and Africa, or Eastern Europe. Yet, religion in societies such as the United States also strongly reflect ethnicity. Catholicism is dominant among Hispanics, and blacks have re-created their own varieties of Protestantism. Ethnicity and religion still are interrelated to a considerable extent in the United States even among immigrant groups, such as Scandinavians, Irish, Poles, and Italians, that largely have been assimilated into the larger society.

In many societies such as the United States religious affiliation is correlated directly with social stratification and, thereby, social power and influence.[11] The higher a person's social-class rank, the more likely they are to belong to one of the liberal, mainline, Protestant denominations, such as the Episcopalian, Presbyterian, or Congregationalist; and, conversely, the less likely they are to belong to a sectarian religion, such as the Jehovah's Witness or Pentecostal. Similarly, Americans who hold positions of power, such as senators and Supreme Court justices, are disproportionately liberal Protestants, while the members of minority, especially sectarian, religions are under-represented in powerful social positions, particularly the national government.

While conservative religious movements are growing, their ability to exercise power usually depends on extrareligious organizations, such as the formation of political alliances. Such alliances are, moreover, fragile, regularly subject to realignment, and hard to sustain for more than a very short period of time. It is difficult to identify a single instance of a new or resurgent religious movement anywhere that has equaled or

---

[11] H. Richard Niebuhr, *The Social Sources of Denominationalism* (New York: Meridian, 1929); Will Herberg, *Protestant, Catholic, Jew: An Essay in American Religious Sociology* (New York: Doubleday, 1955); Andrew M. Greeley, *The Denominational Society: A Sociological Approach to Religion in America* (Glenview, IL: Scott, Foresman, 1972); and Barry A. Kosmin and Seymour P. Lachman, *One Nation under God.*

surpassed the social power of the traditional, socially dominant religion or religions of a nation or society.

Many of the consequential ways that religion impacts the secular society, such as through parochial schools, hospitals, charities, and so on, including politics, depend on conventional religious organizations. Religions without strong organizations for mobilizing human and material resources may influence public opinion, but their ability to exercise social power to affect society thereby is severely limited in the world today.

In stressing signs of religious change and resurgence worldwide today, some observers have neglected much mention of how radically modernization has affected the entire globe. The consequences of modernity are enormous – so globalizing, in fact, that almost everyone feels its impact. When a Coca-Cola bottle falls from the African sky, a Kalahari Bushman concludes – to the amusement of movie goers everywhere – that "the gods must be crazy." Yet, there are very few, if any, traditional societies left on this planet.

When traditional religion achieves dominance over a society, as illustrated by a variety of cases in the Middle East and elsewhere, this usually does not involve a complete repudiation of modernity. Rather, the debates are about how to direct industrialization as well as related social and economic developments while preserving certain traditional ways of life. There are not many places in the world today that have been as radically preserved or transformed by religion as by urbanization, industrialization, rationalization, and the other mechanisms of modernization.

Modernity, furthermore, promotes individualism; and, along with it, a tremendous range of choices among experiences, beliefs, activities, and groups, religious and otherwise. Human existence thereby becomes more fragmented, compartmentalized, and privatized under the conditions of modernization. Modern peoples thereby can be devoutly committed to a traditional religion while participating fully in a wide range of other modern institutions. Religions taking the form of denominations and moderate sects still attract significant followings, while more radical, world-rejecting sects remain relatively small and socially marginal. Although many modern people yearn for greater community and grieve its loss, most of them also desire ample freedom, and they resist the authority and conformity that community demands. When pluralism prevails, traditionalists and conservatives are among the first to demand and defend the freedom to choose.

A third reason for thinking that the secularization thesis was not completely mistaken pertains to scholarly interpretations of trends.

Hypothesized changes must be supported by multiple indicators of events forming consistent patterns over a fairly lengthy period of time.

Even if we accept the evidence cited by Harvey Cox and other contemporary observers against secularization, all of it may represent nothing more than a minor historical blip. In the overall picture, thirty years is a relatively short period of time for deciding that something of genuine and enduring significance has happened in one way or another with human culture and society. Indications of religious change, revitalization, and revival notwithstanding, there also are many signs that modernization has radically transformed social and cultural life, including many forms of religion, almost everywhere in the world today.

Sacralization?

Now, however, Harvey Cox and many other intellectuals reject the secularization thesis because they think that religion has changed dramatically and in unanticipated ways. There, undeniably, have been significant changes in religion and the social world over the last thirty years. Almost no one expected the collapse of the Soviet Union and Communist control of Eastern Europe, the Islamic revival, the growth of conservative Protestantism in the United States and elsewhere, among other frequently discussed indicators of religion's resiliency and vitality.

I wonder, however, whether or not the greater change – then to now – is with the evidence or its scholarly interpretation. Perhaps the evidence against the secularization thesis was there all along.[12] Since modernization commonly is associated with the West, particularly the United States, it provides one of the most extreme cases for testing this possibility. A glance at the history of American religion therefore serves to illustrate and underscore this point.

Over the last fifteen years previous understandings of American religion have been revised substantially.[13] The following general conclusions are representative of revisionist thinking. In the past, Americans were not always as religious as scholars commonly have assumed. Although most Americans probably always have been religious in some sense, the manner in which they expressed it has been

---

[12] This essentially is the position taken by Andrew M. Greeley, *Religion in the Year 2000* (New York: Sheed and Ward, 1969), at the time.
[13] See Jon Butler, *Awash in a Sea of Faith: Christianizing the American People* (Cambridge, MA: Harvard University Press, 1990); Nathan O. Hatch, *The Democratization of American Christianity* (New Haven, CT: Yale University Press, 1989); and D. Laurence Moore, *Religious Outsiders and the Making of Americans* (Ithaca, NY: Cornell University Press, 1986). Also see Jacob Neusner, ed., *World Religions in America: An Introduction* (Louisville, KY: Westminster/John Knox, 1994).

highly variable. Traditional church membership and attendance declined from the early colonial period until the Great Awakening (1741-42). The excitement it produced gradually deteriorated, eventually leading to the Second Awakening (about 1800-1840), particularly on the American frontier. These more traditional forms of religiosity did not preclude folk beliefs, particularly those involving assorted magical practices. In daily life, many Americans freely intermingled more conventional forms of religiosity with magical practices for healing illness, planting and raising crops, and divining future events.

As a consequence of these religious revivals and the intermixing of old and new religious beliefs, American religion was transformed. Americans, therefore, were not religious in the ways that scholars who focused on the European traditions generally have assumed. Most of the religions imported by American immigrants underwent an Americanization process. Through this process they accommodated to secular pluralism, commonly becoming denominational, and contributed to a generic, nonsectarian, religious culture. Denominational religion co-existed with and mixed in elements of civil religions, folk religions, and a host of later religious imports.

Throughout American history, religion has been subject to cyclical ups and downs, as is evident with the previously mentioned awakenings. Furthermore, since the period of the Second World War, Americans increasingly have been attracted to a diverse array of religions, traditional and otherwise. Many scholarly observers think this reflects yet another religious awakening.

The human lifespan also seems to influence evidence of greater and lesser degrees of religiosity at any particular moment in time. Many people seem to be less interested in religion as they become more independent of their family of origin (parents), and then find religion to be of greater interest as they produce children and get older. Among Americans today, a high degree of religiosity seems to be fairly constant when it is viewed across generations.[14]

In all of these ways the everyday life beliefs and practices of Americans differed substantially from the official religion of the mainline denominations that has been the emphasis of conventional thinking. Scholarly neglect of new religions – such as Spiritualism, New Thought, Christian Science, the Jehovah's Witnesses, Seventh-Day Adventism, and Mormonism – compounded previous misunderstanding. Mormonism,

---

[14] See Andrew M. Greeley, *Religious Changes in America* (Cambridge, MA: Harvard University Press, 1989); and Barry A. Kosmin and Seymour P. Lachman, *One Nation under God: Religion in Contemporary American Society* (New York: Harmony Books, 1993).

for example, was expanding exponentially just as scholars were advancing the secularization thesis.[15] By the middle of the next century, Mormonism probably will be a world religion. More recent new religions in the United States, such as Eastern imports, Scientology, as well as Wicca and other forms of Neopaganism, seem to be attracting significant followings.

Making Sense of the Current Situation

The secularization thesis failed, then, because modern societies never were as secular as the theory supposed; and religion, particularly the ways in which people are religious, was different from what scholars thought. Yet, modernization is not a reversible process: it continues to transform the world today. Traditional societies are gone or going fast; and most contemporary societies have become or are becoming more secular.

Even so, this is not to say that religion is no longer important, largely a private matter, or marginal to contemporary culture and society. There is, as Harvey Cox and other scholars have demonstrated, too much evidence to the contrary. Religion changes, but it is not likely to go away anytime soon.

It is exceptionally important, however, to stress that religion commonly aims to bring about substantially different transformations of the social order. Religion sometimes is reactionary, seeking a return to previous ways, actual or imaginary, of ordering human existence. Sometimes it is conservative, resisting change and pursuing the preservation of the past or existing social order. And, sometimes it aims for social reform, or even a revolutionary new order.

What sense is there to make, then, of this complex and confusing situation? In observing some of the ways in which religion has changed over the last thirty years, Professor Cox and other opponents of the secularization thesis have not considered seriously that culture and society have changed too. This is the missing link in the argument.

The modern conviction, of which the secularization thesis was merely a reflection, that science would save us is no longer credible – as Professor Cox notes, but only in passing. This realization is monumental for any consideration of science, religion, or any other form of knowledge that is to serve as a basis for social and cultural life. It has produced a colossal epistemological crisis – a profound skepticism about what can be regarded as truth and knowledge – in modern, Western

---

[15] See Jan Shipps, *Mormonism: The Story of a New Religious Tradition* (Urbana: University of Illinois Press, 1985); and Rodney Stark, "The Rise of a New World Faith," *Review of Religious Research* 26 (1): 118-27.

thought. This change is so radical, so earth shaking, that many scholarly observers now think that modernity has been eclipsed, and that we currently are witnessing the dawn of a new historical epoch, the postmodern age.[16]

Whether or not a new age is upon us, postmodern thought negates absolutism, radically relativizing all knowledge and its authority. In its more extreme forms, postmodernism argues that there are no certain (absolute) grounds for advancing truth claims. All truth claims depend on beliefs and the particular practices supporting them. Therefore, there is no way, independent of any given body of belief and its practices, of deciding with certainty what is or is not true.

If, for example, someone claims that God created the heavens and earth, as specified and sanctioned by the beliefs and practices of a religion, then this claim is true as constituted on these grounds. The contention that the universe was created by a large explosion (the Big Bang theory) also is true insofar as it is supported by another set of beliefs and practices, like those of scientific astronomy. There is no independent way, according to postmodernism, of judging between these seemingly rival contentions. Each of these claims necessarily depends on certain (faith) assumptions; they are different; but there is no way, apart from the beliefs and practices upon which the argument is based, for deciding between them.

Viewed in this way, beliefs and practices, religious or otherwise, are like games. The contention that religion provides a better explanation of the universe than science, or the other way around, therefore is nonsense. It amounts to much the same thing as saying that tennis is superior to golf, or the other way around. A person may prefer one game to another, but there is no way, independent of one's preference for one or the other, of deciding which game is best.

All claims to truth about the nature of reality, according to extreme postmodernism, therefore are nothing more than opinions. There are multiple realities, all of them based on particular beliefs and practices, and no independent way of deciding which one is better or worse, right or wrong. To advance such a claim is like looking into a mirror. All that one thereby sees is one's own reflection; that is, how one set of beliefs and practices look when viewed from the standpoint of the other. Religion, thereby, no longer is an inferior basis for truth or human relationships, as it was for modernism. It has been freed to compete on a potentially equal footing with science, politics, and itself.

---

[16] See Jean-Francois Lyotard, *The Post-Modern Condition* (Minneapolis: University of Minnesota Press, 1985).

This makes sense, it seems to me, of the five major changes in religion – deregionalization, deprivatization, deregulation, dedogmatization, and depatriarchalization – astutely identified by Professor Cox and noted by other contemporary scholars. All of them reflect the radical relativization of knowledge claims as seen from a postmodern standpoint. These changes pertain to religion and society today, and they tell us something about what we may expect from the future.

Religion and Public Life in a Postmodern World

Religion will be a major player in the public life of postmodern societies. It will be a very complex and confusing world, one in which religion stands on its own and for different, sometimes conflicting values: traditional, modern, and postmodern. Just as traditionalism survived modernity, many of modernism's tendencies will continue to influence the world of the future, whether it is postmodern or something else.

Traditional and antimodern religions will have to deal with secular, pluralistic societies. Successful sects tend to become denominations over the long run. Traditional religions may be able to direct, but they probably cannot control, modernization. In a postmodern world, traditional religions and those that have adapted to modernism will have to deal with even greater pluralism and competition. The big issue here involves being different while respectfully acknowledging and valuing enormous cultural and religious diversity.

However things turn out, this is how it should be: Religion is far too important for human existence to be excluded from these discussions, debates, and conflicts. The challenge for religion is to exercise its tremendous potential and power to preserve, recreate, and originate images of what it means to be human together on this little planet in a majestic and mysterious universe.

Part I

ANCIENT ISRAEL

4

Religion, Politics, and the Social Order: The Creation of the History of Ancient Israel

Sara Mandell
University of South Florida

Because the biblical text itself does not deal with the political order, even in the so-called historical books of Primary History (Genesis-2 Kings), until recently scholars have tended to ignore that particular aspect of biblical study, focusing on historical, theological, and literary studies. It is important, however, to recognize that we cannot understand how Israel came to being without understanding the inseparable connection between religion, the social, and the political order at the time of Israel's inception, which does not coincide with that of its description in the biblical narrative. We are, however, at something of a loss in our attempt to deal with this relationship between religion and politics, and between the theo-political and the socio-political order at the beginning of Israelite history because we accept legend and pious fiction as historical data even while indicating that most of our data comes from a far later period than that of Israel's alleged origin.[1]

Basic to an understanding of the representation of formative Israel is the relationship between religion and society or church – as

---

[1] Actually, the depiction of the alleged events in Israel's formative period will themselves lead to an understanding of the socio-theo-political perspective of the respective author/redactors responsible for the various accounts of that same period.

defined by Durkheim – and state. This seems to many modern scholars to be two disparate entities precisely because we have conceptually divorced religion from our own self-understanding of society. Consequently, we expect politics to be peculiar to the latter, whereas we are "unforgiving" when we find it in the former. However, until the beginning of the Industrial Revolution, religion was always basic to a society's self-understanding, and therefore to its political enterprise. But, save when a nation viewed itself as having some sort of manifest destiny vis-à-vis its relationship to foreign nations, that self-understanding was generally viewed as part of the nation's internal development, what we today might construe as its sociology, rather than as part of the totality of its history. And, since history, from the time of the Industrial Revolution onward, has been treated as a "science," modern historians have tended to ignore the religious facet of a nation's development, frequently considering it as worthy of little more than a note if they mention it at all, and only including particular religious events when they are clearly and evidently causal of specific alterations in the course of history. Consequently, in looking at pre-Industrial Revolution societies, it is not always possible to extricate religion from politics, or politics from the exercise of power, each of which is always inextricably intertwined with the course of historical events and their representation.

As George Orwell made abundantly clear in *Animal Farm*, there is no such thing as a society without politics, even in a utopia. It doesn't matter if politics are minimally defined as the necessary civil machinery that enables the society to function, or maximally as the interaction of individuals and where appropriate their followers who are involved in the consciously thought-out or at least intentionally enacted process of ordering their society to suit their own ideology, be it expressed or implied. We cannot divorce religion or its subcomponents – theology, cult, and ritual (both high and popular), or belief (also both high and popular) – from politics or from the exercise and manipulation of power necessary for its exercise within the framework of politics. And, notably, we cannot always be sure that what we construe as high or as popular religion or belief was understood as such by its practitioners, for we human beings tend to mediate what is received in any tradition in light of our own beliefs as did those who transmitted the traditions. For the same reason, we cannot divorce politics, along with the various facets of their power substrate, from history; and, we cannot divorce any one of these factors from the development and ordering of society. Therefore, it is important to ask who transmitted any given tradition and what theo-political stake did the tradent(s) have in the way in which that tradition was handed down.

So it becomes meaningful that the efforts to divorce these foci from one another are actually part of an endeavor to obfuscate that reality in which "social systems," with their inherent "political power" relationships, function as if they were a religion and consequently become the focus of worship. This substitution of what is essentially a secular religion is not necessarily something that is an intentional creation of those seeking to rule or at least to control their fellow men, but it is used by them to that end. As is generally the case with the ideological foci, it represents a subterranean, if you will subconscious, wellspring that itself directs the consciousness of those for whom it is predicated. Berger's formulation that religion is consequent on the formation of society upon which it then operates and consequently alters within the context of his "world building" and culture production,[2] has made it clear that religion cannot be divorced from politics, which themselves cannot be divorced from the entity we call society. So, I classify events within their socio-political construct, which in actuality is a theo-political or better yet a socio-theo-political construct, rather than treat the social, theological, or political construct as separate entities within the larger framework of history. And I distinguish between history and society as represented in the part of the Bible we call Primary History (Genesis-2 Kings) and history and society as represented in the works of the so-called writing prophets. The formative era as represented in Primary History is a theo-political ex post facto construction of the social order of early Israel in accord with each redactor's own utopian vision. And the representations of religion and society in the works of the earlier writing prophets (e.g., Amos, Hosea, and first Isaiah), who themselves may be understood as militant radicals at war with both their society and its basic religious underpinnings, must be understood as at the very best revisionist and unacceptable to all but their own circles. On the other hand, the works of some of the later writing prophets, particularly those of the sixth century (e.g., Ezekiel, Jeremiah, second and

---

[2] Peter L. Berger, *The Sacred Canopy: Elements of a Sociological Theory of Religion*, 2nd ed. (New York: Anchor, 1990), 3-51. This relationship between religion and the social order may be summed up by Berger's statement that "worlds are socially constructed and socially maintained. Their continuing reality, both objective...and subjective..., depends upon *specific* social processes that ongoingly reconstruct and maintain the particular worlds in question" (45). For the precariousness of such a socially constructed world, see Berger, 50.

possibly third Isaiah, et al.), may be understood as coming from within the greater social context, which itself held to the revisionist ideology that characterizes the redactors of Primary History from the Deuteronomist's time onward.

The traditional method of viewing Israelite politics vis-à-vis the development of Israelite History is predicated on the underlying truthfulness of the Bible and the reality of the personae depicted therein, even when the particular events and or personae portrayed are merely paradigmatic and/or nonhistorical in and of themselves. The Hexateuch (Genesis-Joshua) in particular is construed as representing the circumstances in which, or even the world from which, Israel emanated, and Moses and Joshua as being salvation heroes and covenant signatories with whom the deity, at least as depicted, spoke directly.[3] So they as well as the representation of the events in which they are represented as being involved have become paradigmatic exemplars of both people and events even when they and the narrative in which they are depicted are non-historical. Unfortunately, many scholars still try to extract what is historical from the narrative and to treat the figures in it as really having existed. On the other hand, acknowledging that the Hexateuch, in particular, is not historical in its entirety, many scholars still want to see elements of history alongside of what paradigmatic matter is to be found in it. So, they use archaeology to test their material. Unfortunately, they use what artifactual data that can account for what is in the Bible to show that the representation of the Bible is valid, at least in that specific instance. However, many identifications of artifacts are based on what is in the Bible, so that the justification of the biblical text on that basis reflects circular reasoning and cannot be accepted.[4]

We must remember, that the Bible does not give a historical account, but rather an ideological one that itself is its authors'/redactors' respective utopian vision. And this ideological

[3] For Joshua, see, for example, *The Jerome Bible Commentary*, Joshua, Section 6 (Logos Software ed., Logos 2a, 1995).
[4] This has been noted, discussed, and substantiated by a growing number of scholars. See, for example, Philip R. Davies, *In Search of 'Ancient Israel'* (Sheffield: JSOT, 1992); Niels Peter Lemche, *Early Israel: Anthropological and Historical Studies on the Israelite Society before the Monarchy* (Leiden: E. J. Brill, 1985); Thomas L. Thompson, *Early History of the Israelite People: From the Written and Archaeological Sources* (Leiden: E. J. Brill, 1992); et al. For a summary of the supportive data, see my discussion in "Religious and Socio-Political Construction of Early Israel," vol. *Approaches to Ancient Judaism*, ed. Jacob Neusner 10 (Atlanta: Scholars, forthcoming).

account is a construct that not only emanates from the mind of its conceivers, but also and equally meaningfully of its readers (sic). Consequently, its basic meaning, its sense, as well as its interpretation differs as each reader himself differs.[5] So, for example, J. Maxwell Miller and John H. Hayes, as now do a few others, treat Genesis-Joshua as a work of literature that has been influenced by theology.[6] Others, myself included, treat it more radically as a utopian ideology, or even as a theological fiction from which politics cannot be divorced. This is particularly meaningful in light of Berger's model of development, whereby society, which from our perspective must be construed as a political entity, not only forms its religion as part of its culture, but together with the inherent socio-psychological need that *homo religiosus* has to worship something or to have some type of faith, even if its object is society itself, actually causes that religion to come into effect.[7] Therefore, just as the "scholarly 'ancient Israel' lies between literature and history – or rather, it straddles the two,"[8] so the religion and society of "ancient Israel" lies between religious literature, political ideology, and sociology, and in fact "straddles" all three.

What is particularly significant is that the relationship between religion and society, according to Berger, is not a one-way dynamic. Rather it is a back-and-forth flow insofar as the religion formed by society then reflects back, and alters the development of the society that brought it into being.[9] And this does not seem to be what is depicted in the relationship between the religion(s) and society of early Israel from the thirteenth century – that is, from what is ostensibly and from the later redactors' perspective is really the formative period – onward. This is particularly notable in the ideological reconstruction made by the early sixth-century exilic author/redactor, whom we call the Deuteronomistic Historian (Dtr) and who is responsible for the framework of Deuteronomy and the remainder of Primary History. The representation of what he alleges occurred, at least as presented in what is representative of his redaction of the narrative that forms the books of Joshua, Judges, and Samuel, seems to be within a somewhat static system with only hints of variance.

---

[5] In particular, this difference is basic to reader response criticism.
[6] J. Maxwell Miller and John H. Hayes, *A History of Ancient Israel and Judah* (Philadelphia: Fortress, 1986), 78.
[7] P. L. Berger, *The Sacred Canopy*, 3-51.
[8] P. R. Davies, *In Search of 'Ancient Israel,'* 16.
[9] P. L. Berger, *The Sacred Canopy*, 3-51.

In light of this, we must look at the so-called Mosaic period and
the subsequent Conquest and Settlement period, each of which from a
religious perspective falls within the provenience of sacred time and
takes place in part-sacred space, but which from a utopian one falls
within historical time and takes place in geographic space, as
multifaceted political propaganda originating from more than one
group, each of which is aspiring for power. This propaganda is in
fact in accord with the ideological and therefore clearly static,
utopian vision of either the school or the individual redactor, who is
responsible for the narrative in any given redaction. The tenth-
century Yahwistic and the ninth-century Elohistic accounts of Moses
and the Mosaic period are either so folkloristic, so legendary, so
mythical, and/or so fragmentary that it is difficult to extract any
ideological orientation from them. Although the most extensive
presentation of the Mosaic era comes from the hand of the Priestly
Redactor (P), who was writing while in exile in Babylon some time
between 586 and 561 B.C.E.,[10] he is not the only redactor to deal with
it. The Deuteronomist, who was writing at the time of Josiah's
reform (622 B.C.E.) also presents a lengthy "Mosaic" account, albeit
not as lengthy as that of P. And by framing D's work, Dtr, who like
P wrote some time between 586 and 561 B.C.E.,[11] made it his own,
thereby including a lengthy report of the Mosaic era in his narrative.
In the same manner, we say that despite the possibility that Dtr's
account of the Conquest and the Settlement, which is the only extant
account of events once the sons of Israel entered the Land
(Canaan/Palestine), may include earlier materials, or represents a
redaction of earlier writings, this is problematic. They are neither
extensive nor are they to be treated as reflective of earlier ideology
since by including them, Dtr in fact framed, recast, and/or altered
them, just as he had framed D's work, in such a way as to make
them his own. If these accounts really had been composed, be it in
writing or as part of an oral tradition, centuries prior to that of the
late seventh-century D, and the exilic P and Dtr respectively, this
may perhaps suggest why the representation is static. Moreover,
their cutting, rearranging, and in particular their framing by those
same later redactors ipso facto alters their earlier meaning, where

---

[10] This is not the place to deal with the probable of P's antecedents within
priestly circles. There are many academic works treating this difficult
problem.
[11] There is a great body of literature reflecting on whether there was one Dtr
or two. It is my belief that there was only one and he worked during the
early Exile. But, even if there were two, the second would have lived during
the Exile.

we really can ascertain that they had existed at all, in such a way that they reflect the ideology of their "editors" and framers, that is the later redactors, rather than of their own redactor. So, in looking at the Mosaic and the Conquest and Settlement eras, we must never presume that what is represented has anything to do with either the religion practiced during those respective periods or of their socio-theo-political realia. In fact, it is related to that of the various schools or individuals responsible for the individual redactions, or even to that of the final redactor whoever he was.

What is most problematic is that we do not know whether P was the last hand to edit the Pentateuch or whether Dtr was.[12] Nevertheless because the Priestly material is so extensive, and likewise the combined Deuteronomic and the Deuteronomistic material for the Mosaic period is also extensive, we can ascertain something of each of the three redactors ideological representation of the Mosaic period, thereby justifying Engnell's belief that there was only a Deuteronomic and a Priestly document, but not his belief that both of necessity relied on earlier oral traditions. Unfortunately, we can only determine that of Dtr for the period of the Conquest and the Settlement. What I am saying is that representation of the Mosaic figure as well as of the Mosaic era found in the Hebrew Bible is delineated by and in light of the ideology of D, P, and Dtr. And that of the Conquest and Settlement is only presented in light of that of Dtr. In other words, these respective ideologies reflect the theo-political world of the redactors' own times, not of that of the legendary eras they represent.

Moreover both the Priestly Redactor's and the Deuteronomistic Historian's representation of Israel's formative period are more than attempts to depict that formative era and its personae. Each is intended to show its school as the legitimate heirs of Moses and Joshua, to whom we must remember the deity is represented as having spoken directly.

It is precisely because as heirs of Moses and Joshua, they each claim to have a divinely ordained right to administer *the Covenant* concluded at Sinai and/or Horeb, and thereby to be the spiritual as well as the political rulers of the sons of Israel, that these

---

[12] Some think that P was the final redactor, and some that Dtr was. There was some editor who combined the work into one entity, which we call Primary History, but unless he is P or Dtr himself, he only did minor editing and there is no reason to presume that his ideology differs from that of either P or Dtr but not both. I myself think that Dtr was that final editor, however. See Sara Mandell and David Noel Freedman, *The Relationship Between Herodotus' History and Primary History* (Atlanta: Scholars, 1993).

respective accounts must be considered socio-theo-political constructs. Their representation is an attempt to obtain or to hold power over the Israelites, based on fabricated events or stories that had long been part of the folk tradition. They were created or adapted so as to realize the redactor's socio-theo-political goals. The Deuteronomist's representation of the formative era, then, may well be an attempt to correct the ideological faults of Israel's postformative history, by validating Josiah's reform of 622 B.C.E. as a return to "the old-time religion" in which the deity established Israel by the "great," socially defining covenant as well as the fulfillment of what are allegedly yet-earlier covenants given to the legendary patriarchs, granting them the Land.

Our understanding of the formation of Israel must be predicated on the acceptance of Yahwism, since there is no other basis for differentiating between so-called Israelites and other Canaanites prior to the conversion of those who were to define themselves as Israelites to Yahwism. What is clear is that in Dtr's representation of the Southern as well as the Northern kingdom, the two states into which the Monarchy split after the death of Solomon (922 B.C.E.), representative "Israelite" societies were not exclusively Yahwistic, and in fact they were not even primarily Yahwistic at least until Josiah's reform (622 B.C.E.). Furthermore there is no reason to believe that Josiah's reform itself was based on a deeply religious, reformative experience. Rather, it may well represent Judah's attempt at self-protection in light of current international events; it may even reflect Judah's reaction to changes in the Assyrian Empire after Ashurbanipal's death a decade earlier.[13]

In fact, from a historical perspective as well as from a socio-theo-political one, both kingdoms had been part and parcel of the various Canaanite societies found in Palestine, even when their rulers viewed themselves as sons of Israel. And, this is confirmed by Dtr's attack on the ruling kings – who were not exclusively Yahwistic – depicting them as bad precisely because they were not exclusively Yahwistic. And, likewise it is confirmed by prophetic attacks on the sons of Israel, both in Israel prior to its fall in 722 and in Judah alike. Meaningfully these prophetic attacks are themselves frequently directed toward those who were not exclusively Yahwistic, often condemning them for precisely that lack of religious exclusivity.[14]

---

[13] See the *Jerome Bible Commentary*, 1-2 Kings, Section 74.

[14] For the dominant (allegedly Israelite) religious practices as polytheistic between 1020 and 586 B.C.E., see Bernhard Lang, *Monotheism and the Prophetic Minority* (Sheffield: Almond, 1983), 20.

And by integrating a *Rib,* that is, a divine lawsuit, into the narrative, the prophets even act as if it were Yahweh himself who was the "prosecuting attorney." But in addition, as an attempt at political manipulation, the prophets frequently condemned the sons of Israel for class distinctions as well as for socioeconomic situations that were from the prophetic vantage reflective of a situation in which the sufferings of the poor could well be attributed to the actions of the wealthy.

Clearly then, the prophetic presentation, starting in the eighth and holding strong through the greater part of the seventh-century, from the vantage of a radical utopian vision that is itself Yahwistic but one which becomes progressively less radical as the events of the next centuries change Israel's own perspective; and, both Jeremiah's and Dtr's sixth-century presentation from a realized utopian vision whereby Yahwism has become the religion of the sons of Israel,[15] cause both the prophets and Dtr to insinuate that what was in fact social reality and the norm was actually an aberration from the socio-political norm demanded by adherence to a true Yahwism, and it was also theologically inappropriate behavior representative of apostasy from that allegedly Yahwistic norm. Although Dtr tended to "background" these variances precisely because they were inconsistent with his theo-political outlook, they have become "foregrounded," and thereby brought to our attention precisely because they are incongruous within their narratival and their societal context.[16]

The eighth-century prophets in particular are far less constrained, perhaps because until the period of Josiah's reform, they were radicals and outcasts who had much less to lose. We don't even know if the poor, whom they allegedly defended, accepted them. This may be why their attack is not only more open, but it places a far greater stress than does Dtr on the socioeconomic problems as well as on international politics that may well be related to the socioeconomic problems. And, whereas Dtr was most interested in the

---

[15] B. Lang (*Monotheism and the Prophetic Minority,* 36) treats the Yahweh elements alone as later additions to Isaiah and Michah.

[16] For such inconsistencies, see J. Maxwell Miller, "The Israelite Occupation of Canaan," in *Israelite and Judaean History,* ed. John H. Hayes and J. Maxwell Miller (Philadelphia: Westminster, 1977), 215-17 et passim. So, it becomes clear that there is a basis whereby we deem untrustworthy those portions of the narrative that are basic to an acceptance of the biblical text as offering what may be construed as valid data for the reconstruction of formative Israel, such as Josh. 9-10, Judg. 1, et alia. See, Baruch Halpern, *The Emergence of Israel in Canaan* (Chico: Scholars, 1983), 7.

world of the "Royals," particularly their faults in accord with the Deuteronomistic formulation whereby Israel sins, the Lord punishes them, the people cry out to the Lord, the Lord sends a savior/avenger, etc., etc., etc., the prophets were interested in the world of the sons and sometimes even the *daughters* of Israel, and their paradigm did not usually include a savior other than Yahweh himself, or an avenger other than Yahweh himself and/or the international enemies acting as motivated by Yahweh. Notably then, the fact that a savior figure does show up on occasion makes its/his general absence the more striking. What is perhaps more meaningful is that the prophets are reflecting on their own times without a retrospective to the Mosaic, Conquest, Settlement eras whereas D, P, and Dtr either focus wholly on that retrospective (D and P as we have them) and the pertinent portions of Dtr, or in the case of Dtr, he includes the entire gamut of their alleged history from the formative period until his own.

Precisely because we are looking at events in Primary History in light of the ideology of its redactors, it is not surprising that often the various ideologically conformed presentations within the narrative of Primary History are not supported by either artifactual data or confirming literary data.[17] This is particularly serious, for example, in matters "reported" in the ninth-century Mesha Stele, which like Primary History is not totally reliable precisely because of its ideological function, but which nevertheless cannot be construed as presenting a totally or even a mainly "fabricated" scenario. Rather, it serves as political "propaganda," which as others have noted is as much for "internal" consumption as for foreign, and therefore must be viewed as an exaggeration and possibly even a starry-eyed representation of events that in fact really did occur.[18]

---

[17] Gösta W. Ahlstöm (*The History of Ancient Palestine* [Minneapolis: Fortress, 1993], 21) notes that the two primary types of material for reconstructing Syro-Palestinian history are archaeological data and literary materials, but this can be supplemented with geographic and climate-related data. For the rejection of the biblical text precisely because it is out of accord with archaeological data, see, in particular, N. P. Lemche, *Early Israel: Anthropological and Historical Studies on the Israelite Society before the Monarchy*, 1985. For the lack of royal inscriptions, iconic portrayals of monarchs in Syro-Palestinian archaeology, see Frank S. Frick, "*Cui Bono?* – History in the Service of Political Nationalism: The Deuteronomistic History as Political Propaganda," Semeia 66 (1994): 81.

[18] And so we must pay attention to events noted in the Mesha Stele that the Moabites would have deemed dishonorable, since it would not be likely that Mesha would have fabricated events that diminish his or Moab's stature. And this must be taken into consideration even if the representation of his

From the perspective of the narrative of Primary History, this lack of external or artifactual support is notable.[19] The nature of the relationship between the two allegedly disparate groups, the Canaanites and the Israelites, is particularly telling insofar as it suggests that those represented as Israelites and others represented as non-Israelites were far less distinct from one another than the Bible suggests,[20] even at the time in which Israel was said to have come into the Land, and some suggest come into existence as well.[21] So, the theological and ideological precept whereby Israel, led first by the legendary salvation hero and covenant concluder Moses, and then by his legendary successor as both salvation hero and covenant concluder Joshua, left Egypt, concluded the Sinai and/or Horeb covenant with Yahweh,[22] whereby he became their exclusive God and they became his exclusive people, and then took the Land that had been promised them, has more questionable elements than merely that of the reality much less the location of the cosmic mountain. In fact, there are yet other data, both artifactual and literary, of which those who hold to some invasion precept, be it partial or total, or some "Yahweh alone" precept under which the Israelites united once the Sinai and/or Horeb covenant had been concluded, have to take account. In particular, we must note the

---

accomplishments in the face of difficulty would magnify his own greatness. For example, even though Primary History does not refer to Omri's subjugation of Moab, the Mesha Stele takes this as a given. See, for example, Klaas A. D. Smelik, *Writings from Ancient Israel: A Handbook of Historical and Religious Documents* (Louisville: Westminster/John Knox, 1991), 46. There are yet other inconsistencies with the text of Primary History (ibid., 42-43).

[19] As, for example, in the case of Judg. 1, which is closely related to Josh. 15-19 insofar as it lists "Canaanite" city-states in Western Palestine that had not been "conquered" by the Israelites during the so-called early Settlement era.

[20] Mark S. Smith (*The Early History of God: Yahweh and the Other Deities in Ancient Israel* [San Francisco/New York/et alia: Harper & Row, 1990], 21) states: "Some of the older Israelite poems juxtapose imagery associated with El and Baal in the Ugaritic texts and apply this juxtaposition of attributes to Yahweh." Smith (ibid., 23 et passim) believes that there was a "convergence of titles and imagery of deities to the personage of Yahweh" that was "part of a wider religious development of conflation of religious motifs in Israelite tradition." And, although I agree with Smith, I place this syncretistic tendency as a "mainstream" development in a much later time than does he: sometime between Josiah's reform and the Babylonian Exile, or possibly even during the Exile.

[21] For the reciprocal relationships, see Yohanan Aharoni, *The Land of the Bible*, 2nd ed. (Philadelphia: Westminster, 1979), 233.

[22] We must remember that these two cosmic mountains had not always been syncretized with one another.

response or lack of response to the Israelites in Palestine by foreign powers having an interest in, or hegemony or even suzerainty over, any portion of the region.[23]

Of course, we need to determine that what was found should really be deemed Israelite. And here we have a crux of the problem. Many presume that anything new that arises is Israelite, particularly in the central highland region that forms what Miller and Hayes properly call the "center stage" for the enactment and unfolding of the events that delineate the history of ancient Israel and Judah.[24] But such scholars make that assumption because it fits the biblical narrative, which posits an Israelite "Conquest" and then a "Settlement" traditionally thought to have taken place during the thirteenth century, at the end of the Late Bronze and the beginning of the Early Iron Age.

Even were we to grant the assumption that there was either an Israelite Conquest or a specifically Israelite Settlement, which I do not, we cannot then use the data so identified to signify that the biblical narrative is correct. The fact that we date artifactual data, quite properly, to the period we presume to be that of the early Settlement, does not make something characteristically Israelite, it simply means that it comes from the period in question.[25] In any case,

---

[23] So, for example, even Y. Aharoni (*The Land of the Bible*, 232), who consistently tries to harmonize archaeological data with the biblical text, has to admit that "the Israelite penetration did not make a deep impression upon Egyptian sources." Although Aharoni tries to justify this on geopolitical grounds (ibid., 232-33), his argument reflects his desire to accord some validity to at least some of the biblical reports; and at best, it lacks substance. Aharoni, however, does admit to some things particularly when artifactual evidence, or the lack thereof, are in contradistinction to the biblical narrative. Meaningfully, he acknowledges that there are no Late Bronze remains in the Negev, suggesting to him that there was no Canaanite settlement there at the time the alleged conquest took place (Y. Aharoni, *The Land of the Bible*, 216). On the other hand, where there is some destruction, as in Hazor, the pottery which is similar to that attributed to settlements in the Upper Galilee is used by Aharoni, as well as others, to determine that this stratum was Israelite (Y. Aharoni, *The Land of the Bible*, 226-27). When faced with evidence that is clearly contrary to the biblical narrative, Aharoni, like many others, equivocates, as T. L. Thompson (*Early History of the Israelite People*) make abundantly clear.

[24] J. M. Miller and J. H. Hayes, *A History of Ancient Israel and Judah*, 30.

[25] So, J. M. Miller and J. H. Hayes (*A History of Ancient Israel and Judah*, 72) suggest that there is "nothing intrinsically 'Israelite' about either of the two items that have been given most serious consideration as being distinctively Israelite...the so-called 'collared-rim jars' and 'four-room houses.'" Archaeological data does not secure any purely Yahwistic practice. And, it does not even secure a separate material culture for what many

this type of correlation is itself circular reasoning, as others have noted.[26] Malamat's and Halpern's observation, then, that the biblical text blends together events of diverse and/or extended periods,[27] is extremely important. It must be used to invalidate the circular reasoning on which the artifactual data are said to support the text, despite the fact that those same artifacts were identified in light of and in accordance with the identifier's preconceptions, which themselves emanate from the narrative in the Bible. But, even this coalescing and blending of events cannot be taken for granted unless we can presume that what is reported has any relationship to any type of historical reality and is not totally an ideological configuration of a utopian past.[28]

There is no defect of method inherent in the fact that neither Berger's dynamic, whereby religion is formulated by society but then reflects back and alters that very society, nor the social-scientific methodology in general allows us to supply a firm date for this emergence. None of the broad spectrum of analytic tools we use has yet been of substantial help in this particular aspect of the endeavor.

---

archaeologists construe to be Israelite rather than Canaanite villages or cities. As many scholars have observed, the fact that plastered, whitewashed cisterns became more widespread during the Early Iron Age does not mean that this was an Israelite innovation, particularly since they are not a new phenomenon. So, unless they represent a rediscovery of what was used in the Early Bronze Age, their presence merely indicates that the technological skills were not so great in some areas as in others, or that there is some alteration in the culture using it, or that we have not yet found other representative artifacts to establish some continuity. For various artifactual data treated as characteristically Israelite, and therefore signifying a break with contemporary culture, having existed prior to the Early Iron Age, some commencing with the Early Bronze Age and others somewhat later, see G. W. Ahlström, *The History of Ancient Palestine*, 337-42, 351, et passim. Since as Aharoni (*The Land of the Bible*, 107) notes, this development "permitted the establishment of settlements independent of the springs" and, consequently "we find many small villages springing up in regions hitherto unoccupied," there is no reason (pace Aharoni!) to attribute those new settlements to some new invaders, such as the biblically construed Israelites. T. L. Thompson's (*Early History of the Israelite People*) precept that the settlers were "pioneers" is an equally if not more appropriate presumption.

[26] See, in particular, T. L. Thompson, *Early History of the Israelite People.*
[27] B. Halpern, *The Emergence of Israel in Canaan*, 7. For the limitation of sources and the "problem of reliability" vis-à-vis this and yet other constraints, see G. W. Ahlström, *The History of Ancient Palestine*, 26-27.
[28] I cannot agree with B. Halpern (*The Emergence of Israel in Canaan*, 7) that the events presented are "theological (or national-ideological) reformulations of originally disparate events" because there is no basis for predicating the historicity of the events in the first place.

What is significant, however, is that Berger's dynamic in conjunction with this particular type of methodology has led us to reframe our questions, amongst other things, about the process whereby Israel came into being. And it has brought about the reformulation of Israel's history by rejecting the superimposition of the commonly held religious paradigm, whereby there was an Exodus from Egypt in which the *sons* of Israel, the Masoretic Text does not say children of Israel, entered the Land together with their wives, children, etc., which as any feminist would tell you is itself a chauvinistically derived, domination- and control-oriented theo-political statement.

So, the new modeling, if nothing else, has allowed us to cease to take the biblical account as a historical report. But, at the same time, it has prevented us from totally rejecting as ill-founded what few valid data, or perhaps even hints of valid data, are contained within that account; and, it has even allowed us to deconstruct the text, particularly that of DtrH (the Deuteronomistic History [Deuteronomy-2 Kings]), to show the hypertexting that was used so as to present a utopian paradigm for Israelite History. Consequently, it has made secure the premise that what was once construed as historical may now be viewed as some type of pious fiction with an eschatological bent,[29] or it may at least be viewed as ideological, utopian vision that is also reflective of a literary construct.[30] This methodology has also led us to look at certain functions paradigmatically even when the paradigms only loosely fit and cannot be said to be congruent. And, most importantly, it has made us realize that politics do play a major role in the formative period of Israel – but that formative period is not the same as what is represented in the narrative of Primary History. Rather, it is represented in the "creation" of Primary History by its later redactors, particularly the Deuteronomist, the Deuteronomistic

---

[29] As Bernard Batto has so skillfully shown when he delineated the crossing of the Sea of Reeds or the Sea of Death as forthrightly eschatological, in B. F. Batto, "The Reed Sea: *Requiescat in Pace*," JBL 102 (1983), 27-35. See also *Mythmaking in the Biblical Tradition: Slaying the Dragon* (Louisville: Westminster/John Knox, 1992), 102-52 et passim.

[30] As P. R. Davies, amongst many others, has shown in his pursuit of the valid historical origin of "ancient Israel." See P. R. Davies, *In Search of 'Ancient Israel,'* passim. See especially p. 52, for an explicit statement of the people of Palestine, who must be "regarded as the historical *counterpart* to biblical 'Israel,'" as attested to by archeological data although we do not have much information about them. And likewise for the biblically defined Israel as a "literary concept about whom we know everything (since everything that pertains to them falls inside the Bible!)." There is an enormous and continuously growing body of literature dealing with this.

Historian, and the Priestly Redactor, who themselves may reflect the pressure toward Yahwism emanating from the eighth-century prophets and their successors.

5

Reading Archaeological and Literary Evidence: A Response to Sara Mandell

James F. Strange
University of South Florida

I wish to thank my honored colleague Dr. Sara Mandell for a strikingly direct and clear presentation of her ideas about the formation of the ancient constructs "Israel" and the modern scholarly constructs "history and religion of Israel." Her first point is one we can all probably agree with, namely, that we cannot understand how Israel came to being without understanding the inseparable connection between religion, the social order, and the political order at the time of Israel's inception. Although modern scholars often emphasize one of these, namely the social, the political, and the religious elements, in their descriptions of biblical Israel, it now more a less a commonplace for scholarship to take note of their inseparable character.

Her second point, that the time of Israel's inception does not coincide with its description in the biblical narrative, is more problematic, but it lies at the heart of disputes about the historicity of the biblical narrative which have characterized current scholarship. Earlier in this century we have seen the arguments of Albrecht Alt,[1] Martin Noth,[2] and others that the biblical narratives are in the main theological fictions interlarded with legend and myth. On the other hand we have seen the arguments

---

[1] Alt and Albrecht, "The Settlement of the Israelites in Palestine," in *Essays on Old Testament History and Religion* (Garden City: Doubleday, 1968).
[2] Martin Noth, *A History of Pentateuchal Traditions* (Englewood Cliffs: Prentice Hall, 1972).

of John Bright[3] and G. Ernest Wright[4] and others that the Bible is "salvation history," a theological interpretation of history, not simply fictive events. Interestingly enough the proponents of "salvation history" did not argue for the historicity of all the political and other events enshrined in the biblical narrative.

Of course if we accept legend and pious fiction, even "utopian vision," as historical data, then we will be confused in our attempt to deal with Israelite history, and therefore with the relationship between religion and politics. To be sure this requires us to have these literary categories at ready before our critical eyes as an appropriate filter for sifting out the legendary chaff from the kernels of history. If we sift out all events as fictive which serve the interests of the theological, political, and even ideological ideas of the text, then certainly we have little choice but to identify as fictive Moses, the Conquest, and the Settlement, as by definition these form the framework of Israel's confession or confessions of God's dealings with Israel.

In other words, Americans, for example, much like the citizens of any other country, ancient or modern, frame their "confessions" with idealized history. We believe in the Bill of Rights because of the Constitutional Convention and because of those wonderful essays in the Federalist. We believe in the thirteenth amendment to the Constitution because of the Civil War and its aftermath. We discarded (non credamus) the ideals of Prohibition because of certain unforeseen and perhaps untoward events that marked those heady days in national politics in the past.

The idea of a "utopian vision" is very interesting, and I might enjoy following it, except that I need to move to an area more within my competence. I am referring to the relationship of literary evidence to archaeological evidence.

In order to move to that relationship I will mention another of Dr. Mandell's points, namely, that in the case of Israel particularly, we cannot distinguish religion from politics and politics from the exercise of power. Indeed, I would say that this is so not only for Israel, but for any political entity past or modern. The exercise of power, and the sanctioning of that exercise, is the unique content of politics in human life. After all, it is still true that the state is the only entity in our lives which legally seizes our property and takes our lives. That is power.

I recapitulate Professor Mandell's argument for the midsection of the paper as follows: Biblical events are to be classified within their own socio-theo-political constructs. The operative constructs that Dr. Mandell

---

[3] John Bright, *A History of Israel* (Philadelphia: Westminster, 1981).
[4] George Ernest Wright, *Biblical Archaeology* (Philadelphia: Westminster, 1962).

sees are presented first in Primary History, namely, in Genesis-2 Kings. Second, this construct of history, religion, and society is to be distinguished from the revisionist history and society of the "writing prophets," which was "unacceptable in their own time except among their own circles" (sic). On the other hand, and third, the biblical history and society of some of the later writing prophets, namely Ezekiel, Jeremiah, and Second and possibly Third Isaiah, held to the revisionist ideology that characterized the redactors of Primary History from the Deuteronomist's time forward.

I will not recapitulate her argument about traditional and recent biblical scholarship, as I wish to remain with her presentation of Israel's self-understanding. She notes that Israel's religion and society, within the biblical narrative, is only presented as a static system in which neither forms the other. This forms an curious exception to Peter Berger's point that religion forms society, and society in turn forms religion.[5] In other words, Israel's self-understanding, at least in the several forms in which we have it in the Bible, if she is right, does not cohere with our modern understanding of what happens between society and religion. Furthermore, the static system is the work of the seventh century B.C.E., namely, that of D, P, and Dtr, all of whom presented (again) a curiously static construct of religion and society under Moses. Likewise Dtr presented a static portrait of the Conquest and Settlement, that is, a portrait of religion and society which do not form one another back and forth, but which stand in more or less unchanging relationship. This portrait is that of Dtr's own times, not of the time of the legendary Conquest and Settlement.

Now, it seems to me that a religio-political conclusion follows which remains unstated in Dr. Mandell's paper. I will be so bold as to state it.

In fact, if it is true that religion and society are presented by the biblical authors, particularly in the Primary History, as not forming one another, then we must ask why such an arresting exception to the general rule pertains. To follow the anthropologist Roy Rappaport, we expect to find in a holy text holy utterances which regulate or sanction, that is, which *sanctify* the power structures of the society, specifically which *sanctify* the power position of certain elites.[6] In other words we expect to find utterances of sages, seers, and prophets which serve to endorse and support theologically the special position of the power elites of ancient Israel or which conversely withhold endorsement and

---

[5]Peter L. Berger, *The Sacred Canopy: Elements of a Sociology of Religion* (New York: Anchor Books, 1990-67).

[6] Ray A. Rappaport, "Ritual, Sanctity, and Cybernetics," *American Anthropologist* 73 (1971): 59-76.

support, that is, which withhold sanction, of other power elites of ancient Israel. But that is precisely what we find, namely, a set of utterances (stories, laws, anecdotes, aphorisms, etc.) which make plain that the real power elite is precisely the authorship of each document. The authors or final redactors, or the authorship of the Primary History, is composing, redacting, or narrating the Primary History precisely in the sense of those who are establishing, endorsing, and in general sanctioning (sanctifying) proper power elites in Israel, that is, themselves. If this is so, then we have in the biblical narratives examples of religious, political, and social reasoning which establish, that is, sanction, the power elites which are speaking.

This is an interesting solution to the problem of where religion and politics are to be found in the Primary History. I would say, however, that the attribution of the sanctioning power to the authorship of a document is true of any document. But, since Dr. Mandell did not come to this conclusion explicitly, it seems inappropriate to say more.

Now I would like to turn to another of Dr. Mandell's points. Dr. Mandell insists that the various ideological presentations of the narrative of Primary History, namely of Moses – and the Exodus – are not supported by either positive artifactual data or confirming literary data. This point suggests that the proper approach to artifactual and external literary data, such as excavation data or the Moabite Stone, for instance, or the recent "House of David" inscription from Tell Dan,[7] is that of "support." That is, one establishes the plausibility of one's understanding or theory of the biblical data by appealing to external literature and internal excavation data, namely, excavation data from the realm of Israel's Conquest and Settlement according to Joshua and Judges. I take this to mean that one tests a hypothesis of Israel's religion and history formed from the Bible precisely against external literary data (inscriptions) and again precisely against internal excavation data. If I have understood her point properly, then I agree that any interpretative hypothesis must be testable, preferably against new data.

Yet, if I follow her argument correctly, she agrees with certain recent historical scholarship that it is impossible to prove that any given archaeological data is exclusively Israelite and not Canaanite. So, for example, Miller and Hayes have claimed that neither collared-rim jars nor four-room houses are inescapably Israelite.[8] This may be so, but it is not the first time we have had to appeal to evidence which is not without

---

[7] Avraham Biran and Joseph Naveh, "An Aramaic Stele Fragment from Tel Dan," *Israel Exploration Journal* 43 (1993): 81-98.
[8] J. Maxwell Miller and John Hayes *A History of Ancient Israel and Judah* (Philadelphia: Westminster, 1986), 72.

ambiguity in order to engage in historiography. More to the point, must we abandon archaeological data as a resource to test our historical hypotheses? I think the only answer is no.

I beg your indulgence while I set the archaeological and cultural scene.[9] If we had no biblical narrative, we would still know that there was a major dislocation of peoples in the eastern Mediterranean at the end of what we call the Late Bronze Age, which corresponds to the beginning of the Early Iron Age, or the beginning of the twelfth century B.C.E. The Late Bronze walled cities were, in many cases, violently destroyed, but those who destroyed them did not always live in the emptied city immediately. When they did, they built smaller houses in a poorer architectural tradition. In general the rebuilt settlements were on a plan that ignored the previous plan, orientation, and even size of settlement. The new settlements were generally smaller. The new people had new pottery, weapons, jewelry, and tools. In the pottery, for instance, although they prepared their clay in a ceramic technology virtually identical to the Late Bronze ceramic traditions, they manufactured different forms of vessels from those that we know and admire in the Late Bronze repertoire. Furthermore these new settlers planned their settlements differently from the Late Bronze peoples, they used different installations, such as grain silos, and they planned their houses differently.

But it is not the case that new people lived only in old, destroyed settlements. New settlements on virgin soil sprang up in the area between Hebron and Shechem, for example. The density of settlement went up by a factor of five. Furthermore a wave a new settlers swept over the central hill country, the hills of Ephraim, from northeast to southwest, leaving scores of small, unfortified settlements of less than five acres.[10] Lawrence Stager has called this process the opposite of urbanization, that is, ruralization.[11]

In terms of reconstructing the power landscape of the period, we notice that there are no large city-states from Hebron to Shechem in this Early Iron Age period. That is, there are no recognizable political units

---

[9]I owe much of this to Amihai Mazar, "The Israelite Settlement in Canaan in the Light of Archaeological Excavations," in *Biblical Archaeology Today: Proceedings of the International Congress on Biblical Archaeology, Jerusalem, April, 1984* (Jerusalem: Israel Exploration Society, The Israel Academy of Sciences and Humanities in cooperation with the American Schools of Oriental Research, 1985), 61-71; see also idem, *Archaeology of the Land of the Bible* (New York: Doubleday, 1990).

[10] Moshe Kochavi, "The Israelite Settlement in Canaan in the Light of Archaeological Surveys," in *Biblical Archaeology Today* (Jerusalem: Israel Exploration Society et al., 1985), 54-60.

[11]*Biblical Archaeology Today* (Jerusalem: Israel Exploration Society, 1985), 83-87.

to administrate this large territory so densely settled with farming villages. That in itself is an interesting observation, for it implies that this landscape was not united by city-state administration, as appears to have been the case before the end of the Late Bronze Age, particularly during the Amarna Age of the 14th century B.C.E.

To return to our description: In some cases the newcomers built their villages away from traditional sources of water. The newcomers cut cisterns into the bedrock beneath the houses to store water after the rainy season. Joseph Callaway noticed that often the cisterns were cut into the bedrock before the houses were built.[12] This suggests that their inhabitants were carefully planning and building the villages according to a village-planning technology which they brought with them. The new people also terraced the hillsides for their agriculture, which meant that they could exploit steep land heretofore not tillable to grow their food resources. The new people also subsisted on small animal husbandry, namely, the raising of sheep and goats. It is noticeable, even surprising, that these new peoples, with the exception of those on the Mediterranean coast, seem to have brought no art of any kind, unless it appeared on perishable media such as bark and cloth.

Let me give you two examples. One is from Tell el-Qadi, which we identify with ancient Dan. In this case the great, walled city was destroyed in a general conflagration by military action. That is, invaders breached the city wall, then set fires in every room of almost every house after they looted the rooms. Some lengthy time after the destruction, the new people rebuilt what they could on new plans. It is not clear that they reused and repaired the city wall nor that they rebuilt the gate. They brought with them the new collared-rim jars, which otherwise hardly occur in the Galilee. The excavator, Avraham Biran, does not hesitate to identify this conquest with the events of Judg. 18.

On the other hand, in the case of Tell el-Far'ah (N), the new visitors seem to have used architectural and other material traditions traceable to Syria. For example, the new pillared houses at Tell el-Far'ah (N) seem to be most similar, according to recent scholarship, to those found at Ugarit on the Mediterranean shores of Syria. These and other examples from the new material culture of the Iron Age at this site tend to suggest that at least these new comers were from Syria, or at least had their last long acculturation in Syria.

In the course of ordinary archaeological interpretation we would say that a new factor has entered the picture, namely, a new people or peoples. It is not unambiguously clear from the archaeological evidence that there is only one set of new people, but the new peoples sometimes

---

[12]*Biblical Archaeology Today* (Jerusalem: Israel Exploration Society, 1985), 72-78.

seem to come from the south, but a few of them seem to come from Syria. Those on the coast are less unambiguously traceable. Either they have just come from some place near Mycenean Greek cities or they are themselves Mycenean Greeks, given their pottery and art forms.

Where do we look for evidence of the origins of these peoples? First, we look for areas outside the boundaries of Canaan where such technologies were available. That is, where can we find people with tools for cutting house pillars, the tradition of pillared houses with enclosures inside the houses for keeping small animals, who know cistern technology, and who understand hillside, agricultural terracing?

Moshe Kochavi[13] and J. Balensi[14] have suggested that we should look to the north and northeast for the origins of these newcomers. Joe Callaway has suggested that we look to the coastal plans and the Shephelah of Canaan, below the hill country, for their root. Amihai Mazar has suggested that these are seminomads, who had lived at the edges of settled, Late Bronze culture for a century and gradually adopted the LB material culture. Norman Gottwald has suggested that we should look no further than the plains and hills of ancient Canaan itself.[15]

Now that we have a descriptive picture from the archaeological remains, what do we do as historians, that is, how do we engage in historiography? How do we place these events that I have described above in the general history of the ancient Near East?

This is no idle question, for it asks how one engages in the hermeneutics of material culture, that is, archaeological remains. The answer is that normally one looks around in the ancient literature of the period to see if that helps. The Bible is one such source. Therefore it seems to me that one MUST use the method of correlation with known literary sources in order to shed light on who these people might be. This method is called "historical archeology" in this country or even "literary archeology" in other circles, but it is simply a truism that literary sources are in fact real sources that aid in interpreting archeological remains.

Here I must make an important point that Tom Thompson and others have not understood.[16] If one works from archaeological remains to literary sources and back again in constructing a narrative of what

---

[13]See footnote 10 above.

[14]*Biblical Archaeology Today* (Jerusalem: Israel Exploration Society, 1985), 94.

[15]Norman K. Gottwald, "The Israelite Settlement as a Social Revolutionary Movement," in *Biblical Archaeology Today* (Jerusalem: Israel Exploration Society, 1985), 34-46; idem, *The Tribes of Yahweh: A Sociology of the Religion of Liberated Israel, 1250-1050 B.C.E.* (Maryknoll: Orbis, 1979).

[16] Thomas L. Thompson, *The Settlement of Palestine in the Bronze Age* (Wiesbaden: Reichert, 1979).

happened, the reasoning is not necessarily circular.   When R. G. Collingwood wrote the history of the Roman period in Britain, he relied on archaeological reports as much as he did the classical texts. He also took a close look at the evidence of numismatics and water resources, to name two other classes of evidence.[17] No one accused him of circular reasoning when he identified Celtic village remains with destruction layers and Roman arrowheads in the destruction with sites mentioned in certain Latin texts. It is a method of correlation, but it is not necessarily circular. Circular reasoning would consist of at least three steps: First, identify a major battle and the sacking of a Celtic village from archeological remains. Second, select from the Latin narrative a battle at a specific site and identify it with the remains. Third, insist that the archaeology now confirms the text. (Of course one could logically take the other tack and insist that the text now confirms the archaeology.) But, in spite of what some scholars may have said in the past, we are not in the confirming business, only in the business of constructing the most reasonable, elegant, and coherent historical narrative that appears to account for all the evidence.

I would like to approach this point yet another way. If one develops a theory of the history of Israel which disallows any historicity to the Conquest as reported in Joshua and Judges, then ipso facto one must ignore Joshua and Judges in any account of what happened at the end of the Bronze Age. In the case of disallowance we may suggest that the dislocations in ancient Canaan at the end of the Late Bronze Age were simply part and parcel of the same dislocations in Greece, Turkey, Syria, Mesopotamia, and Egypt. If so, then do we apply the same hermeneutics of suspicion which we apply to the Bible to Mesopotamian and Egyptian literature and disallow the historicity of the Egyptian texts, for example? After all, it is tempting to explain that Thutmosis III made no incursion at all into ancient, Late Bronze Canaan, as his report of such an incursion served his own propaganda purposes at home against pretenders to the throne.

It is fascinating to realize that the Greeks "remember" that the Dorians came into Achaea at the beginning of the Heroic Age. Are we to use this as a historical datum, or are we forced to deny the historicity of the text on the grounds that it serves to support the political ambitions of the Achaeans? My point is that we cannot escape the problem of correlation of inferred archaeological events with literary events or the problem of the historicity of texts by moving elsewhere in the Late Bronze and Iron IA Near East. Some kind of method of correlation is inevitable, and it need not be circular reasoning, contra Thompson et al.

---

[17]*Roman Britain,* rev. ed., (Oxford: Clarendon Press, 1970).

I now reserve space for one final comment on the following remarks made by Dr. Mandell:

> Malamat's and Halpern's observation, then, that the biblical text blends together events of diverse and/or extended periods is extremely important. It must be used to invalidate the circular reasoning on which the artifactual data are said to support the text, despite the fact that those same artifacts were identified in light of and in accordance with the identifier's preconceptions, which themselves emanate from the narrative in the Bible. But, even this coalescing and blending of events cannot be taken for granted unless we can presume that what is reported has any relationship to any type of historical reality and is not totally an ideological configuration of a utopian past.

I take this to mean that the heterogeneity of the biblical text or perhaps its mixed character would seem to undercut the attempt to identify any historical period as the period of the text. If the text is a mixture of events drawn from various periods or from extended periods, then the attempt to place the text within a historical or archaeological context is doomed from the start.

On the other hand, the assertion that the text is mixed suggests that the critic has at hand a clear typology, century by century, or perhaps "period by period" whatever that might mean, of biblical history. But where did this typology come from? From linguistic analysis? D. N. Freedman has observed that the language of the Bible reveals a northern and a southern dialect. Freedman has observed further that the southern or Judah-ite dialect dominates the Bible. Finally Freedman has said that the Judah-ite dialect and Yahwism come from the same place, the south, without saying where that is, except that it is not within Canaan.[18] What is missing from these interesting observations is anything that would give us a linguistic clue to unravel the putative mixed character of the texts a la Malamat and Halpern. If indeed these texts are mixed, as they say, then we need a literary and historical theory to account for that, since they would stand out against other such texts from Egypt and Mesopotamia, which, in the main, seem to keep periods separate. But, if we can detect that the text is mixed, that suggests that we know the history of Israel from other sources. What are these sources?

Whatever the case, we do have a fixed terminus about 1207 B.C.E., according to the best Egyptian chronologies. I refer first to the victory stele of Merenptah, Pharaoh of Egypt. Furthermore in the battle reliefs of Merenptah, formerly attributed to Ramses II, the Israelites wear the same clothing and hairstyles and beards as Canaanites. In this case we are

---

[18]*Biblical Archaeology Today* (Jerusalem: Israel Exploration Society, 1985), 95.

seeing Egyptian records of a revolution in Canaan, and it is a revolution against Egypt by Canaanites and Israelites.[19]

This, too, is evidence that must be factored into our historiography of ancient Israel alongside the excavation evidence and that of the Bible, if we can grant any portion of it historicity, and thereby deduce anything about religion and politics in ancient Israel.

---

[19]F. Yurco, "Merenptah's Palestinian Campaign," *Society for the Study of Egyptian Antiquities Journal* 8 (1978): 70.

Part II

JUDAISM

6

Why and How Religion Speaks through Politics: The Case of Classical Judaism

Jacob Neusner
University of South Florida

A religious system sets forth a theory of the social order, encompassing three main components: a worldview, a way of life, and an account of the character of the social entity that realizes the way of life and explains that way of life through the specified worldview. That religious statement of the social order then presents a theory of how the social group embodies an account of cosmic reality and through its everyday affairs embodies that reality. In theory, religious systems may well utilize every available medium to make their statement, utilizing music and art, theology and myth, gesture, dance and song, rules of clothing, food, sexual relationships, modes of building buildings and organizing cities, rationalizing time and space, family nurture, economic action – every mode and possibility of human action and express will serve. Through all things, systems will say the same thing. But as a matter of fact, religious systems will lay stress on some few media, even while exploiting the expressive potentialities of them all. To state matters in a crude but current way, Judaism is hung up about food, Catholicism about sex, so that piety in the one religion comes to expression at the dining table, and the other, at what happens, or does not happen, in bed.

When religious-system framers seek appropriate media for the expression of the system they propose to put forth, politics and the framing of public policy present themselves as candidates – but no more than that. For some religious systems find urgent the expression of their systemic statement through political media – political symbols, political institutions, the formation of public policy – and others do not. Or, at a given period, for particular circumstances, politics will appear irrelevant, while at another period, under different conditions, political action will take on critical importance and central expressive potentiality. Christianity for its first three centuries framed no vision of the political order, but in the fourth century confronted a new reality and formulated a theory of politics that made space for both church and state, with the Christian theory of the social order fully exposed through a large account of the interplay of religious and political institutions and the tasks of each. One result familiar to all of us is the profound reflection of Augustine on the city of God, in which the political metaphor served to convey a deeply supernatural theory of the social order.

Now, as a matter of fact, we in the West have long ago formulated a theory of the social order that distinguishes religion from politics, church or synagogue or mosque from institutions of state. We define politics in an acutely secular way as the theory of the legitimate exercise of violence, and reserve for the state the power of physical force, assigning to religion the moral force of persuasion. This is expressed in a clear way by Brian Mitchell, when he says:

> In the West, the rightful employment of coercion is generally reserved for political powers, the civil and military authorities at their various levels. Persuasion, on the other hand, is generally left to the social powers, consisting of the many voluntary associations that influence individual behavior (church, family, community, etc.). Primitive tribes...recognize no distinction between the social and the political. The tribe functions as an extended family, organized in a strictly hierarchical fashion....Everyone has his place in the pyramid, and every social subgroup is a subordinate part of the whole. Some societies have maintained a unified, hierarchical, and essentially tribal structure....Most Western nations are still political societies, with a political system easily distinguishable from the rest of society, and a political hierarchy representing just one way in which the society is organized.[1]

Mitchell underscores that in the West, political power is limited, and the social powers stand on their own: "Christianity...confirmed the distinction between political rule and social life, providing

---

[1] Brian Mitchell, "The Distinction of Powers: How Church and State Divide Us," *Religion and Public Life* 29 (1995) 2.

Western civilization with both a cosmological basis for the distinction and a powerful new social order to counterbalance the political order." One may speculate that the first three centuries of Christian history, with the Church confronting a hostile state, introduced the distinction between the Church as an autonomous social entity and the empire: "It claimed for itself the right to function free of government interference and made itself responsible for many matters of public welfare and moral, at the same time leaving the use of coercion to civil authorities alone." The theory of the two masters conveys that distinction. The systemic message of earliest Christianity appropriated a politics of division, perhaps turning necessity into the occasion for a restatement of the systemic perspective on the coming of God's kingdom under Christ.

Now it is easy for us to miss the extreme and radical character of that theory of distinction between church and state, religion and politics, for that distinction is not only familiar in the politics of our own country but also a given of the Christian civilization that defines Western civilization. As a result, we in this country find exceedingly difficult the task of understanding a different utilization of politics from the Christian and Western, secular one, with its critical distinctions, as Mitchell has expressed them in most current form. And that difficulty persists even though the foundation document of Christianity, the Old Testament, portrays politics as integral to the religious structure of ancient Israel, with the prophet, Moses, portrayed also as the king of Israel, lawgiver and head of state. The pentateuchal books are so set forth as to formulate the systemic statements that they wish to make through an acutely political account of the social order. Moses rules as God's prophet but also as God's political agent, and Israel takes shape as God's people: a kingdom of priests and a holy people. When by contrast, the Gospel of John portrays Jesus as king and prophet, or the Gospel of Matthew sets Jesus on the mountain forth as Moses at Sinai, the clear distinction between king and prophet, Caesar and Christ, forms the premise of all discourse.

The upshot of the character of Western Christian and secular politics, with its critical distinction between and among power in various modes, political from prophetic, for instance, is simple: we find exceedingly difficult the task of making sense of a politics that serves for systemic purposes in religious systems. We have no theory that encompasses a politics embedded in the religious theory of the social order, shaped by that theory, given legitimacy and purpose through that theory. Hence we cannot hear the religious messages that politics, when embedded in an encompassing, religious theory of the social order, wishes to set forth.   And we miss the deep congruences between those messages when stated politically and the same, identical messages when stated gastronomically or sexually, to revert to the Judaic and Catholic matters to which I alluded earlier. We not only are unable to make sense of those enormous portions of the world in which politics and religion cohere and deliver a single, uniform and cogent statement, but we also cannot formulate in our own context a theory that will explain to us the political aspirations of religious societies, with the result that important components of the political order in this country, on both right and left (the Christian Coalition, the National Council of Churches, for example) come to the public square with pronouncements on public policy that invoke theological principles and express them.   Consequently, religious groups appear to speak a kind of gibberish, intelligible only to themselves, when in fact they mean to make a statement not only to, but about, the social order that encompasses us all. They address the definition of what it means to be a human being, what God wants of us, how we are to relate to one another and assume public responsibilities – deeply religious categories of thought. But the rest of us hear, and fear, yet another pressure group, but an illegitimate one.

If, as I maintain, we cannot understand religious discourse within the political structures of society, it is because we have no model, deriving from Western Christian and secular life, of how political discourse may convey that same religious systemic statement that theological or mythical or liturgical discourse conveys. We do not grasp that what religions may say about the political order, they also say about every other dimension of human existence, and we have no useful examples of how such a global discourse takes place. My contribution to the solution to the problem at hand – one of trying to understand a kind of thinking about politics that proves alien at its deepest premises to the one that predominates among us – is then to show how in a particular case the theory of politics will itself form a statement of a religious theory of the social order, not to be distinguished from all other statements of that same theory of the social order, in whatever media they are made, under whatever circumstances they reach concrete expression and produce practical consequences.

I speak in particular of the politics of a particular Judaism, the one set forth in the Mishnah, a second-century A.D. law code that expresses a coherent philosophical program. Like the Pentateuchal Judaism, this was a Judaic system that found it necessary to utilize matters of politics and public policy in the full formulation of its systemic message.[2]

Politics within the Judaic Myth

The principal structural components of this Judaism's politics are easily defined. Just as a systemic myth expresses the teleology of a worldview, telling people why things are the way they are, a political myth expresses that element of a social entity's worldview that instructs people why coercive power is legitimate in forcing people to do what they are supposed to do. It presents the narrative equivalent of legitimate violence, because it means through the force of its teleological apologia to coerce conformity with the social order and its norms. As we shall see, the political institutions envisaged by a politics convey details of the way of life of the same entity that, in theory at least, exercises the coercive power to secure compliance with the rules. Finally, the management of politics delineates, within the social entity's ongoing affairs, how the institutions secure suitable and capable staff to carry out their public tasks. Politics defines the concrete and material component of the conception of a social system, and the theory of politics, defining both how things should be and also how they should be done, forms the critical element in a religious system.

The task undertaken by the political myth of Judaism is not only to make power specific and particular to cases. It is especially a labor of differentiation of power, indicating what agency or person has the power to precipitate the working of politics as legitimate violence at all.[3] When, therefore, we understand the differentiating force of myth that imparts to politics its activity and dynamism, we shall grasp what everywhere animates the structures of the politics and propels the system. In the case of the politics of Judaism, we shall work our way downward, into the depths of the system, toward a myth of taxonomy of power. Appealing to a myth of taxonomy, the system accomplishes its tasks by explaining why this, not that, by telling as its foundation story a myth of classification for the application of legitimate violence. The myth appeals in the end to

---

[2] What follows reviews some of my findings in *Rabbinic Political Theory: Religion and Politics in the Mishnah* (Chicago: University of Chicago Press, 1991).

[3] A fundamental premise of my mode of systemic analysis is that where a system differentiates, there it lays its heaviest emphasis and stress. That is how we may identify what particular questions elicit urgent concern, and what other questions are treated as null.

the critical bases for the taxonomy, among institutions, of a generalized power to coerce. Let me make these somewhat abstract remarks more concrete.

Specifically, we analyze the mythic foundations of sanctions. And when we move from sanctions to the myth expressed and implicit in the application and legitimation of those sanctions, we see a complex but cogent politics sustained by a simple myth. This somewhat protracted survey of sanctions and their implications had best commence with a clear statement of what we shall now uncover.

The encompassing framework of rules, institutions, and sanctions is explained and validated by appeal to the myth of God's shared rule. That dominion, exercised by God and his surrogates on earth, is focused partly in the royal palace, partly in the Temple, and partly in the court. For us, the issue here is the differentiation of power, which is to say, which part falls where and why? Helpfully, the political myth of Judaism explains who exercises legitimate violence and under what conditions, and furthermore specifies the source for differentiation. The myth consequently serves a particular purpose – which is to answer that particular question. Indeed, the Judaic political myth comes to expression in its details of differentiation, which permit us to identify, and of course to answer, the generative question of politics.

Moving from the application of power to the explanation thereof, we find that the system focuses upon finding answers to the question of who imposes which sanction, and why. And those answers contain the myth, nowhere expressed, everywhere in full operation. So we begin with cases and end with cases, only in the midstages of analysis uncovering the narrative premises for our diverse cases that, when seen together, form the myth of politics in the initial structure of post-Temple Judaism. Through the examination of sanctions, we identify the foci of power. At that point we ask how power is differentiated.

In spelling out what the reader may now find somewhat enigmatic, I have skipped many stages in the argument and the examination of the evidence. So let us begin from the very beginning. How, exactly, do I propose to identify the political myth of Judaism? And precisely what data are supposed to attest to that myth?

Institutions of political persuasion and coercion dominate not only through physical but also through mental force, through psychological coercion or appeal to goodwill. So my inquiry's premise is not far to seek. I take as a given that a political myth animates the structure of a politics. But the authorship of the Mishnah has chosen other media for thought and expression than narrative and teleological ones. It is a philosophical, not a historical (fictive) account; it is conveyed through masses of detailed rules about small things. While the Mishnah through its cases amply informs us on the institutions of politics, the mythic framework within which persuasion and inner compliance are supposed to bring about submission to legitimate power scarcely emerges, remaining only implicit throughout.[4] But it is readily discerned when we ask the right questions. If we were to bring to the authorship of the Mishnah such questions as who tells whom what to do? they would point to the politics' imaginary king and its equally fictive high priest, with associated authorities. Here, they would tell us, are the institutions of politics – represented in personal rather than abstract form, to be sure. But if we were to say to them, tell us the story (in our language: the myth) that explains on what basis you persuade people to conform, they would find considerable difficulty in bringing to the fore the explicit mythic statements made by their writing.

How then are we to identify, on the basis of what the Mishnah does tell us, the generative myths to which the system is supposed to appeal? The answer derives from the definition of politics that governs this entire study. A myth, we recall, explains the exercise of legitimate power. Now, we know, power comes to brutal expression when the state kills or maims someone or deprives a person of property through the imposition of legal sanctions for crime or sin.[5] In the absence of a myth of power, we therefore begin with power itself. We shall work our way back from the facts of power to the intimations, within the record of legitimately violent sanctions, of the intellectual and even mythic sources of legitimation for the exercise and use of that legitimate violence. For it is at the point of imposing sanctions, of killing, injuring, denying property, excluding from society, that power operates in its naked form. Then how these legitimate exercises of violence are validated will set before us such

---

[4] Given the authority of Scripture and the character of the Pentateuch as a design of a holy state, on holy land, made up of holy people, living a holy life, we should not be surprised by silence, on the surface at least, about the reason why. People everywhere acknowledge and confess God's rule and the politics of the Torah, in its written form as the Pentateuch, claiming legitimacy attained through conformity to the law and politics. But we cannot take for granted that Scripture has supplied a myth.

[5] I do not distinguish crime from sin, since I do not think the system does. At the same time our own world does make such a distinction, and it would be confusing not to preserve it. That accounts for the usage throughout.

concrete evidence of the myth. And, so far as there is such evidence, that will identify the political myth of Judaism.[6]

Since the analysis of sources will prove somewhat abstruse, let me signal in advance the main line of argument. Analyzing myth by explaining sanctions draws our attention to the modes of legitimate violence that the system identifies. There we find four types of sanctions, each deriving from a distinct institution of political power, each bearing its own mythic explanation. The first comprises what God and the heavenly court can do to people. The second comprises what the earthly court can do to people. That type of sanction embodies the legitimate application of the worldly and physical kinds of violence of which political theory ordinarily speaks. The third comprises what the cult can do to the people. The cult through its requirements can deprive people of their property as legitimately as can a court. The fourth comprises conformity with consensus – self-imposed sanctions. Here the issue is, whose consensus, and defined by whom? Across these four types of sanction, four types of coercion are in play. They depend on violence of various kinds – psychological and social as much as physical. Clearly, then, the sanctions that are exercised by other than judicial-political agencies prove violent and legitimately coercive, even though the violence and coercion are not the same as those carried out by courts.

On this basis we can differentiate among types of sanctions – and hence trace evidences of how the differentiation is explained. Since our data focus upon who does what to whom, the myth of politics must explain why various types of sanctions are put into effect by diverse political agencies or institutions. As we shall see, the exercise of power, invariably and undifferentiatedly in the name and by the authority of God in Heaven to be sure, is kept distinct. And the distinctions in this case signal important differences which, then, require explanation. Concrete application of legitimate violence by (1) Heaven covers different matters from parts of the political and social world governed by the policy and coercion of (2) the this-worldly political classes. And both sorts of violence have to be kept distinct from the sanction effected by (3) the community through the weight of attitude and public opinion. Here, again, we find a distinct set of penalties applied to a particular range of actions.

---

[6] It goes without saying that appeal to Scripture at this point is irrelevant. People used Scripture in building their system; they did not begin their system building by perusing Scripture. But when our analysis of the application of power invites attention to Scripture, we surely are justified in seeing what we find there.

When we have seen the several separate kinds of sanction and where they apply, we shall have a full account of the workings of politics as the application of power, and from that concrete picture we may, I think, identify the range of power and the mythic framework that has to have accommodated and legitimated diverse kinds of power.

Our task therefore is to figure out on the basis of sanctions' distinct realms, Heaven, earth, and the mediating range of the Temple and sacrifice, which party imposes sanctions for (in modern parlance) what crimes or sins. Where Heaven intervenes, do other authorities participate, and if so, what tells me which party takes charge and imposes its sanction? Is the system differentiated so that where earth is in charge, there is no pretense of appeal to Heaven? Or do we find cooperation in coextensive jurisdiction, such that one party penalizes an act under one circumstance, the other the same act under a different circumstance? A survey of the sanctions enables us to differentiate the components of the power structure before us. So we wonder whether each of these three estates that enjoy power and inflict sanctions of one kind or another – Heaven, earth, Temple in between – governs its own affairs, without the intervention of the others, or whether, working together, each takes charge in collaboration with the other, so that power is parceled out and institutions simultaneously differentiate themselves from one another and also intersect. The survey of sanctions will allow us to answer these questions and so identify the myth of politics and the exercise of power that Judaism promulgated through the Mishnah.

What has been said about the relationship of the Mishnah to Scripture – the system makes its own choices within the available revelation – imposes the first task. We must address this obvious question: Can we not simply open the Hebrew Scriptures and choose, therein, the operative political myth? No, we cannot. Why? First, the system builders choose what they find useful and ignore what they do not. Second, Scripture presents for a political myth pretty much everything and its opposite; it allows for government by the prophet (Moses), the king (David), the priest (Ezra). So if we are to appeal to Scripture in our search for myth, we can do so only by showing that, in the very context of the concrete exercise of power, the framers of the Mishnah turn to Scripture. They then will tell us where to look and why. In fact, our authorship does represent the entire system as the realization of God's dominion over Israel. And this representation is specific and detailed. It thus justifies an inquiry, once we have identified the questions the myth must answer, into how, in Scripture, we find responses to just those questions.

Here, then, is one instance of the way in which Scripture provides a detail of a myth accompanying a detail of legitimate coercion. The following lists the number of law violations that one commits by making a profit, which is to say, collecting interest:

> Those who participate in a loan on interest violate a negative commandment: these are the lender, borrower, guarantor, and witnesses.
>
> Sages say, "Also the scribe."
>
> They violate the negative commandment, "You will not give him your money upon usury" (Lev. 25:37); "You will not take usury from him" (Lev. 25:36); "You shall not be a creditor to him" (Ex. 22:25); "Nor shall you lay upon him usury" (Ex. 22:25); and they violate the negative command, "You shall not put a stumbling block before the blind, but you shall fear your God. I am the Lord" (Lev. 19:14)

M. Baba Mesia. 5:11

We appeal to the Torah to justify law obedience and to impose sanction for disobedience. But where is the myth that sustains obedience? Let me explain this question, which is critical to all that follows. On the basis of the passage just cited, we do not know what actually happens to me if I do participate in a loan on interest and so violate various rules of the Torah. More to the point, we do not know who determines that penalty or effects it. That is to say, the generalized appeal to the law of the Torah and the assumed premise that one should obey that law and not violate it hardly tell me the morphology of the political myth at hand. They assume a myth that is not set forth, and they conceal those details in which the myth gains its sustaining vitality and power.

Clearly, simply knowing that everything is in accord with the Torah and that God wants Israel to keep the laws of the Torah does not reveal the systemically active component of the political myth. On the one hand, the propositions are too general; on the other hand, they do not address the critical question. The sequence of self-evident premises that runs (1) God revealed the Torah, (2) the political institutions and rules carry out the Torah, and therefore (3) people should conform, hardly sustains a concrete theory of *just* where and how God's authority serves the systemic construction at hand. The appeal to Scripture, therefore, reveals no incisive information about the Mishnah's validating myth.

This conclusion is reinforced by the references we find here and there to "the kingdom of Heaven"[7] that appeal to God's rule in an everyday framework. These form a mere allegation that, in general, what the political authorities tell people to do is what God wants them to do, and this illuminates not at all. For example, at M. Ber. 2:5, to Gamaliel is attributed the statement, "I cannot heed you to suspend from myself the kingdom of Heaven even for one hour." Now as a matter of fact that is not a political context[8] – there is no threat of legitimate violence, for instance – for the saying has to do with reciting the *shema*. No political conclusions are drawn from that allegation. Quite to the contrary, Gamaliel, head of the collegium of sages, is not thereby represented as relinquishing power to Heaven, only as expressing his obedience to divine rule even when he does not have to. Indeed, "the kingdom of Heaven" does not form a political category, even though, as we shall see, in the politics of Judaism, all power flows from God's will and law, expressed in the Torah. In this Judaism the manipulation and application of power, allowing the impositions of drastic sanctions in support of the law, for instance, invariably flow through institutions, on earth and in Heaven, of a quite concrete and material character. "The kingdom of Heaven" may be within, but violate the law deliberately and wantonly and God will kill you sooner than you should otherwise have had to die. And, as a matter of fact, the Mishnah's framers rarely appeal in the context of politics and the legitimate exercise of violence to "the kingdom of Heaven," which, in this setting, does not form a political institution at all.

Indeed, from the pentateuchal writings, we can hardly construct the *particular* politics, including the mythic component thereof, that operates in the Mishnah's (or any other) Judaism. First of all, the

---

[7] In line with the Mishnah's usage, I refer to God and God's heavenly court with the euphemism of "Heaven," and the capital H expresses the simple fact that "Heaven" always refers to God and God's court on high. The Mishnah is not clear on whether its authorship thinks God personally intervenes throughout, but there is a well-established belief in divine agents, for example, angels or messengers, so in speaking of Heaven or Heaven's intervention, we take account of the possibility that God's agents are meant.

[8] I am puzzled by the fact that in the Mishnah "kingdom of Heaven" never occurs in what we should call a political context, rather, it occurs in the context of personal piety. My sense is that this usage should help illuminate the Gospels' presentation of sayings assigned to Jesus concerning "the kingdom," "my kingdom," "the kingdom of God," and the like. Since the Mishnah presents a highly specific politics, the selection of vocabulary bears systemic weight and meaning (something I have shown in virtually every analytical study I have carried on); these are in context technical usages.

Pentateuch does not prepare us to make sense of the institutions that the politics of Judaism for its part designs – government by king and high priest, rather than, as in the Pentateuch, prophet. Second, and concomitantly, the pentateuchal myth that legitimates coercion – rule by God's prophet, governance through explicitly revealed laws that God has dictated – plays no active and systemic role whatsoever in the formulation and presentation of the Mishnah's politics of Judaism. Rather, of the types of political authority contained within the scriptural repertoire, the Mishnah's philosophers reject prophetic and charismatic authority and deem critical authority exercised by the sage's disciple who has been carefully nurtured in rules, not in gifts of the spirit. The authority of sages in the politics of Judaism does not derive from charisma (revelation by God to the sage who makes a ruling in a given case, or even from general access to God for the sage). The myth we shall presently explore in no way falls into the classification of a charismatic myth of politics.

True, everybody knows and believes that God has dictated the Torah to Moses. But the Mishnah's framers do not then satisfy themselves with a paraphrase of what God has said to Moses in the Torah. How might they have done so? The answer to that question provides perspective on what our authorship has done. The following allows us to see how matters might have been phrased – but never were:

M. Rosh Hashshanah 3:8

A. *Now it happened that when Moses held up his hand, Israel prevailed, and when he let his hand fall, Amalek prevailed* (Ex. 17:11).

B. Now do Moses' hands make war or stop it?

C. But the purpose is to say this to you:

D. So long as the Israelites would set their eyes upward and submit their hearts to their Father in Heaven, they would grow stronger. And if not, they fell.

E. In like wise, you may say the following:

F. *Make yourself a fiery serpent and set it on a standard, and it shall come to pass that everyone who is bitten, when he sees it, shall live* (Num. 21:8).

G. Now does that serpent [on the standard] kill or give life? [Obviously not.]

H. But: So long as the Israelites would set their eyes upward and submit to their Father in Heaven, they would be healed. And if not, they would pine away.

M. Rosh Hashshanah 3:8

The silence now becomes eloquent. We look in vain in the pages of our systemic writing for a *single* example in which authorities ask people to raise their eyes on high and so to obey what said authorities command. Such a political myth may, however, be implicit. But when made explicit and systemically active, not left in its inert condition, the myth we seek by definition precipitates not obedience in general, but rather concrete decision-making processes, to be sure inclusive of obedience to those decisions once made. And we shall know the reason why.

More to the point, is God's direct intervention (for example, as portrayed in Scripture) represented as a preferred or even available sanction? Yes and no, but mostly no. For in our system what is important is that the myth of God's intervention on an ad hoc and episodic basis in the life of the community hardly serves to explain obedience to the law in the here and now. What sort of evidence would indicate that God intervenes in such wise as to explain the obedience to the law on an everyday basis? Invoking God's immediate presence, a word said, a miracle performed, would suffice. But in the entirety of the more than five hundred chapters of the Mishnah, no one ever prays to have God supply a decision in a particular case. More to the point, no judge appeals to God to put to death a convicted felon. If the judge wants the felon killed, he kills him. When God intervenes, it is on the jurisdiction assigned to God, not the court. And then the penalty is a different one from execution.

It follows that an undifferentiated myth explaining the working of undifferentiated power by appeal to God's will, while relevant, is not exact and does not explain this system in its rich detail. How the available mythic materials explain the principles of differentiation now requires attention. The explanation must be both general and specific. That is to say, while the court orders and carries out the execution, the politics works in such a way that all three political institutions, God, the court, and the Temple, the three agencies with the power to bestow or take away life and property and to inflict physical pain and suffering, work together in a single continuum and in important ways cooperate to deal with the same crimes or sins. The data to which we now turn will tell us who does what to whom and why, and, in the reason why, we shall uncover the political myth we seek.

Predictably, when we work our way through sanctions to recover the mythic premises thereof, we begin with God's place in the institutionalization and execution of legitimate violence. Of course, the repertoire of sanctions does encompass God's direct intervention, but that is hardly a preferred alternative or a common one. Still,

God does commonly intervene when oaths are violated, for oaths are held to involve the person who invokes God's name and God. Further, whereas when faced with an insufficiency of valid evidence under strict rules of testimony, the earthly court cannot penalize serious crime, the heavenly court can and does impose a penalty. Clearly, then, God serves to justify the politics and account for its origin. Although God is never asked to join in making specific decisions and effecting policy in the everyday politics of the state, deliberate violation of certain rules provokes God's or the heavenly court's direct intervention. Thus obedience to the law clearly represents submission to God in Heaven. Further, forms of heavenly coercion such as we shall presently survey suggest a complex mythic situation, with more subtle nuance than the claim that, overall, God rules would indicate. A politics of rules and regulations cannot admit God's ad hoc participation, and this system did not do so. God joined in the system in a regular and routine way, and the rules took for granted God's part in the politics of Judaism.

Precisely how does the intervention of God into the system come to concrete expression? By appeal to the rules handed down at Sinai as an ultimate reference in legal questions, for instance. This is the case in the story about R. Simeon of Mispah, who sowed his field with two types of wheat. Simeon's problem is that he may have violated the law against sowing mixed seeds in a single patch. When the matter came before Rabban Gamaliel, the passage states:

C.   They went up to the Chamber of Hewn Stone and asked [about the law regarding sowing two types of wheat in one field].

D.   Said Nahum the Scribe, "I have received [the following ruling] from R. Miasha, who received it from his father, *who received [it] from the pairs, who received [it] from the prophets, [who received] the law [given] to Moses on Sinai,* regarding one who sows his field with two types of wheat...."

M. Peah. 2:6 (my emphases)

Here, the law's legitimacy clearly depends on its descent by tradition from Sinai. But that general principle of descent from Sinai was invoked only rarely. Indeed, R. Simeon's case undermines the Mishnah's relation to God's intervention. R. Simeon's problem is minor. Nothing important requires so drastic a claim to be made explicit. That is to say, it is a mere commonplace that the system appeals to Sinai.

But this is not a politics of revelation, for a politics of revelation consistently and immediately appeals to the myth that God works in the here and now, all the time, in concrete cases. That appeal is not common in the Mishnah's statement of its system, and, consequently, that appeal to the myth of revelation does not bear important political tasks and is not implicit here. Indeed I do not think it was present at all, except where Scripture made it so (for example, with the ordeal inflicted on the wife accused of adultery). Why the persistent interest in legitimation other than through the revelation of the Torah for the immediate case? The answer to that question draws upon the traits of philosophers, who are interested in the prevailing rule governing all cases and the explanation for the exceptions, rather than upon those of historian-prophets, who are engaged by the exceptional case which is then represented as paradigmatic.[9] Our philosophers appeal to a myth to explain what is routine and orderly, and what they wish to explain is what is ordinary and everyday: institutions and rules, not cases and ad hoc decisions yielding no rule at all.

The traits of the politics of Judaism then emerge in the silences as much as in the acts of speech, in the characteristics of the myth as much as in its contents. The politics of Judaism appeals not to a charismatic but to a routine myth, in which is explained the orderly life of institutions and an administration, and by which are validated the rules and the workings of a political structure and system. True, as I have repeatedly emphasized, all of them are deemed to have been founded on revelation. But what kind of revelation? The answer derives from the fact that none of the political institutions appeal in the here and the now to God's irregular ("miraculous") intervention. Treatment of the rebellious elder and the false prophet as we shall see tells us quite the opposite. The political institutions not only did not invoke miraculous intervention to account for the imposition of sanctions, they would not and did not tolerate the claim that such could take place.

It is the regularity and order of God's participation in the politics that the character of the myth of the politics of Judaism maintains we have to understand and account for. Mere allegations in general that the law originates with God's revelation to Moses at Sinai do not serve to identify that middle-range myth that accounts for the structure and the system. If God is not sitting at the shoulder of the judge and telling the judge what to do (as the writers of Exodus 21ff. seem to suppose), then what legitimacy attaches to the judge's decision to give Mr. Smith's field over, or back, to Mr. Jones?

---

[9] A fine distinction, perhaps, but a critical one, and the distinction between charisma and routine is not a fine one at all.

And why (within the imaginary state at hand) should people support, sustain, and submit to authority? Sages' abstract language contains no answers to these questions. And yet sages' system presupposes routine and everyday obedience to power, not merely the utilization of legitimate violence to secure conformity. That is partly because the systemic statement to begin with tells very few stories. Matters that the pentateuchal writers expressed through narrating a very specific story about how God said thus and so to Moses in this particular case, rewarding the ones who obeyed and punishing those who did not, in the Mishnah come to expression in language of an allusive and philosophical, generalizing character.

Here, too, we discern the character of the myth even before we determine its contents. While we scarcely expect that this sort of writing is apt to spell out a myth, even though a myth infuses the system, we certainly can identify the components of the philosophical and theological explanation of the state that have taken mythic form.

Even here, to be sure, the evidence proves sparse. First, of course, in the mythic structure comes God, who commands and creates, laying out what humanity is to do, exercising the power to form the social world in which humanity is to obey. God then takes care of God's particular concerns, and these focus upon *deliberate* violation of God's wishes. If a sin or crime is inadvertent, the penalties are of one order, if deliberate, of a different order. The most serious infraction of the law of the Torah is identified not by what is done but by the attitude of the sinner or criminal.[10] If one has deliberately violated God's rule, then God intervenes. If the violation is inadvertent, then the Temple imposes the sanction. And the difference is considerable. In the former case, God through the heavenly court ends the felon's or sinner's life. Then a person who defies the laws – as these concern one's sexual conduct, attitude toward God, relationships within the family – will be penalized either (if necessary) by God or (if possible) by the earthly court. This means that the earthly court exercises God's power, and the myth of the system as a whole, so far as the earthly court forms the principal institutional form of the system, emerges not merely in a generality but in all its specificity. These particular judges, here and now, stand for God and exercise the power of God. In the latter case, the Temple takes over jurisdiction; a particular offering is called for,

---

[10] The distinction between secular felony and religious sin obviously bears no meaning in the system, useful as it is to us. I generally will speak of "felon or sinner," so as not to take a position on a matter unimportant in my inquiry.

as the Book of Leviticus specifies. But there is no need for God or the earthly court in God's name to take a position.

Now come the data of real power, the sanctions. We may divide sanctions just as the authorship of the Mishnah did, by simply reviewing the range of penalties for law infraction as they occur. These penalties, as we mentioned above, fall into four classifications: what Heaven does, what political institutions do, what religious institutions do, and what is left to the coercion of public opinion, that is, consensus, with special attention to the definition of that "public" that has effective opinion to begin with. The final realm of power, conferring or withholding approval, proves constricted and, in this context, not very consequential.

Let us begin with the familiar, with sanctions exercised by the earthly court as they are fully described in Mishnah-tractates Sanhedrin and Makkot. We will review at length the imposition of sanctions as it is represented by the earthly court, the Temple, the heavenly court, the sages. This review allows us to identify the actors in the system of politics – those with power to impose sanctions, and the sanctions they can inflict. Only from this perspective will the initial statement of Judaism, in its own odd idiom, be able to make its points in the way its authorship has chosen. When we take up the myth to which that statement implicitly appeals, we shall have a clear notion of the character of the evidence, in rich detail, on which our judgment of the mythic substrate of the system has been composed.

The most impressive mode of legitimate violence is killing; it certainly focuses our attention. The earthly court may justly kill a sinner or felon. This death-dealing priority accorded to the earthly court derives from the character of the power entrusted to that court. The earthly court enjoys full power to dispose of the property and life of all subject to its authority – in the context imagined by Judaism, of all residing in territory that comes under the state's control.

Imposing the death penalty is described in the following way:

Mishnah-tractate Sanhedrin 7:1-3

A.   Four modes of execution were given over to the court [in order of severity]:

B.   (1) stoning, (2) burning, (3) decapitation, and (4) strangulation.

C.   R. Simeon says, "(2) Burning, (1) stoning, (4) strangulation, and (3) decapitation."

M. San. 7:1

The passage leaves no doubt that the court could put people to death. Only the severity of suffering imposed by each mode of execution is in question. Thus, Simeon's hierarchy of punishments (C) differs from that of B in the degradation and suffering inflicted on the felon, not in the end result. The passage details four modes of execution, that is, four forms of legitimate violence. In the account, the following is of special interest. I have emphasized the key words.

A. The religious requirement of decapitation [is carried out as follows]:

B. They would cut off his head with a sword,

C. just as the government does.

D. *R. Judah says, "This is disgusting.*

E. "But they put the head on a block and chop it off with an ax."

F. *They said to him, "There is no form of death more disgusting than this one."*

G. The religious requirement of strangulation [is carried out as follows]:

H. They would bury him in manure up to his armpits, and put a towel of hard material inside one of soft material, and wrap it around his neck.

I. This [witness] pulls it to him from one side, and that witness pulls it to him at the other side, until he perishes.

M. San. 7:3

In among all the practical detail, Judah's intervention stands out. It leaves no doubt that carrying out the law ("way of life") realizes a particular worldview. Specifically, his language implies that the felon remains a human being, in God's image. Clearly, then, at stake in the theoretical discussions at hand is how to execute someone in a manner appropriate to his or her standing after the likeness of God. This problem obviously presupposes that in imposing the penalty in the first place and in carrying it out, the court acts wholly in conformity with God's will. This being the case, a political myth of a dominion belonging to God and carrying out God's plan and program certainly stands behind the materials at hand.

But that observation still leaves us struggling with a mere commonplace. On the strength of our knowledge that God stands behind the politics and that the consideration that human beings are in God's image and after God's likeness applies even in inflicting the death penalty, we still cannot identify the diverse media by which power is carried out. More to the point, we can hardly distinguish one medium of power from another, which we must do if we are to gain access to the myth that sustains what we shall soon see is the fully differentiated political structure before us. We do well at this turning point to remember the theoretical basis for this entire inquiry: a politics is a theory of the ongoing exercise of the power of coercion, including legitimate violence.[11] Sanctions form the naked exercise of raw power – hence will require the protection and disguise of a heavy cloak of myth.

How to proceed? By close attention to the facts of power and by sorting out the implications of those facts. A protracted journey through details of the law of sanctions leads us to classify the sanctions and the sins or crimes to which they apply. What precisely do I think requires classification? Our project is to see who does what to whom and, on the basis of the consequent perception, to propose an explanation for that composition. For from these sanctions of state, that is, the legitimate exercise of coercion, including violence, we may work our way back to the reasons adduced for the legitimacy of the exercise of coercion, which is to say, the political myth. The reason is that such a classification will permit us to see how in detail the foci of power are supposed to intersect or to relate: autonomous powers, connected and related ones, or utterly continuous ones, joining Heaven to earth, for instance, in the person of this institutional representative or that one. What we shall see is a system that treats Heaven, earth, and the mediating institution, the Temple, as interrelated, thus, connected, but that insists, in vast detail, upon the distinct responsibilities and jurisdiction accorded to each. Once we have perceived that fundamental fact, we may compose for ourselves the myth, or at least the point and propositions of the myth, that accounted for the political structures of Judaism and persuaded people to obey or conform even when there was no immediate threat of penalty.

A survey of (1) types of sanctions, (2) the classifications of crimes or sins to which they apply, and (3) who imposes them, now yields these results. First come the death penalty on earth and its

---

[11] Weber defines a state as a political association with access to the use of physical force: "a human community that (successfully) claims the monopoly of the legitimate use of physical force within a given territory" (PV, 77, 78). A political question, then, means "that interests in the distribution, maintenance, or transfer of power are decisive for answering the questions and determining the decision." But there were political questions that far transcend the narrow limitations of power, yet that by any definition of politics involve politics. Politics then and now as well derives from the larger social order and cannot be interpreted outside of the larger system that expresses itself, also, through politics. To use violence to achieve one's will forms too narrow a definition of politics, because it ignores a variety of other ongoing, institutionally founded, media by which the system appeals to coercion that is effective yet in no way based upon violence, for one thing.

counterpart, which is extirpation (death before one's allotted time) imposed by Heaven:

HEAVEN	EARTH	TEMPLE	COMMUNITY
EXTIRPATION	*DEATH PENALTY*	*DEATH PENALTY*	

for deliberate actions
sexual crimes:	sexual crimes:		
incest	in improper		
violating sex taboos	relationships:		
(bestiality,	incest		
homosexuality)			
religious crimes	*religious crimes*		
against God	*against God:*		
blasphemy	blasphemy		
idolatry	idolatry		
magic	magic		
sorcery	sorcery		
profaning Sabbath	profaning Sabbath		
	religious sins		
	against family:		
	cursing parents		
	social crimes:		
	murder		
	communal		
	apostasy		
	kidnapping		
	social sins:		
	public defiance of		
	the court		
	false prophecy		

religious sins, deliberately committed, against God
unclean person who ate a Holy Thing
uncleanness in sanctuary
violating food taboos
making offering outside of Temple
violating taboos of holy seasons
replicating Temple incense or oil outside

Next we deal with court-inflicted sanctions carried out against property or person (for example, fines against property, flogging or other social or physical violence short of death for the felon or sinner):

HEAVEN	EARTH	TEMPLE	COMMUNITY
	flogging *exile*	*obligatory offering and/or flogging for inadvertent action*	*shunning or approbation*
	manslaughter incest violation of menstrual taboo marriage in violation of caste rules	uncleanness eating Temple food in violation of the law	repay moral obligation (debt canceled by Sabbatical Year)
		replicating Temple oil, incense outside violating Temple food taboos	stubbornly rejecting majority view opposing majority will
		violating taboos of holy days (Passover, atonement)	opposing patriarch
			obedience to majority or patriarch
	violating food taboos	uncleanness (Zab, mesora, etc.) Nazirite sex with bondwoman unclean Nazirite false oath of testimony false oath of deposit	
	removing dam with offspring violating negative commandments		

The operative distinction between inflicting a flogging and requiring a sacrifice (Temple sanctions against person or property), and the sanction of extirpation (heavenly death penalty), is made explicit as follows: "For those [transgressions] are people liable, for deliberately doing them, to the punishment of extirpation, and for accidentally doing them, to the bringing of a sin-offering, and for not being certain of whether or not one has done them, to a suspensive guilt-offering."

(That distinction is suspended in a few instances, as indicated at M. Ker. 2:1-2.)

This summary yields a simple and clear fact, and on the basis of that simple fact we may now reconstruct the entire political myth on which the politics of Judaism rested. Let me emphasize: *Some of the same crimes or sins for which the heavenly court imposes the penalty of extirpation are those that, under appropriate circumstances (e.g., sufficient evidence admissible in court) the earthly court imposes the death penalty.* That is, the heavenly court and the earthly court impose precisely the same sanctions for the same crimes or sins. The earthly court therefore forms down here the exact replica and counterpart, within a single system of power, of the heavenly court up there. This no longer looms as an empty generalization; it is a concrete and systemically active and indicative detail, and the system speaks through its details.

But this is not the entire story. There is a second fact, equally indicative for our recovery of the substrate of myth. We note that there are crimes for which the earthly court imposes penalties, but for which the heavenly court does not, as well as vice versa. The earthly and heavenly courts share jurisdiction over sexual crimes and over what I classify as serious religious crimes against God. The heavenly court penalizes with its form of the death penalty religious sins against God, in which instances a person deliberately violates the taboos of sanctification.

And that fact calls our attention to a third partner in the distribution and application of power, the Temple with its system of sanctions that cover precisely the same acts subject to the jurisdiction of the heavenly and earthly courts. The counterpart on earth is now not the earthly court but the Temple. This is the institution that, in theory, automatically receives the appropriate offering from the person who inadvertently violates these same taboos of sanctification. But this is an odd choice for the Mishnah, since there is now no Temple on earth. The juxtaposition appears then to involve courts and Temple, and the upshot is that both are equally matters of theory. In the theory at hand, then, the earthly court, for its part, penalizes social crimes against the community that the heavenly court, on the one side, and the Temple rites, on the other, do not take into account at all. These are murder, apostasy, kidnapping, public defiance of the court, and false prophecy. The earthly court further imposes sanctions on matters of particular concern to the heavenly court, with special reference to taboos of sanctification (for example, negative commandments). These three institutions, therefore, exercise concrete and material power, utilizing legitimate violence to kill someone, exacting penalties against property, and inflicting pain. The sages' modes of power, by contrast, stand quite apart, apply mainly to their own circle, and work through the intangible though no less effective means of inflicting shame or paying honor.

The facts we have in hand draw us back to the analysis of our differentiation of applied and practical power. In the nature of the facts before us, that differentiation tells us precisely for what the systemic myth will have to give its account. Power flows through three distinct but intersecting dominions, each with its own concern, all sharing some interests in common. The heavenly court attends to deliberate defiance of Heaven, the Temple to inadvertent defiance of Heaven. The earthly court attends to matters subject to its jurisdiction by reason of sufficient evidence, proper witnesses, and the like, and these same matters will come under heavenly jurisdiction when the earthly court finds itself unable to act. Accordingly, we have a tripartite system of sanctions – Heaven cooperating with the Temple in some matters, with the court in others, and, as noted, each bearing its own distinct media of enforcing the law as well. What then can we say concerning the systemic myth of politics? The forms of power and the modes of mediating legitimate violence draw our attention to a single political myth, one that we first confronted, if merely as a generality and commonplace to be sure, at the very outset. The unity of that myth is underlined by the simple fact that the earthly court enters into the process right alongside the heavenly court and the Temple; as to blasphemy, idolatry, and magic, its jurisdiction prevails. So, as I have stressed, a single myth must serve all three correlated institutions.

It is the myth of God's authority infusing the institutions of Heaven and earth alike, an authority diffused among three principle foci or circles of power, Heaven's court, the earthly court, and the Temple in between. Each focus of power has its own jurisdiction and responsibility, Heaven above, earth beneath, the Temple in the position of mediation – transmitting as it does from earth to Heaven the penalties handed over as required. And all media of power in the matter of sanctions intersect at some points as well: a tripartite politics, a single myth drawing each component into relationship with a single source and origin of power, God's law set forth in the Torah. But the myth has not performed its task until it answers not only the question of why, but also the question of how. Specifically, the details of myth must address questions of the details of power. Who then tells whom to do what? And how are the relationships of dominion and dominance to compliance and obedience made permanent through myth?

We did not require this sustained survey to ascertain that God through the Torah has set forth laws and concerns. That generality now may be made quite specific, for it is where power is differentiated and parceled out that we see the workings of the political myth. So we ask, how do we know who tells whom to do, or suffer, what sanction or penalty? It is the power of myth to differentiate that defines the generative question. The key lies in the criterion by which each mode of power, earthly, mediating, and heavenly, identifies the cases over which it exercises jurisdiction. The criterion lies in the attitude of the human being who has done what he or she should not: did he act deliberately or unintentionally?

I state the upshot with heavy emphasis: *The point of differentiation within the political structures, supernatural and natural alike, lies in the attitude and intention of a human being.* We differentiate among the application of power by reference to the attitude of the person who comes into relationship with that power. A person who comes into conflict with the system, rejecting the authority claimed by the powers that be, does so deliberately or inadvertently. The myth accounts in the end for the following hierarchization of action and penalty, infraction and sanction: (1) If the deed is deliberate, then one set of institutions exercises jurisdiction and utilizes supernatural power. (2) If the deed is inadvertent, another institution exercises jurisdiction and utilizes the power made available by that same supernatural being.

A sinner or criminal who has deliberately violated the law has by his or her action challenged the politics of Judaism. Consequently, God or God's surrogate imposes sanctions – extirpation (by the court on high), or death or other appropriate penalty (by the court on earth). A sinner or criminal who has inadvertently violated the law is penalized by the imposition of Temple sanctions, losing valued goods. People obey because God wants them to and has told them what to do, and when they do not obey, a differentiated political structure appeals to that single hierarchizing myth. The components of the myth are two: first, God's will, expressed in the law of the Torah, second, the human being's will, carried out in obedience to the law of the Torah or in defiance of that law.

Have we come so far and not yet told the story that the myth contains? I have now to explain and spell out the story that conveys the myth of politics in Judaism. It is not in the Mishnah at all. Do I find the mythic foundation in Scripture, which accounts for the uses and differentiation of power that the Mishnah's system portrays? Indeed I do, for, as we realize, the political myth of Judaism has to explain the differentiation of sins or crimes, with their associated penalties or punishments, and so sanctions of power. And in Scripture there is a very precise answer to the question of how to differentiate among sins or crimes and why to do so. Given the position of the system of the Mishnah, the point of differentiation must rest with one's attitude or intentionality And, indeed, I do have two stories of how the power of God conflicts with the power of humanity in such wise as to invoke the penalties and sanctions in precisely the differentiated modes we have before us. Where do I find such stories of the conflict of wills, God's and humanity's?

The first such story of power differentiated by the will of the human being in communion or conflict with the word of the commanding God comes to us from the garden of Eden.[12] We cannot too often reread the following astonishing words:

> The Lord God took the man and placed him in the garden of Eden...and the Lord God commanded the man, saying, "Of every tree of the garden you are free to eat; but as for the tree of knowledge of good and bad, you must not eat of it; for as soon as you eat of it, you shall die."
> ...When the woman saw that the tree was good for eating and a delight to the eyes, and that the tree was desirable as a source of wisdom, she took of its fruit and ate; she also gave some to her husband, and he ate....
> The Lord God called out to the man and said to him, "Where are you?"
> He replied, "I heard the sound of You in the garden, and I was afraid, because I was naked, so I hid."
> Then He asked, "Who told you that you were naked? Did you eat of the tree from which I had forbidden you to eat?"
> ...And the Lord God said to the woman, "What is this you have done!"
> So the Lord God banished him from the garden of Eden....

------

[12] This is not to suggest that the distinction behind the system's differentiation is important only in the myth of Eden. Quite to the contrary, the authorship of the laws of Leviticus and Deuteronomy repeatedly appeals to that same distinction in speaking of the "Israel" that they wish to bring into existence – an Israel in the Eden of the Land of Israel. But our interest is in myth, and I find in the myth of Eden the explanation for the point of differentiation that the political myth of Judaism invokes at every point. So, as I have said, the sanctions lead to the systemic question that requires mythic response, and once we know the question, we can turn to Scripture for the myth (as much as we can find in Scripture ample expansion, in law, of that same myth).

Now a reprise of the exchange between God, Adam, and Eve tells us
that at stake was responsibility: who has violated the law, but who
bears responsibility for deliberately violating the law:

> "The woman You put at my side – she gave me of the tree, and I
> ate."
> "The serpent duped me, and I ate."
> Then the Lord God said to the serpent, "Because you did this...."

The ultimate responsibility lies with the one who acted
deliberately, not under constraint or on account of deception or
misinformation, as did Adam and Eve.   Then the sanction applies
most severely to the one who by intention and an act of will has
violated God's intention and will.

Adducing this story by itself poses several problems.   First, the
storyteller does not allege that Adam intended to violate the
commandment; he followed his wife.   Second, the penalty is not
extirpation but banishment.   That is why to establish what I
conceive to be the generative myth, I turn to a second story of
disobedience and its consequences, the tale of Moses' hitting the rock:

> The community was without water, and they joined against
> Moses and Aaron....Moses and Aaron came away from the
> congregation to the entrance of the Tent of Meeting and fell on their
> faces.   The Presence of the Lord appeared to them, and the Lord
> spoke to Moses, saying, "You and your brother Aaron take the rod
> and assemble the community, and before their very eyes order the
> rock to yield its water.   Thus you shall produce water for them from
> the rock and provide drink for the congregation and their beasts."
> Moses took the rod from before the Lord as He had commanded
> him.   Moses and Aaron assembled the congregation in front of the
> rock; and he said to them, "Listen, you rebels, shall we get water for
> you out of this rock?"   And Moses raised his hand and struck the
> rock twice with his rod.   Out came copious water, and the community
> and their beasts drank.
> But the Lord said to Moses and Aaron, "Because you did not trust
> me enough to affirm My sanctity in the sight of the Israelite people,
> therefore you shall not lead this congregation into the land that I
> have given them."
> Those are the waters of Meribah, meaning that the Israelites
> quarreled with the Lord – through which He affirmed His sanctity.
>   Num. 20:1-13

Here we have not only intentional disobedience, but also the penalty
of extirpation.   Both this myth and the myth of the Fall make the
same point.   They direct attention to the generative conception that
at stake in power is the will of God over against the will of the
human being, and in particular, the Israelite human being.

The political myth of Judaism now emerges in the Mishnah in all of its tedious detail as a reprise – in now-consequential and necessary, stunning detail – of the story of God's commandment, humanity's disobedience, God's sanction for the sin or crime, and humanity's atonement and reconciliation. The Mishnah omits all explicit reference to myths that explain power and sanctions, but invokes in its rich corpus of details the absolute given of the story of the distinction between what is deliberate and what is mitigated by an attitude that is not culpable, a distinction set forth in the tragedy of Adam and Eve, in the failure of Moses and Aaron, and in countless other passages in the Pentateuch, Prophetic Books, and Writings. Then the Mishnah's is a politics of life after Eden and outside of Eden. The upshot of the matter is that the political myth of Judaism sets forth the constraints of freedom, the human will brought to full and unfettered expression, imposed by the constraints of revelation, God's will made known.

Since it is the freedom of humanity to make decisions and frame intentions that forms the point of differentiation among the political media of power, we are required, in my view, to return to the paradigmatic exercise of that same freedom, that is, to Eden, to the moment when Adam and Eve exercise their own will and defy God. Since the operative criterion in the differentiation of sanction – that is, the exercise of legitimate violence by Heaven or by earth or by the Temple – is the human attitude and intention in carrying out a culpable action, we must recognize the politics before us rehearses the myth of Adam and Eve in Eden: it finds its dynamic in the correspondence between God's will and humanity's freedom to act however it chooses, thus freely incurring the risk of penalty or sanction for the wrong exercise of freedom.

At stake is what Adam and Eve, Moses and Aaron, and numerous others intend, propose, plan, for that is the point at which the politics intervenes, making its points of differentiation between and among its sanctions and the authorities that impose those penalties. For that power to explain difference, which is to say, the capacity to represent and account for hierarchy, we are required, in my opinion, to turn to the story of the Fall of Adam and Eve from Eden and to counterpart stories. The reason is that the political myth derives from that same myth of origins its points of differentiation and explains by reference to the principal components of that myth – God's and humanity's will and power – the dynamics of the political system at hand. God commands, but humanity does what it then chooses, and in the interplay of those two protean forces, each power in its own right, the sanctions and penalties of the system apply.

Power comes from two conflicting forces, the commanding will of God and the free will of the human being. Power expressed in immediate sanctions is also mediated through these same forces, Heaven above, human beings below, with the Temple mediating between the two. Power works its way in the interplay between what God has set forth in the law of the Torah and what human beings do, whether intentionally, whether inadvertently, whether obediently, whether defiantly. That is why the politics of Judaism is a politics of Eden. And that further explains why sages' systemic statement turned to politics as the necessary medium for its full formulation. Quite how matters were to be phrased as this Judaism crossed the frontier from the realm of theory and theology to practical issues of public policy is not to be predicted on the basis of the systemic statement we have examined, which, we now see, in no way made provision for the complexities of an ordinary, diverse society. But, then, systems never do.

7

The Politics of the Mishnah in Its Contemporary Setting

Alan J. Avery-Peck
College of the Holy Cross

Jacob Neusner's paper illustrates the supposition that underlies this volume, that a statement of politics and public policy is as appropriate and powerful a vehicle for the articulation of a religious system as are ritual, theology, prayer, or any of the other categories of behavior or thought that we commonly think of as "religious." Within this construction, he addresses the more specific question of *how* we are to make sense of the politics of a religion, and he portrays the extent to which the examination of such a politics provides important insights for our interpretation of a religion as a whole.

His specific example, that of the Mishnah, is appropriate to this task. For while the Mishnah encompasses ideas that are central to political discourse, it lacks some of the primary features we expect to find in a political system. The Mishnah, for instance, contains no discussion of how sovereignty is acquired and appropriately exercised. Nor does it provide a general theory of the characteristics of good and bad government.[1] Perhaps most important, when viewed as a whole, the Mishnah clearly is not about politics at all. Its politics emerges as only one aspect of its authorship's broadly utopian social and religious vision, not as a fully articulated program for governance of a real community.

Neusner's confronting of these characteristics of the Mishnah leads to the paper's two central theoretical contributions. First, the absence here of topics normally central in the discussion of politics leads him to

---

[1] Jacob Neusner, *Rabbinic Political Theory* (Chicago: University of Chicago Press, 1991), 8.

identify a rather unexpected point of entry into the politics of the
Mishnah.[2] Taking as foundational the notion that "state power is unique
in its acknowledged right to exercise force, even to kill,"[3] Neusner
comprehends the Mishnah's politics as emerging from its theory of
sanctions, that is, from the rabbis' determination of the agency or person
who has the power to act legitimately against another. Through their
theory of sanctions, he argues, the rabbis directly express their political
theory and reveal their underlying mythic conception of the nature and
source of political power.

The paper's second major contribution emerges from Neusner's
dealing with the fact that the Mishnah is a *religious* statement that
incorporates discourse about politics as only one aspect of its description
of the social order. In light of this characteristic of the Mishnah, he
points out that an inquiry into the Mishnah's politics, and into the
politics of religious systems in general, primarily yields insights into the
underlying *religious* myth of the system. In the case at hand, the
authorship of the Mishnah speaks through politics as but one way of
reflecting on a broader set of issues that we commonly perceive as
religious or theological. The rabbis' discussion of politics contributes to
their larger program, a program that explains how a certain group of
believers, living in a certain time and place, can make sense of their
human situation and of their relationship to God. The study of a
religion's politics thus provides insights into that religion. This is without
regard for whether or not that politics was intended to or could function
as an actual system of governance.

Approaching the politics of the Mishnah in this way, Neusner notes
that central in the rabbis' conception is not simply the notion that God
shares power with certain human surrogates. This, after all, is a
commonplace. Rather, at the heart of the Mishnah's politics is the
rabbinic notion that, as a result of this shared authority, God's own
ability to act in the earthly realm is severely circumscribed. According to
the Mishnah, God acts only in response to a person's deliberate violation
of certain laws. The authorities of the Temple and the earthly court, by
contrast, respond to inadvertent defiance. The Mishnaic system thus
rejects the charismatic, prophetic, or miraculous, through which God
interjects himself at will into the human sphere. It sees these as
inappropriate foundations for a political system. In place of such modes
of God's uncontrolled activity in the human sphere, the rabbis of the
Mishnah painstakingly describe a judicial system immune to
intervention even from the divine.

---

[2] Ibid., 6.
[3] I. M. Finely, cited in ibid., 1-2.

Neusner locates the foundation of the Mishnah's approach in passages in Scripture in which God responds to sin in exactly the way the Mishnah portrays. In the story of the garden of Eden, the most severe punishment applies to the party who acted deliberately; in the tale of Moses' striking the rock, intentional defiance of God leads to a sanction of extirpation, early death. Yet, while these scriptural foundations of the Mishnah's political myth are striking, they should not obscure the extent to which, at its heart, the Mishnah's politics in fact rejects the central premise of the Hebrew Bible.

For alongside these and other clear parallels, we can point to a broad divergence of the rabbis' thinking in the Mishnah from the ideology of the Bible. For in Scripture, unlike in the Mishnah, knowledge of God's qualities and understanding of God's demands upon Israel are acquired primarily through God's acts of self-revelation in history, including God's direct statement of the law to Moses at Sinai. Emerging in the Exodus story, which negates any notion of an inactive deity and asserts instead the reality of a God who is intimately involved in the political life of the world, this theme is mentioned over 120 times in the Hebrew Bible, more than any other historical event or theological concept.[4] In Scripture, unlike in the Mishnah, this is to say, the charismatic, prophetic, and miraculous are the *primary* ways of knowing God, on the one side, and are the central modes of God's political activity, on the other.

This point is well illustrated by Exod. 18:14-26's story of how, following the theophany at Sinai, Moses established a system of judges. Scripture reports that Moses' father-in-law saw Moses sitting before the people all day, inquiring of God regarding the correct resolution of each legal question (Exod. 18:14). Insisting that Moses did not have the strength to bear this responsibility alone, Jethro instructed him to teach the law to the people themselves, so that they could begin to bear personal responsibility for correct behavior. At the same time, Moses was to appoint judges ("rulers of thousands, of hundreds, of fifties, and of tens" [Exod. 18:21]) to help in settling disputes. But as Exod. 18:19, 22, and 26 make clear, this commission of judges would not in any way impinge upon God's absolute authority. For these men were to handle only the easy matters, in which the law already was clear. Any hard case, in which there was a question of law, by contrast, still needed to be brought to Moses, who would continue as before to "represent the people before God and bring their cases to God" (Exod. 18:19).

We see that even in the earthly judicial system imagined by the Book of Exodus, God alone retains the power to interpret and apply the law. How far this is from the theory of the Mishnah and from the developing

---

[4] Nahum Sarna, "Exodus, Book of," in *Anchor Bible Dictionary*, 2: 698-699.

rabbinic ideology expressed so clearly, for instance, in the often-cited story of the Oven of Akhnai (Babylonian Talmud Baba Mesia 59b). That passage instructs that even God's attempt to determine the law through direct, miraculous intervention into the human sphere can safely be ignored. The law, rather, is defined only by a vote of the majority of sages, who determine proper conduct based upon their wisdom and knowledge, and who give no heed to supernatural interference. In the rabbinic theory, rabbis alone have the power to establish the meaning and application of the law, because, having already been transmitted to humans at Sinai, that law is no longer in Heaven at all. It is, rather, in the people's mouth and heart. They are empowered to engage in reasoned debate and then to vote, thereby taking over the role of God in revealing Torah and in establishing courts that wield legitimate political power.

Since the Mishnah's authors surely understood their work as continuous with Judaism's scriptural heritage, comprehending their ideology entails understanding why they chose to reject the biblical idea of a politics dependent at base upon God's absolute right to intervene in human affairs. To answer this question, let us turn briefly to the world in which the Mishnah was formulated and in which its vision of the social order was to operate. For, indeed, in defining a system of sanctions primarily in the hands of the human court, the rabbis appear to have responded to the pivotal theological question of their age, a period in which the destruction of the Second Temple and the Bar Kokhba revolt had dramatically altered both the political and theological contexts in which Judaism existed.[5]

The question to which all contemporary theologies of Judaism had to respond was phrased succinctly and emotionally shortly after the destruction, when the author of IV Ezra asked (3:32-34, 6:59):

> Have the deeds of Babylon been better than those of Zion? Has any other nation known You besides Zion?...If the world has indeed been created for our sakes, why do we not enter into possession of our world? How long shall this endure?

The issue facing the rabbis thus concerned what could be expected of God, how God could be found, and what would be the role of God in international and national affairs.[6] They responded to this question by reshaping it and asking more specifically what it means to "enter into

---

[5] On the following, see Alan J. Avery-Peck, "Judaism without the Temple: The Mishnah," in Harold W. Attridge and Gohei Hata, eds., *Eusebius, Christianity, and Judaism* (Detroit, 1992), 409-31.

[6] On the social and political issues facing Jews in the Land of Israel in the first centuries see Sean Freyne, *The World of the New Testament* (Wilmington, 1985), 122-23.

possession of the world." The Mishnaic authorship answered with an innovative understanding of the primacy of human beings, who, they proposed, through the use of intellect and intention, could themselves shape and give meaning to – and in this way exercise dominion and control over – the world in which they lived. In this understanding, God was inert in the political sphere not because he had failed the people or withdrawn from history. Rather, God appeared to be hidden because God's direct intervention on earth was not really legitimate in the first place. For the rabbis comprehended that, to express their essential humanity, to possess their world, people needed themselves to determine good from evil, to sort out right from wrong, to create a world as they wished it to be and knew it could be. Within this construction of reality, the court on earth needed and deserved complete and unalienable political power.

The Mishnaic authorship thus rejects the notion that God rightly forces people into obedience through voices from heaven, miracles, or divine messengers, the earthly vehicles for God's exercise of political power. Stating that the earthly court speaks in the voice of God, the rabbis reject the coercion implicit in a system in which God holds all the political power, in which assent to God's will results from God's coercive behavior in history rather than from human contact with and consideration of the compelling divine word – that is, Torah. In this system, just as the human court determines right and wrong and imposes appropriate sanctions, so the individual comes to acceptance of the law through his or her own recognition of the value and correctness of that law, not in response to spectacular displays of God's power. It is their own pursuit of justice and promotion of good that leads people to appreciate the presence of God and to find strength in the knowledge that they are following God's path.

To this end, the rabbinic system holds that knowledge of God's will – in all religions, the ultimate source of legitimate political power – results not primarily from God's self-revelation in history. It depends rather upon the Jew's proper grasp of the Torah, acquired through active engagement with the details of revelation, through human sagacity, erudition, and intelligence.[7] God acts in the case of deliberate sexual crimes and other crimes purposely committed directly against God. But in a period in which God clearly did not generally enter into the human sphere to assure justice, the rabbis reject the notion that authority over the broader system of criminal law belongs primarily to God in the first place. They say instead that achieving justice is a human responsibility,

---

[7] On this point, see Jacob Neusner, "God: How, in Judaism, Do We Know God," *Formative Judaism*, 7th series (Atlanta, 1993), 209.

accomplished when people, through the use of their intellect and will, act as partners of God in returning the world to the state of perfection that God had always meant it to take.

In the context of such thinking, the Mishnah's authorship insists that the earthly court, in using its own intellect to define the law and determine appropriate sanctions, exercises a legitimate political power that reveals God's will on earth. Through this political myth, the Mishnah insists that individual Jews have the ability and the obligation themselves to define and then to create a new and better world, a world of holiness and sanctification, a world as they know it should be, wish it to be, and, if they only imagine intently enough and work hard enough, will assure that it someday will be. Thus, as Jacob Neusner so aptly stated,[8] the Mishnah's principal message, expressed so clearly in its politics, is that humans stand at the center of creation, at the head of all creatures upon the earth, corresponding to God in Heaven, in whose image they are made. Whereas Scripture asks, What can God do? the question of the Mishnah's authorship concerns, What can people do? And the rabbis' answer is that, by force of their will and deed, people – the Israelite nation – can do everything. They are the masters of the world, the crafters of their own destiny. In the aftermath of the two wars, the message of the Mishnah's politics could not have been more poignant.

---

[8] These final sentences paraphrase Neusner, *Rabbinic Political Theory*, 226.

8

Mysticism and Politics in the State of Israel

Ithamar Gruenwald
University of Tel Aviv

In what follows an attempt will be made to describe as objectively as possible the role and place religion, in general, and mysticism, in particular, have in the sociopolitical life of the Jewish People, in the past and in the modern State of Israel. As everyone following recent events in Israel knows, Israel is in the middle of a complicated peace process. This process has to overcome many difficulties, and many people feel deep frustration at having to face political moves that are likely to shatter for them strong beliefs and deep hopes. For those who saw in the "great Israel" the realization of their religious expectations and the materialization of essential political convictions, the giving up of territories resulted in deep distress. For them, it is a cause of fear at having to give up basic strongholds of their physical security. We have to bear all this in mind, when discussing issues that, as we shall see, are sometimes hard to predict and understand.

In any event, attempts were made at disrupting the peace-making process. The means that were used in bringing about such a disruption were many. People staged violent street demonstrations; they procured Halakhic decrees prohibiting the handing over of any part of the Holy Land to non-Jewish hands; and in some extreme cases even had recourse to acts of magical cursing. We shall try to describe what happened in terms that will make clear the role that religion, or religious institutions, played in this state of affairs.

I am well aware of the fact that an academically objective assessment of any situation can be given only when the needed historical and mental distance is established between the scholar and the subject of his research. We are still too close to the events discussed in this paper to allow for a definitive statement regarding their overall meaning. We have to keep that reservation in mind, especially because the events discussed here can hardly go without engaging an element of personal view and criticism in their description and analysis. It is to be expected that the time factor will assist future scholars in drawing a somewhat more detached picture, one in which the personal view will not be the glue that sticks the pieces together. Distance is indeed required in matters the description of which is likely to result in a rather disturbing picture. In short, from an epistemological point of view, I would admit that my presentation of the material is clearly marked by a personal engagement with the events described.

On a more general level, my approach to examining the situation will be marked by my scholarly· interests. I am convinced that the scholarly study of religion is an important tool in assessing the nature of current social, political, and cultural events. A proper understanding of human life and culture cannot be attained without a serious consideration of their religious components and points of connection. In my own areas of research, mysticism, apocalypticism, and other forms of enthusiastic religious behavior receive intensive attention. I am also interested in the messianic manifestations related to these areas of religious experience and behavior.

It is still an open, but certainly a tantalizing, question: How much of the millenarian spirit is at work in current political events? We are approaching not only the turn of the century but also of the millennium. The winding up of time spans of a thousand years has a special meaning in Jewish and Christian mysticism and apocalypticism. Above all, they mark intensified messianic expectations. In the framework of these expectations, all kinds of unexpected things can either happen or be brought about to happen. A millenarian spirit can make itself felt in many ways, some of which may not be present in a fully conscious manner in the minds of the people motivated by them. We shall, thus, examine the role that mysticism, in the wide sense of the term, played in the events the details of which must in their essentials be familiar to you.

A

The subject of mysticism and politics can be treated in two ways. In the first one, scholars would examine the events of the past, namely, the role mysticism used to play in certain political appointments and processes of decision making in the past. In the second one, attention is directed toward more recent events and developments. Here, as indicated above, those events and developments relating the political life of the State of Israel and the Jews living in the Diaspora are of major interest to us. For various and obvious reasons, not least among them being the fact that there is not much to say on the first aspect of the subject, the major thrust of our discussion falls on the second one.

As for the question, How much political involvement was there in ancient Jewish mysticism? the answer is clear. The political freedom that Jews were allowed to enjoy in the past was practically limited by their exilic existence. Where there is little political freedom, mysticism can have only restricted claims in matters relating political issues. One mystical text, though, mentions the fact that appointments to a certain ruling position among the Jews in Babylonia of Talmudic times depended on the mystical merits of the people seeking the positions in question, or else deciding the appointment. But this is roughly all that is said in the mystical texts in our possession about the political strength, or aspirations, of Jewish mystics in antiquity. In any event, political strength in this connection means something that is basically limited to congregational decisions in a purely Jewish context.

As a rule, mystics are socially withdrawn people. They seek neither the limelights of political life nor the power that comes with it. However, in Tannaitic (that is, in early Christian) times, some of the rabbinic leaders were described as engaging in mystical lore. If the relevant stories can be trusted historically – and that is not only a matter of subjective trust but also of methodological principle – then one may argue that some masters of the Mishnah consolidated their authority and status among their colleagues and coreligionists by claiming for themselves mystical accomplishments.

From a socio-historical point of view, what is at stake here is the question, How much publicity did Jewish mystics seek and how strongly voiced were their complementary claims to social status? This is a question that concerns mystics in all ages. As a rule, there is little of the polemical tone in the writings of the early mystics that could serve as an indication to the presence of a political power struggle. When, for instance, Qabbalists in the Middle Ages strongly criticize those who are unable to read Scripture in a way revealing the secrets of the Qabbalah, this is not a political power game but an attempt to establish the Qabbalistic ways of interpreting Scripture. Qabbalists can be very sarcastic in their debates against their intellectual opponents, particularly among the medieval Jewish philosophers. However, neither they nor the philosophers who came under their attack had any social or political aspirations, in the modern sense of these terms.

In brief, mystics were rarely involved in public debates and struggles. When their writings or ideas were condemned, this was rarely the result of civil disobedience or moral anarchy on their part. The issue usually was a purely intellectual, or theological, one. The polemics against the Qabbalah, or *mutatis mutandis*, against the philosophers, was largely confined to doctrinal issues. Political power games were, if at all, played out on other planes and with other means.

Matters received a sharper political edge in the eighteenth and nineteenth centuries (sometimes also in the twentieth century) when East European Hasidism (piety) and its opponents, the so-called Mitnaggdim engaged in fierce polemics. In many cases, the Hasidim even split among themselves over sociopolitical, that is dynastic, hegemony. In their private Hasidic Courts, concern for the larger Hasidic movement often gave way to particularistic interests. However, as a general rule, unless provoked to polemical stances, mystics kept to their pacifying positions. The reason for that was, as we saw, the lack of political aspirations and interest on their part.

B

However, as indicated above, the strifes of the past are of lesser concern to us here than the ones enacted on the current social and political scene. In the rest of the place allotted to us here we would like to describe the political scene in present day Israel, where "mysticism," in the wide sense of the term, is allowed to play an interesting, though sometimes bewildering, role.

We shall begin our discussion with a few remarks on religion in the modern world. Two points have to be made in this respect. The first concerns the place religion occupies in the modern state. The second relates to the place religion is allowed to have in the minds of secularly oriented people. One may argue, not without justice, that the two points are interrelated. Although the modern state professedly keeps a separation between "state and church," the church plays a role on the main stage as well as behind the scenes of modern political life. Similarly, although the modern mind is basically oriented by secular ideas, religion, as an intellectual and social factor, is very much present in the minds of many people. It appears that against all reasonable odds, religion still is an endemic cultural factor that cannot be removed from the state and the minds of people.

In many cases, though, religion does not appear in its traditional forms as accepted by the religious establishment, but rather in the form of idiosyncratic trends in which mysticism, magic, and enhanced messianism play an important role. In other words, modern society and culture are still very much under the influence of various forms of religious thinking and activity. In all this, irrational factors play a strong role.

In line with modern trends enacted on a large international scene, mystical ideas and practices today have a greater appeal in the eyes of the general public than they used to have in the past. Thus, for instance, *Qabbalah* has become an amazingly widely winged cover term for all kinds of spiritual trends. Because these trends lack any specific and homogeneous structure or system, they seek legitimization in a term that has a long and respectable history. Those who know what Qabbalah is all about, often ask themselves what makes so many people seek refuge in beds still warm from the previous sleeping person. In fact, the use of the word *Qabbalah* in the jargon of modern spirituality makes many knowledgeable onlookers raise a wondering eyebrow. Does this usage of the term betray a romantic urge to seek refuge in obscurity? Obscurity, to be sure, is like a womb: its darkness provides security. However, as we all know, the term one enjoys in the womb is measured by weeks. The day soon comes, when exposure to day light inevitably marks a crisis.

Long before *Qabbalah* became a term for all seasons, Timothy Leary spoke of the "politics of ecstasy." What he meant by this phrase need not bother us here. Briefly, though, it advocated, among other things, the use of hallucinogenic drugs produced from what people thought were sacred mushrooms. Here, in the case of Timothy Leary, "Qabbalah" hardly was an issue at all. But other people transposed certain notions from the mystical inventory of Timothy Leary into a modern "Qabbalistic" key. All this would not have bothered us here, unless we found that the internationalization of Qabbalah affected also certain circles in the State of Israel.

Before we proceed with our discussion, a word is due on the influence Qabbalah had on messianism. Since Qabbalah offers its advocates and believers a mode of spiritual redemption, no great distance had to be covered before spiritual entities could be translated into political hopes. As we know from their Christian counterparts, Jewish manifestations of messianism could easily be geared toward the realization of political ends. Thus, scholars would often debate the question, How much messianism in Jewish Qabbalah? Different answers, expressing a variety of views, were given to the question. They need not concern us here. However, it is interesting to notice that one scholar even found a basically messianic structure in the Zohar, the mystical scripture of the Qabbalists.

Be that as it may, mystical notions easily translated into messianic ones. On the historical scene, the movement of Shabbatai Tsvi in the sixteenth century is a master model in which mystical ideas are the fountainhead from which a messianic movement draws its ideological waters. For those seeking a larger comparative framework, the mystical components in the writings of St. Paul could be referred to as an enlightening parallel.

A few scholars have argued that the messianic zeal of Sabbataism was one of the precursors of modern secular Zionism. However, the indebtedness of modern secular Zionism to the messianic movement mentioned above is a debatable issue. It is interesting to notice, though, that Qabbalah played, and still plays, an important role in modern Israeli life. Here, secularism and orthodox religiousness sound almost the same instruments, though with slightly different tunes.

On the secular side, the line of argumentation takes this direction. Since Qabbalah allegedly entails a direct affront to traditional rabbinism, its use in countermining modern forms of rabbinism becomes an irresistible temptation. Taking such a position can amount to gross cultural manipulation. Still, it had a strong appeal to those engaged in the controversy about the nature of Israeli Judaism. Secular Jews in the modern State of Israel found it an attractive solution, when identifying themselves as "Israelis" rather than "Jews." "Jews" implied a cultural affiliation with traditional Judaism, while "Israelis" could signify anything that was secularly oriented and liberal in its basic forms of thinking and expression.

Gershom Scholem, who for many years acted as the undisputed nestor of Qabbalah studies, openly sided with modern secular Zionism. In his later years, though, Scholem admitted that any kind of Jewish theology could not be severed from its traditional components. However, in the eyes of his prejudiced readers his scholarly achievements were read as a manifesto of a secular type of Judaism that was growing out of the anarchic and polemical stances taken in Qabbalah. In the eyes of Scholem's prejudiced readers, secularism could be presented as a transformed type of the alleged anarchic component in certain Qabbalistic writings.

Things were never as explicitly and loudly said as one could expect them to be, in that respect. Their function, though, appeared clear and simple. Qabbalah is the spiritual forerunner of a rebellious, hence also secular, type of Judaism. It is interesting to notice, in this connection, that some of the major spokesmen reformulating Judaism for their basically secular purposes are the same people that carry out the scholarly legacy of Gershom Scholem, and also posthumously publish his writings!

In some ways, then, mystical notions and ideas were operative in creating the new secular Zionist ethos upon which the State of Israel was to build its future. However, in a more direct manner, the name of Rav Kook comes to mind in this connection. Rav Kook, who acted as Chief Rabbi until his death in 1935, dedicated his intellectual efforts to finding the dialectic of what may paradoxically be called sacred secularism. The pioneers (*Halutsim*), as the new settlers of the Land of Israel were called after a favored American model, came to their old/new homeland fulfilling something that in their eyes had no religious dimension at all. In point of fact, their departure from their previous homeland in Eastern Europe marked an escape from the grips of what seemed to them a dying and oppressing tradition. In this respect, their pioneering activity meant to them the final breach with the exilic past and its religious traditions and institutions. Paradoxically, however, in coming to the Holy Land and joining the heroic efforts of rebuilding it, they inadvertently enacted old hopes that used to sustain Judaism for a long time. These hopes often had a messianic configuration.

The question, then, was asked: How could these rebels be aligned with the traditional aspirations of the Jewish People? Several answers were given to that question. The most systematic one, though, was given by Rav Kook. Using an old notion, that was also taught by many a philosopher in the Platonic tradition, Rav Kook argued that in the life and activity of those Pioneers appearance and reality should consistently be held apart. Allegedly, what looked to be an act of secular rebellion was in reality an inverted type of enacting holiness, or holiness in disguise. The day would soon come, thus went the argument, and true holiness will show its glitter in unblemished purity.

Viewing modern secularism as holiness in disguise is certainly a tour de force of dialectical thinking. It has its philosophical roots in post-Hegelian philosophy, with which Rav Kook was familiar. It also has its origins in the Gothic structure of Jewish Qabbalah. According to the Qabbalah, the quality of things can almost abruptly change in line with certain processes paradigmatically coming about in the divine realms of the Sefirot. In this respect, the same entity can appear in two antagonistic aspects within a very short period of time. There is no need to bother the reader with the details of this Qabbalistic dialectic. Suffice it here to say that this type of dialectic worked well for those who satisfied themselves with the solutions that it provided them with. However, many people, particularly those belonging to the extreme Orthodox circles, had no use for it. In fact, these circles outrightly rejected Rav Kook's writings. They went even as far as excommunicating their author. For a few, however, these writings still provided the needed nostalgia filling the space between a problematic reality and an expected future.

Matters radically changed in this respect after the Six Days' War. With a magical wand in hand, the few heirs of Rav Kook were all of a sudden able to point out in his writings the cornerstones upon which a new messianic ideology could be built. Among other things, that ideology, or messianic dimension, supplied them with the magical spell that turned a masterfully won military campaign into an act of divine redemption. While the official spokesmen of the government pragmatically declared that territories would be traded in for true peace, the new advocates of Rav Kook saw in his writings the pledge for eternally regaining the Holy Land for its divinely appointed owners, the People of Israel. The conquests were no longer viewed as a military inevitability, but the fulfillment of long-standing messianic promises.

In short, military victory was turned into a redemptive, that is, messianic, act. Messianic acts, as we all know, tend to be viewed in their irreversibility. Rav Kook was quoted as the prophet that foresaw everything, and – what is even more important – as theologically justifying every political act that strengthened the Jewish holding over the Holy Land.

It is amazing to notice that among his new interpreters there were some notorious falsifiers. It is one of the utterly strange phenomena in the history of book publishing in modern Israel that the writings of Rav Kook were ideologically tampered with so as to make them fit the new messianic trends and fashions. The original manuscripts are in the hands of people who will never tolerate an objective scholarly eye to scrutinize their contents.

Thus, not before long, the dialectic mysticism of the father was successfully turned into a positivist ideology in the hands of his son, Rabbi Tsvi Yehudah Kook and his followers. Overnight, the yeshivah that carried the name of one of the great rabbinic minds of the twentieth century became a stronghold of messianic politics. The great rabbinic minds in the country usually preferred other rabbinic study houses. In their eyes, Yeshivat Merkaz Ha-Rav – Ha-Rav being the shorthand for Ha-Rav Kook – was no rabbinic jewel. It used to produce political and ideological leaders, but no great rabbinic minds. All of a sudden this yeshivah flourished with students many of whom were later on appointed as heads of the yeshivot, mostly located in the "occupied territories," in which a new type of religiousness evolved.

In the past, a considerable number of the religious population joined the secular sections in a common effort at materializing general Zionist aspirations. The new spirit that evolved in those yeshivot was shaped in such a way that it turned the Zionist aspirations into an exclusively religio-political issue. The political tone and orientation here were markedly right-wing. Before long, attempts were made at altogether delegitimizing secular left-wing Zionism. Moderate, or left-wing, Zionism was treated as offensively un-Jewish. It was presented as the overnight shelter for the infidels, the heretics, and the ignorant people. A former Chief Rabbi of the country recently said in a mass rally: Jews in the State of Israel are divided between the knowing religious and the

Godless unknowing. Religious people who maintained a left-wing position were given the feeling of being under an ideological siege.

I am well aware of the fact that the picture that I am drawing is a gloomy and sad one. Unfortunately, it is as true as it is disturbing, at least in regard to the positions taken by the extreme right-wing sector of the religious population in Israel. Many people identified with that line, some more actively, a few in a more passive manner. Only a small section in the religious population saw that the atmosphere was conducive to an outburst of the unexpected. In a sense, the Jewish settlements and the yeshivot that flourished in them were the ideologically protected greenhouses in which the seeds of religious fundamentalism were sown and the plants of religious extremism were safely growing. Those who had eyes to see could predict the inevitable outcome. The outcome, though, was too bewildering to be taken as a real threat.

In short, almost in spite of themselves the writings of Rav Kook became an important tool in the hands of manipulating religio-political spokesmen. We should mention again the fact that this could not happen before Rav Kook's writings were tampered with so as to serve as the new gospel of the sanctified land. A new sense of holiness was attached to the Land of Israel. A new myth was created. Unusually great financial and human resources were invested in making that myth a political reality.

C

Who were the people that took part in these developments? Generally speaking, they represented a cross section of the religious establishment in the country. Many of them came from middle-class homes where a modern education was standard and economic means were not close to the poverty line. Many of them had academic training, and jobs that were reserved for the upper-middle class. Morally speaking, they were law-abiding people, with a strong commitment to maintain congregational and community welfare. They served in the army, and in many cases as its elite. In short, everything was there to make these people a positive social class, strengthened by its strong ideological affiliation and social commitment.

What turned many of them into a potentially, if not actually, extreme and violent group? There are a number of reasons that can be given by way of an answer to that question. We have already mentioned the distress and the fear that these people felt themselves exposed to, when they realized that the peace process will ultimately force many of them to leave their homes. In addition, the Palestinian "Uprising," *Intifada* as it was called in Arabic, exposed them, and the rest of the population, to daily physical dangers. Under such daily threats people are easily driven into a struggle for survival. This is particularly the case when people come to the conclusion that their government has deserted them, or else does not fulfill its duties in maintaining order and security in the country.

Last but not least of all was the ideological factor. These people deeply believed in the religious significance of the present history of the Jewish People. The ingathering of the Jewish People from all parts of the world, Ethiopia and Russia being unexpected models, convinced many people that the promises of the ancient prophets regarding the future ingathering of the People of Israel are materializing before their eyes. The Land, too, has returned to its original owners. Thus everything was there to show that the days of the Messiah are at hand.

Thus, when new winds began to blow and even Menachem Begin, of all people, gave back territory for peace with Egypt, many people felt that the land under their feet was beginning to shake. Along with it came the fear that the recently revived messianic hopes were likely to collapse long before they had their chance of being fully materialized. As long as the right-wing Likkud was in political power, fears of the future were reasonably contained. However, when the Labor party came to power, the political strategy and tactics changed. One way of fighting the new spirit of peace making was in discrediting, or delegitimizing, the government and its Judaic affiliation and commitment. The rhetoric of political propaganda became extremely hostile. But not only the political rhetoric accelerated its pace; the "language of the street" changed, too. Brutal and dehumanizing street posters were only one side of this street-gang-like warfare. Another aspect was enacted in street demonstrations of the most violent nature. They culminated in severe clashes with the police, and left a shattering impression in the eyes of many people, both in Israel and around the world.

As mentioned before, the political parties of the Left were declared as utterly antireligious and anti-Jewish. Here, the extreme religious parties collaborated with the right-wing secular parties. Since the political system in Israel is secular, serious attempts had to be made to compromise between the religious claims and the political reality. This, however, did not happen in a way conducive to cultural understanding. A fusion between religious and political aims came about only for right-wing political ends. The left wing was exposed to a head-on clash between traditional rabbinic norms and its own political orientation.

When the above-mentioned messianic zeal was superimposed on traditional Halakhic norms, an instant recipe fell into the hands of those wishing to concoct something that in the eyes of many was tantamount to civil disobedience. Halakhic decrees and homiletic pamphlets were constantly circulating in which people were told that giving back any piece of land contradicts the Law of the Torah. In fact, those who were eager to obey rabbinic opinions on the matter had a large amount of learned opinions at their disposal, all of which urged them to disobey any attempt to hand over any part of the land into Palestinian hands. One could even hear the voice of one of the heads of the rabbinic study houses advising people to set booby traps so as to prevent the turning over of Jewish army camps in the West Bank to Palestinian hands. Whatever one makes of such views and injunctions, they create a public atmosphere in which everything becomes possible.

Thus, in face of the imminent threat of losing some land to Palestinian ownership, a horror atmosphere was created in which people learned that peace making that involves the giving up of land is tantamount to betraying one's country. In Jewish Halakhic terms, the political leaders who were directing the peace negotiations, and Yitzhak Rabin at their top, were declared people whose blood was let free. People like Yitzhak Rabin were defined as "pursuers," that is, people caught in pursuing other people to kill them or to hand them over for sexual abuse. Jewish Halakhah maintains that such people can be killed without incurring any indictment on the killer. It is indeed difficult not to see in all this something that amounts to a horror story. Restlessness at such manifestations of theologically motivated violence is the least that could be expected of the left-wing onlookers.

Those who issued the decree that Yitzhak Rabin was a "pursuing person" deserving death, are in one way or another affiliated with the circles of Merkaz Ha-Rav, that yeshivah that bears the name of Rav Kook. In their messianic zeal, the students of Rav Kook found an interesting ally. They were inadvertently assisted by the non-Zionist Lubavitchers, who ardently helped the process of delegitimizing the government and its policy.

The Lubavitchers earned their renown as a modern type of Hasidism, engaged worldwide in acts of social welfare, education, and fighting drug addiction. In many respects, their members created a master model of volunteer work that engaged in the most exciting rescue activities. Long before the gates of the Soviet Union had been opened for emigration, the Lubavitchers established there a wide network of Jewish education. In other parts of the world, they built community houses for socially deprived people. However, their political orientation was strongly motivated by messianic notions. They did not lose an opportunity to give expression to their views, urging the government of Israel not to give in to Arabic and Palestinian territorial claims.

At the end of a very long career of important activity as a charismatic leader, the Lubavitcher "Rebbe," as Menachem Schneorsohn was called, was declared Messiah by his followers. His physical death some time later on was enacted on a Christian model: He would soon be resurrected from the dead and come again! The Lubavitcher mourners persisted in their belief, even when told that a Christological theology could be detected between the lines of their own. In short, the Lubavitchers and the students of Rav Kook were the two channels through which the modern messianism of Gush Emunim, the extreme groups of "settlers," and some other extremists, received their ideological waters. Qabbalah provided the rhetoric and the ideological foundations not only for the ideological declarations of the Lubavitcher Hasidim, but also for the violent street demonstrations in which they, and others, were engaged.

Part of the religious literature that was published on these matters was circulated in synagogues every Friday evening. These were leaflets, or flyers, that discussed various issues relating to the weekly reading of the Torah portion. They all had the appearance of edifying homiletical sermons. In reality, however, they quite often read like yellow papers, in which black and white were the only colors in which the discourse could be held. Rabbis competed with one another in finding hints for the present situation in the weekly Torah readings. The notion of the sacredness of the Land, the obligation to keep to it under all circumstances, and the futility of the secular position – were all easily discovered under every word in Scripture.

In our synagogue, for instance, one could find a weekly output of at least three or four such pamphlets. When alerting people to the intellectual manipulation that was enacted in these pamphlets, I was told that it was useless, if not counterproductive, to censor their publication. In fact, nobody even admitted to placing them there for circulation in the synagogue. With all the tones of legalistic objectivity and homiletic piety, these pamphlets literally provided the groundwork for civil disobedience.

Not many people cared to pay attention to the ominous tones contained in these publications. As in the case of David Koresh, the General Secret Service, in Israel, was completely out of focus. Lacking any kind of expert ability to assess their nature, the General Secret Service ignored these printed materials. The fact that these pamphlets, and rabbinic decrees, were openly circulating blindfolded people as to their potential quality as instigators of civil disobedience. In short, the legend on the wall was clear and simple. However, only few understood its implications. Those who should have noticed the legend and drawn the necessary conclusions were simply unqualified for that job.

In the months preceding the assassination of Yitzhak Rabin, thousands of religious demonstrators – mostly young people affiliated with the settlers and the Zionist religious youth movement Bnei Akiva –

filled the streets and road junctions in violent demonstrations against the peace-making policy of the government. The atmosphere in the air was that of an imminent civil war. Nothing could stop the situation from snowballing into the abyss where the deadly bullets were shot. Paradoxically, though, the three gunshots that were aimed at Rabin quintessentially consummated the inevitable civil war. The shock was too great for that civil war to be carried any further.

D

If we look back and try to see what was the rabbinic contribution to the situation, as well as the mystical component in the crucial developments, the following observations can be made:

1. The rabbinic system is such that it places in the hands of the rabbis, and particularly the heads of yeshivot, absolute power. Halakhic legislation is in their hands. Disobedience to the rabbinic view is tantamount to religious blasphemy. In other words, people disobeying the rabbis are guilty of the worst kind of religious offense. In its own terms of reference, the power of those rabbis is unlimited. In Jewish tradition, people are encouraged, or urged as the case might be, to "make themselves a rabbinic master." They are to accept one religious authority to guide them in all their religious affairs and transactions. Once a person acquires for himself such a rabbinic authority, total and unreserved obedience to that authority is required of him.

2. The rabbis think and believe that what they do is directed by the will of God as implied in the various forms in which that will is manifested in the divine word. In this respect, the word of God is that of the King of the Kings, whereas the voice of the earthly regime is that of the kings, only. When a clash of interests between these two "monarchical orders" arises, priority is automatically given to that of the King of the Kings. In other words, God stands above all political regimes, modern democracy that tolerates the religious institutions and sustains them economically included. There is no need to specify all the antidemocratic consequences that such an attitude entails.

3. Since the rabbis have no penal system to enforce their views and will on those who disobey their decrees, alternative forms of legally imposing the rabbinic law are applied. Among them one can find social excommunication, magical cursing, and legal discreditation. In the case of magical cursing, we, once again, come close to mysticism. For, phenomenologically speaking, mysticism and magic share important aspects in their practice, though for completely different

purposes. In the kind of magical cursing called *Pulsa di-Nura* (Lashes of Fire), which was applied in the case of Yitzhak Rabin, the well-being and the life of the cursed person are literally exposed to the worst kinds of physical harm.

Magical cursing evidently is the most outlandish measure in this power game. It is a measure taken in cases, or moments, of extreme stress and crisis. The question here is not of believing or disbelieving in the efficacy of magic, but in the atmosphere that is created by such acts of alternative violence as invoked by magic. Since magic belongs to the irrational, people may see in it something that supersedes the measures applied in normal conditions. Phenomenologically speaking, magic is used when other means of handling a difficult and critical situation fail. Viewed from the outside, its application marks weakness and despair. When magic is applied against one's enemy, its brutality has no limits. When malevolently applied, it is believed to be as forceful a means as any other unconventional weaponry.

In many respects, the history of the State of Israel has reached a crucial turning point. What forces will prevail in the country is still an open question. At the moment, the answer is not clear. Hopefully, practical needs and the will of survival will help common sense to prevail. What still gives me concern is the fact that so far only a very small fraction of the religious population has openly spoken out against recent developments of political violence. In many ways people prefer not to speak their minds, even when their disagreement and resentment cannot be doubted.

Hopefully, that will soon change. Otherwise physical and moral survival may be in danger. Too much is at stake to let common sense and good will wait for their eventual chance. There is too much to be gained from a different future to let it pass by unnoticed.

9

Religious Resources for Political Culture: The Case of Judaism

William S. Green
University of Rochester
and
Gary G. Porton
University of Illinois

I

Religion is fundamentally about power.[1] Therefore, religion cannot avoid politics. Religion has the ability to ground the use of force in a cosmic and moral order. Therefore, religion is perhaps the strongest legitimator of any political system. Politics has the ability to compel behavior with force and thus to shape immediate collective experience. Therefore, politics has an unusual capacity to reinforce or undermine a religion's worldview. A religion cannot persist if it cannot explain how the exercise of coercive power in the world of immediate experience conforms to, is encompassed by, or at least does not refute, the religion's own theory of how things are or ought to be. Whether or not a religion itself can legitimately deploy force to compel behavior, it must be able to explain how such force in its own world is used. It must show its adherents that it is not mistaken about the world.

The need for a theory of politics is greater for religions that are out of power than for those that are in power. If ordinary, repeated experience

---

[1] Part 1 of this paper was written by William Green. Part 2 was written by Gary Porton as a response to and extension of part 1. Each of us has read and endorsed the contribution of the other.

in everyday life disconfirms what a religion says, then the religion can lose credibility and membership. Religions that do not govern must explain why, since they are not running the government, the government is not running them. Thus, the relationship between religion and politics is both unavoidable and systemically uneasy – a volatile mix. The political philosopher Stephen Smith rightly claims that the "theologico-political question" is basic to Western culture. "Should religion rule politics, or should politics rule religion?...To some degree the entire history of Western political thought can be seen as an answer to that question."[2]

The Jews and Judaism are essential components in any discussion of how the West answered the theologico-political question. The Jews' economic success, educational accomplishment, and cultural assimilation – particularly in America – easily help us to forget that the Enlightenment cut its teeth on the Jewish Question. The Jews, and therefore Judaism, were at the center of the liberalism that has shaped so much of modern Western political life, particularly in America. The stakes for the Jews in political emancipation were high, as Pierre Birnbaum and Ira Katznelson point out:

> At its core, Jewish emancipation was concerned with three sets of issues about citizenship and rights: (1) whether broadly liberal and republican doctrines and institutional arrangements grounded in Enlightenment values would come to govern transactions between the state and civil society to provide fresh potential bases for Jewish citizenship; (2) whether such innovative formulas for political participation, once in place, would prove sufficiently encompassing to include the Jews; and (3) whether the terms of admission to the polity these arrangements countenanced would permit a far-reaching or narrowly gauged pluralism for Jews seeking both to take up the offer of citizenship and remain meaningfully Jewish.[3]

The Jews took up the emancipation's "liberal offer" with a zeal and a faith unmatched by any other modern group. At the core of the liberal program – alongside its concern for the values of free speech and opinion, tolerance of different ideas, the autonomy and dignity of the individual, and constitutional government – is an articulated distinction between religion and politics. Liberalism places sovereignty in the

---

[2] Stephen Smith, *Spinoza, the Enlightenment, and the Jewish Question* (New Haven: Yale University Press, forthcoming). I am grateful to Professor Smith for allowing me to draw on the manuscript version of his book.
[3] Pierre Birnbaum and Ira Katznelson, "Emancipation and the Liberal Offer," in Pierre Birnbaum and Ira Katznelson, eds., *Paths of Emancipation: Jews, States, and Citizenship* (Princeton: Princeton University Press, 1994), 5

collectivity of the people, and it moves to neutralize the importance of religious authorities in the realm of governance.[4]

We tend to explain the Jews' attraction to liberalism in political and social terms. In Western Europe, at least, liberalism allowed the Jews to participate in politics despite their religion. But the persistent role of religion in defining the Jews as a group in Western history surely justifies a broader inquiry into the relationship between Jewish religion and the political behavior of Jews. This paper is a draft of a preliminary first step in that inquiry.

First, some definitions are in order. For the purposes of this paper, politics does not mean small-scale social interaction and does not refer to families and villages. Rather, politics here means governance and statecraft, the power to tax, to wage war, to produce money, to enforce public order, and the ability to make the institutions of that power work for your own ends. For religion, the definition of Melford Spiro serves well: "an institution consisting of culturally patterned interaction with culturally postulated superhuman beings."[5] Finally, the definition of political culture comes from Peter Kaufmann: "any set of doctrines, images, and institutions used by apologists and administrators to distribute or redistribute their government's powers to intervene and control."[6]

What are Judaism's resources for political culture? Do the interactions with God described in the sources of Judaism produce doctrines, images, and institutions that have influenced Jews in their response to governmental power? Do Scripture and the Mishnah contain what Kaufmann calls "enduring categorical structures" that offer a theory of politics? What are Judaism's religious guidelines for the exercise of political power? These questions are obviously heuristic, and the answers supplied below – in fulfillment of the assignment for this paper – are suggestive, speculative, and schematic rather than systematic and probative.

To approach our question we must, in the first instance, see the biblical and rabbinic documents whole, as they appear in their final form, for that is how they have been appropriated by the tradition. To probe the Hebrew Bible's outlook on politics, it will be useful to consider a particularly salient example. If politics is about statecraft and

---

[4] I have based this description of liberalism on Smith, *Spinoza.*
[5] Melford E. Spiro, "Religion: Problems of Definition and Explanation," in Benjamin Kilbourne and L. L. Langness, eds., *Culture and Human Nature: Theoretical Papers of Melford E. Spiro* (Chicago: University of Chicago Press, 1987), 187-222.
[6] Peter Iver Kaufmann, *Redeeming Politics* (Princeton: Princeton University Press, 1995), 5.

governance, then the Bible's attitude toward Israel's ruler, and the king of Israel in particular, is a useful and tractable starting point. Monarchy is a potent symbol in Judaism because it is associated both with Jewish political autonomy and with Jewish messianism.

On the matter of who should govern Israel, the Hebrew Bible is far more ambivalent about native kingship than about imperial domination. Indeed, biblical texts seem to prefer foreign to native rule. The biblical tradition holds the idea of a native Israelite king at arm's length. As Moshe Halbertal and Avishai Margalit explain, "The demand for the establishment of a monarchy in Israel is directly connected with the problem of God's exclusivity as Israel's sovereign."[7] In Gideon's words, "I will not rule over you myself, nor shall my son rule over you; the Lord alone will rule over you" (Judg. 8:23). A native Israelite king is possible only if "both the king and the people understand that they are still subject to God and that the king is nothing but an agent."[8] In apparent contrast to the priesthood and other ancient Near Eastern kings, the Israelite monarchy "is not...rooted in the cosmic order, and is not part of the primordial structure of the world."[9] It "is not essential for the existence of order in nature or in the political sphere. The gap between the king and the cosmos also is expressed by the fact that the Israelite king has no special role in divine worship, and he is not responsible for rainfall or the success of the crops."[10] To these arguments we can add the redaction of the Hebrew Bible, which severs the Deuteronomic history from the Pentateuch and thereby decisively separates kingship from the founding narrative of Israel's engagement with God. The priestly editing defers the stories of the Israelite kings to the middle of Israel's epic, and the text itself ends in 2 Chronicles with the hope for a renewed Temple cult, but no kingship. The Hebrew Bible thus denies the king of Israel any fundamental role in maintaining Israel's relationship to God.

By contrast, Jeremiah and Second Isaiah depict the leaders of foreign imperial powers as willing agents of Israel's God. Second Isaiah calls the Persian emperor Cyrus God's "anointed." Prophetic literature distinguishes Israel's submission to Nebuchadnezzar or Cyrus from a political alliance with another power. Indeed, the prophets appear to regard surrender to imperialism not as politics, but as obedience to God.[11] The approval of foreign rule is more pronounced in other biblical texts. Consider, for example, 2 Chron. 36:22-23:

---

[7]Moshe Halbertal and Avishai Margalit, *Idolatry* (Cambridge: Harvard University Press, 1992), 218.

[8] Ibid., 219.

[9] Ibid., 220.

[10] Ibid.

[11] Ibid., 224.

> And in the first year of King Cyrus of Persia, when the word of the Lord spoken by Jeremiah was fulfilled, the Lord roused the spirit of King Cyrus of Persia to issue a proclamation throughout his realm by word of mouth and in writing, as follows: "Thus said King Cyrus of Persia: 'The Lord God of Heaven has given me all the kingdoms of the earth, and has charged me with building Him a House in Jerusalem, which is in Judah. Any one of you of all his people, the Lord his God be with him and let him go up.'"[12]

The books of Ezra-Nehemiah explicitly make the rebuilt Temple, and thus the Temple cult, an extension of the Persian imperial regime. As Joseph Blenkinsopp notes, "The requirement that sacrifices and prayers for the royal family be incorporated into the liturgy (Ezra 6:10) reinforced the point that the temple and all it stood for was understood to be part of the apparatus of imperial control."[13] The contrast between the Israelite king and the Persian royal house could not be more stark. The king has no fundamental role in Israel's worship, but the Persian regime is essential to the Temple's establishment and the cult's persistence. Ezra-Nehemiah thus legitimate imperial control over the Land of Israel and deny to the cult any mission or meaning of Jewish political autonomy.

As for rabbinic literature, Jacob Neusner shows in this volume and elsewhere that the Mishnah is a utopian document and that it offers no recipe for statecraft or political rule. The absence of a concern for statecraft is evident in Talmudic literature as well. The famous, though infrequently cited, dictum of the Babylonian *amora* Samuel, *dina' de-malkhuta' dina'* (the law of the land is the law), assumes that *malkhuta'* does not refer to a Jewish institution.[14]

Scripture and the Mishnah envision a cult without a king or kingdom. They therefore conceive of what we would call religion ("culturally patterned interaction with culturally postulated superhuman beings") as independent of Jewish (or Israelite) political autonomy. In this sense, both the biblical and rabbinic records appear to reflect an incipient native distinction between religion and politics.[15]

---

[12] Translation from *TANAKH: A New Translation of The Holy Scriptures* (Philadelphia: Jewish Publication Society, 1985).

[13] Joseph Blenkinsopp, "Temple and Society in Achaemenid Judah, " in P. R. Davies, ed., *Second Temple Studies*, vol. 1, *The Persian Period*, JSOT Supplement Series 117 (Sheffield: JSOT Press, 1991), 39.

[14] I owe this observation to my colleague Ayala Emmett.

[15] This is not to suggest that historically religion and politics operated in antiquity in separate spheres. Rather, it is to say that the textual worlds of Scripture and the Mishnah understand a distinction between the two and reflect it in the construction of the textual record. I do not claim isomorphism between text and society.

To begin to explain this point of view, it helps to recall that Jewish religious life in the ancient Mediterranean developed and persisted in large measure because of the policies of imperial powers, most notably Persia and Rome. In the first instance, it was the Persian state that permitted and enabled the construction of the second Temple. Consider the testimony, for example, of Neh. 2:1-9:

> [1]In the month of Nisan in the twentieth year of King Artaxerxes, wine was set before him; I took the wine and gave it to the king – I had never been out of sorts in his presence. [2]The king said to me, "How is it that you look bad, though you are not ill. It must be bad thoughts." I was very frightened, [3]but I answered the king, "May the king live forever! How should I not look bad when the city of the graveyard of my ancestors lies in ruins, and its gates have been consumed by fire?" [4]The king said to me, "What is your request?" With a prayer to the God of Heaven, I answered the king, "If it please the king, and if your servant has found favor with you, send me to Judah, to the city of my ancestors' graves, to rebuild it." [6]With the consort seated at his side, the king said to me, "How long will you be gone, and when will you return?" So it was agreeable to the king to send me, and I gave him a date. [7]Then I said to the king, "If it please the king, let me have letters to the governors of the province of Beyond the River, directing them to grant me passage until I reach Judah; [8]likewise, a letter to Asaph, the keeper of the King's Park, directing him to give me timber for roofing the gatehouses of the temple fortress and the city walls and for the house I shall occupy." The king gave me these, thanks to my God's benevolent care for me. [9]When I came to the governors of the province of Beyond the River, I gave them the king's letters. The king also sent army officer and cavalry with me.

Historians debate the meaning of the Persians' and the Jews' actions. Pierre Briant claims that the Persian permission to the Jews to return to the Land of Israel suggests no particular affection for Yahwism (and, by extension, political privilege for the Jews?) and was "a common and banal event for the Persian political establishment."[16] Alternatively, Shaye Cohen suggests that the Jews' restoration of their ancestral religious center was exceptional under imperial rule: "Of all the nations exiled from their lands by the Assyrians and Babylonians, only the Jews returned to their homeland in order to rebuild their ancient temple."[17] In either case, it is unthinkable that the Persians would have placed the Temple's reconstruction in the hands of Jews it deemed unreliable or hostile to the imperial regime. Later, Judaism also benefited from both

---

[16] Pierre Priant, "Persian Empire," in *Anchor Bible Dictionary* (New York: Doubleday, 1995), 5:236-44. Also see Blenkinsopp, 24.

[17] Shaye J. D. Cohen, *From the Maccabees to the Mishnah* (Philadelphia: Westminster Press, 1987), 27.

Ptolemaic and Seleucid policies, which exempted the Jews "from putting a royal cult in their Temple and public places."[18]

In the case of Rome, Julius Caesar granted privileges to the Jewish religion that lasted for three centuries. To see precisely how the Roman imperial establishment enabled Judaism, it is worth listing Caesar's privileges in detail. The Jews

> were granted the right of assembly for worship and common meals, the right to observe the Sabbath and festivals and to follow the other requirements of their Law, and the right to hold funds, and they were authorized to build synagogues. The Jews' communal property was safeguarded by a ruling that theft of the Temple tax or of the rolls of the Scriptures from a synagogue by a gentile should count as sacrilege and be punished by the confiscation of property, and that the envoys taking the money to Jerusalem should not be molested; and their religious liberties as individuals was protected by exemption from summonses to law on the Sabbath, when they would not attend and so would lose their cases by default.[19]

These facts underscore a familiar but sometimes unappreciated reality. In the ancient Mediterranean, Jewish religion took shape and developed almost entirely under foreign political domination. This means that Judaism in all its forms was not a religion of free people. Rather, Judaism was a colonial religion, a religion of political dependence. Thus, we must read the sources of Judaism as a species of the literature of the unfree, as repressed writing, as the expression of people whose control of their lives, environments, and destinies – for most of the time – was extremely limited. How shall we develop such a mode of reading?

The established scholarly interpretation understands this record, and the behavior that allegedly derived from it, as a form of accommodation:

> The base political stance of the Jews of both the land of Israel and the diaspora was not rebellion but accommodation. The Jews must support the state until God sees fit to redeem them. This was the counsel of Jeremiah in the sixth century BCE, of Josephus in the first century CE, and of the rabbis of the second through the twentieth centuries CE.[20]

This accommodationist interpretation casts the Jews as politically passive and quiescent. Moreover, it seems to hold the position that, for people

---

[18] Doron Mendels, *The Rise and Fall of Jewish Nationalism* (New York: Doubleday, 1992), 24.

[19] E. Mary Smallwood, *The Jews under Roman Rule* (Leiden: E. J. Brill, 1981), 234-35. Judaism apparently was not the only religion to receive some support and protection from the Romans, but its exemption from the imperial cult surely makes its privileges noteworthy.

[20] S. Cohen, 34.

under political domination, anything short of rebellion is not political action. Contemporary work in political science, however, suggests that the alternatives rebellion/accommodation are both too extreme and too limiting. Political resistance can take other forms.

For example, James C. Scott's *Domination and the Arts of Resistance*[21] challenges the notions of hegemony and false consciousness as explanations of the behavior of oppressed people, castes, or classes. Scott argues against the widely held views that oppressed people accept domination because they either come to believe the ideology of the dominant group or regard their own oppressed condition as natural and inevitable. To overturn these established ideas, he develops the concepts of the "public transcript" and the "hidden transcript." These two transcripts – which include both discourse and behavior – describe the relations between the dominant and the dominated and help to expose the political character of the discourse of the oppressed. The public transcript is a "self-portrait of dominant elites as they would have themselves seen...a highly partisan and partial narrative. It is designed to be impressive, to affirm and naturalize the power of dominant elites, and to conceal or euphemize the dirty linen of their rule."[22] The hidden transcript "consists of those offstage speeches, gestures, and practices that confirm, contradict, or inflect what appears in the public transcript."[23] It is "a substitute for an act of assertion directly in the face of power."[24] The relationship between these two transcripts, Scott suggests, is complex but supplies a more accurate account of political relations between the dominant and dominated than does the public transcript alone:

> Every subordinate group creates out of its ordeal a "hidden transcript" that represents a critique of power spoken behind the back of the dominant. The powerful, for their part, also develop a hidden transcript representing the practices and claims of their rule that cannot be openly avowed. A comparison of the hidden transcript of the weak with that of the powerful and of *both* hidden transcripts to the public transcript of power relations offers a substantially new way of understanding resistance to domination.[25]

A key point in Scott's analysis is that subservient groups participate in the construction of the public transcript. Thus, for instance, the

---

[21] I am grateful to my colleague Curt Cadorette for bringing Scott's work to my attention.
[22] James C. Scott, *Domination and the Arts of Resistance: Hidden Transcripts* (New Haven: Yale University Press, 1990), 18.
[23] Ibid., 5.
[24] Ibid., 115.
[25] Ibid., xii.

masters are not inaccurate when they report that their slaves love them because, when they are with the masters, that is how the slaves act. But when the dominated classes are alone, away from their rulers and overlords, the dominated classes express – and thereby act out – their resistance to political control in the hidden transcript. Each group, the dominant and dominated, has both transcripts. In addition to acts of theft or violence, the hidden transcript typically exhibits the traits of anonymity, disguised speech, unrestrained behavior, utopianism, and apocalypticism. Utopianism and apocalypticism – which need carefully to be distinguished from one another – demonstrate the subservient group's ability to imagine a "counterfactual" political order. The capacity mentally to construct things as other than they are is a basic component in Scott's rejection of theories of ideological hegemony and false consciousness as adequate explanations for the apparently politically quietistic behavior of subordinate groups.

Scott uses the two transcripts to discern "at least four varieties of political discourse among subordinate groups." The first, "the safest and most public form of political discourse, is that which takes as its basis the flattering self-image of elites." With this discourse, subordinate groups can appeal to the elites' own self-image as a means of achieving their goals. The "second and sharply contrasting form of political discourse is that of the hidden transcript itself." The traits of the hidden transcript have been described above. Scott posits "a third realm of subordinate group discourse that lies strategically between the first two. This is a politics of disguise and anonymity that takes place in public view but is designed to have a double meaning or to shield the identity of its actors." Scott includes the folk culture of subordinate groups in this category and argues that "a partly sanitized, ambiguous, and coded version of the hidden transcript is always present in the public discourse of subordinate groups." Finally, there is "the rupture of the political *cordon sanitaire* between the hidden and the public transcript."[26]

Scott's analysis of hidden and public transcripts provides a useful lens to expose aspects of the political culture in the sources of Judaism. Let us focus briefly on the Hebrew Bible. In its structure and redaction, and perhaps in content as well, the Hebrew Bible is not a gradualist text, an accretion of centuries of Israelite history. Rather, it is a product of the Second Temple period. Robert Carroll puts it distinctly:

> The Hebrew Bible was the product of the Second Temple period, though how much of it was produced in the Persian era cannot be determined....Elements of the Hebrew Bible may have been produced in writing before the Persian era, but there is no concrete evidence for this

---

[26] Ibid., 18-19.

presupposition, nor is it possible to say which parts existed in writing
before the destruction of the temple. It is logical to locate the framing of
the various scrolls and the production of the bulk of the biblical books in
the period of the Second Temple because one of the most dominant
traits of that period is the production of writings which later became
scripture for many religious communities. Temple and texts are
therefore two of the key elements in the understanding of this period.[27]

As such, the Hebrew Bible reflects the political realities of a context of
domination. Again, Carroll states matters bluntly:

> The controlling ideological myth of the Hebrew Bible produced in the
> Second Temple period (that is, that Yahwism was as old as Abraham)
> needs to be read as a direct indication of the fact that Yahwism came
> from Mesopotamia, but not in the distant past of the Bronze age.
> Rather, it came out of Babylonia as a direct consequence of an elite's
> experiences arising out of the deportation. Only the Jerusalem territory
> in Palestine, however, afforded the Persian group the opportunity to
> impose their ideology on whatever factions would support them.[28]

If the worldview of the Hebrew Bible is "a direct consequence of an
elite's experiences arising out of the deportation," then what sorts of
political readings do Scott's hidden and public transcripts enable?

Let us take a very preliminary probe of the Pentateuch, the
foundation text of a colonial religion. One of the Pentateuch's principle
goals is to establish the ideological and behavioral bases of Israel's
collective life. It wants to explain why Israel is, who Israel is, and how
Israel is to behave. The Pentateuch is a constitutional document. Since
the Pentateuch was redacted, promulgated, and initially read and
understood under the duress of deportation and political domination, it
must be effective – indeed, persuasive – on two fronts. On the one hand,
it must appear innocent to the conquerors. It must participate in the
public transcript of the imperial regime by exhibiting no political threat.
On the other hand, it must appear savvy to the conquered. It must
participate in the hidden transcript of its adherents – actual and potential
– in order to secure their loyalty and allegiance. In this sense, the
Pentateuch – for all its literary artistry – resembles Scott's "third realm of
subordinate group discourse," which encodes the hidden transcript in
the public one.

From this perspective, the exclusion of native kingship from the
Pentateuch is no accident. It makes a point. The absence of kingship
from a core text could appeal to the imperial authorities by explicitly
denying any agenda of Jewish political autonomy. The priestly editors

---

[27] Robert P. Caroll, "Israel, History of (Post-Monarchic Period)," in *Anchor Bible
Dictionary*, 3:572.
[28] Ibid., 574.

made a strategic decision. By choosing cult over monarchy, they affirmed a preference for tithes over taxes and purity over politics. By keeping the king away from the altar and thereby making the Pentateuch's discourse seem politically nugatory, they participated in the public transcript of the imperial regime. Like Nehemiah, the Pentateuch is "never out of sorts with the king" (Neh. 2:1).

To grasp the political message of the Pentateuch, we need only compare its picture with the behavior of the Hasmonean dynasty. In developing and maintaining their Jewish state, the Hasmoneans ultimately[29] combined native kingship and priesthood into a single office, to the detriment of both. Within the pentateuchal framework, that behavior is at best unpredictable, at worst nonsensical.

Further, the Pentateuch exhibits what Scott calls the "repressed speech" of politically dominated peoples, for a fundamental contradiction appears to lie at the text's core. On the one hand, the Pentateuch claims that the God of Israel is the power of the cosmos, the creator of Heaven and earth, and it strongly implies that all other gods are unreal. On the other hand, in the pentateuchal redaction, the formation of God's people and the exercise of God's cult take place in the desert – that is, in no state – and thus constitute no political threat to any pagan king. Thus, the Pentateuch appears to swallow the political implications of its own bold theological assertions.

The Pentateuch blunts monotheism's political edge in at least two basic ways. First, as we have seen, it separates the king from the cult and the cult from the land. Second, it makes monotheism familial. The Pentateuch tells the story of a single family that forms a relationship with the only God there is. But the relationship stays primarily in the family. The "ethnic" monotheism of Second Temple Judaism and the particularistic terminology of Ezra-Nehemiah – the notion of the "holy seed," for instance – are often portrayed in the scholarly literature as a falling away, a disappointing retreat, from an allegedly more universalistic vision of the prophets. But maintaining distinct group identities was part of the Persian strategy toward its captives.[30] In such a context, the "ethnicizing" of Judaism would have been one important way for the Jews to participate in the public transcript of their captors and demonstrate political reliability. That is, the Jews (or, better: some Jews) in exile played to the hilt the role assigned to them by the public transcript of the Persian regime, and they were able to call upon, perhaps even justifiably claim, the regime's favor as a result. Through this lens, the alleged exclusivism of the returnees, the "children of the exile,"

---

[29] See Mendels, 60.
[30] See the papers collected in Davies.

displays not theological arrogance or ethnic segregation but extremely effective political manipulation. To maintain the privileges it received from a succession of imperial regimes, Judaism had to be plausible as no threat to imperial political rule. The "ethnicizing" of Judaism may have been one way to make that claim credible.

Finally, Scott's transcripts are especially useful because they also show us how to understand the Pentateuch as a form of resistance. The Pentateuch's story of the creation of the altar and the cult – the focus of Israel's relation with God – constitutes an outright denial of the political realities discussed in the Prophets and Ezra-Nehemiah. There are no Persians in the Pentateuch, no controlling powers to whom one needs to kowtow and with whom one needs to cut deals. Indeed, the only deal cutter in the Pentateuch is God himself. From this perspective, the pentateuchal picture of the cult emerges as a utopian hidden transcript, the picture of a world populated only by God and his chosen people. As Neusner has shown, a similar utopianism shapes the Mishnah, which hardly recognizes the domination of Rome.

To be sure, the Pentateuch, the Hebrew Bible, and the Mishnah are not the only versions of Jewish hidden and public transcripts in antiquity. Different groups of Jews adopted different literary, imaginative, and political strategies for dealing with foreign domination. Hellenistic Jewish novels, such as 3 Maccabees, can easily spin scenarios in which pagan kings become Jews.[31] And the literature of Qumran – replete with apocalyptic, veiled language, and the lexicon of war and conquest – is a powerful, and enraged, hidden transcript of Jewish political emotion. But the Second Temple Judaism of the Pentateuch – which became the foundation of all Judaisms – is both cosmic and parochial, but neither territorial nor governmental. Its religious resources for political culture contributed substantially to centuries of toleration of Judaism by imperial regimes in antiquity.

If this preliminary reading is plausible, then the separation of religion from politics, from governance, is fundamental to the biblical and rabbinic traditions, at least insofar as they are read whole as the sources of a religion. These traditions do not offer much advice on how to run a state. But they do establish an enduring model on how to be subordinate to a state without its running you.

II

The struggles between the rabbinic masters and the Jewish political leaders, the *nasi* in Palestine and the *resh galuta* in Babylonia, forced the

---

[31] I am grateful to my new colleague Sarah Johnson for a particularly insightful paper on 3 Maccabees.

sages of late antiquity to delimit clearly the rabbinic institutions which controlled the public arenas of activity, while at the same time justifying their inability to control fully internal governmental affairs.[32] The realities of the distribution of power in late antiquity led Samuel to formulate his doctrine of *dina' de-malkhuta 'dina,'* (the law of the land is the law).[33] Within the Babli's context, the principle establishes the Persian government's presumptive ownership of land, and the government's right to sell Jewish land for nonpayment of taxes, even when these acts run counter to rabbinic Halakhah.[34] But, what really mattered, the rabbis tell us, was what occurred in the marketplace and in the schoolhouses,[35] and it is important to note that both Talmuds say very little of a positive nature about the exilarch or the patriarch as political leaders. The legal basis for Samuel's ruling has never been established in the traditional Jewish sources, although it has been debated since the time of the *geonim*, reflecting its ambiguity in the hidden transcript. Nevertheless, the principle has played a major role in the history of the relationship between Jewish communities and the non-Jewish governments.[36]

Within the context of the premodern *kehillah*, the *mara d'atra*, the rabbinic authority of each particular location, validated the economic, social, and religious *minhagim* of each locality, while the *parnassim* controlled the nonreligious daily activity of the people. But even here, or perhaps especially here, the political mythologies of late antique Judaism found their fullest expressions, for the community through its various legal procedures could exercise various forms of coercive power, such as the *herem*.[37] Ultimate power rested in the hands of the non-Jewish authorities, but salvific power was in the hands of the Jewish authorities. Although fully aware that they needed constantly to negotiate with the non-Jewish political powers, as the creation institution of the *shtadlan*, the formal Jewish negotiator at the court of the gentile ruler, evidences, these communities still saw themselves as unified wholes held together by the

---

[32] On the exilarch and the rabbis see Jacob Neusner, *A History of the Jews in Babylonia* (Leiden: E. J. Brill, 1968-70), 2:119-25; 3:41-94; 4:73-124; 5:45-60, 124-27, 248-59. See also David Goodblatt, *The Monarchic Principle: Studies in Jewish Self-Government in Antiquity* (Tübingen: J. C. B. Mohr, 1994), 176-311.
[33] See Neusner, 2:64-72.
[34] The phrase actually occurs only four times in the Babylonian Talmud: Nedarim 28a, Gittin 10b, Baba Qama 113a, Baba Batra 54b-55a.
[35] Neusner, 2:151-287; 3:95-338.
[36] Shmeul Shile, "Dina de-malkhuta dina," in *Encyclopedia Judaica*, 6:51-55. "Dina de-malkhuta dina," in *Talmudic Encyclopedia*, 7:295-308. David Biale, *Power and Powerlessness in Jewish History* (New York: Schocken Books, 1986), 54-57.
[37] Jacob Katz, *Tradition and Crisis: Jewish Society at the End of the Middle Ages* (New York: Schocken Books, 1961), 99-102.

mythologies of Rabbinic Judaism, of which Samuel's dictum was an essential element, along with the mythology of the rabbis as heirs of *moshe rabbenu*.[38] The gentile governments collected taxes from the *kehillot*, but the Jewish communities seem to have functioned, or at least to have described their activities, in terms of the Babylonian Talmud's mythology.

These political theories were challenged within the Jewish community at the same moment that the mythology of the rabbi was questioned.[39] The rise of Hasidism marks a new point in Judaism's political theory. The anti-intellectual, personal mysticism which formed the basis of early Hasidism posed a threat to the hegemony of traditional rabbinic power.[40] Hasidim challenged the integrity and worthiness of the rabbinic class to be the leaders of the Jewish community, for the zaddik offered a new theory of leadership which was independent of the rabbinic mythology.[41] As the Besht's followers spread his teachings into White Russia, the rabbinic community, under the leadership of Wilna Gaon mounted vigorous opposition. At first the rabbinic Jewish community employed its own political power by issuing bans and sanctions against the followers of the new sect, but eventually the Hasidim, followed soon afterward by the Mitnaggdim, turned to the coercive powers of the non-Jewish authorities for support.[42] These activities breached the boundaries which Samuel's dictum had established, for now the non-Jewish authorities were brought in to exercise their power within the context of struggles over ritual, dogma, and leadership which were being fought by different factions within the Jewish community. The same breach occurred in Germany with the rise

---

[38] Katz's *Tradition and Crisis* is the best book on the *kahal*.

[39] The best outline of this mythology is found in Jacob Neusner, *There We Sat Down: The Story of Classical Judaism in the Period in Which It Was Taking Shape* (Nashville and New York: Abington Press, 1972).

[40] In this we follow Scholem's claim that Hasidism is part of the Jewish mystical tradition; Gershom Scholem, *Major Trends in Jewish Mysticism* (New York: Schocken Books, 1961), 325-50.

[41] Samuel Dresner, *The Zaddik* (New York, Toronto, London: 1960). Benzion Dinur, "The Origins of Hasidism and Its Social and Messianic Foundations," in Gershon David Hundert, ed., *Essential Papers on Hasidism: Origins to Present* (New York and London: New York University Press, 1991), 145-52. Ada Rapoport-Albert, "God and the Zaddik as the Two Focal Points of Hasidic Worship," in Hundert, 299-329.

[42] For a brief description of the struggle between the Hasidim and the Mitnaggdim see Mordecai L. Wilensky, "Hasidic-Mitnaggeddic Polemics in the Jewish Communities of Eastern Europe: The Hostile Phase, " in Hundert, 244-71. The turning to the Russian government is discussed on 244-46.

of Reform Judaism, which also challenged the classical mythologies.[43] In both cases, the results were disastrous. Shneur Zalman of Lyady, the found of HaBaD Hasidism spent time in prison, and below we shall see the control which some German states attempted to exercise over the Reform rabbinate.

As we noted above, with the Enlightenment the Jewish community and Judaism changed forever, for both the mythological unity of the Jewish community and the cohesiveness created by the rabbinic mythology were destroyed forever. As a result, any clear possibility of the rabbinic authorities exercising coercive power over significant elements of the larger Jewish community was lost. No longer was there even in theory one Jewish community united by a belief in God the Creator, Revealer, and Redeemer or the rabbi as God's representative on earth. This dissolution of the mythological unity of the Jewish community is illustrated by the rise of Reform Judaism in Germany and the responses by the Orthodox community and the Positive Historical Movement.[44] The end of the rabbis' control over the Jewish community is symbolized by the acts of the Paris Sanhedrin in 1806 in which the rabbinical authorities formally accepted the government's control of some aspects of the Jews' life which were formerly under rabbinic jurisdiction, such as marriage and divorce.[45] As David Biale explicitly notes, Samuel's principle was employed by the rabbis of the Paris Sanhedrin as justification for their limiting some of the rabbis' traditional communal authority.[46] Moses Mendelssohn even provided philosophical underpinnings to the removal of the synagogue and church from the political sphere by eliminating from the religious community and institutions any coercive power to force their will and opinions upon people: "Civil society," he wrote, "...has the right of coercion; in fact, it has secured this right through the social contract. Religious society neither demands the right of coercion nor can it possibility obtain it by any conceivable contract."[47] This new formulation of Samuel's dictum

---

[43] David Philipson, *The Reform Movement in Judaism* (New York: Macmillan Co., 1907), 33-37.

[44] In addition to Philipson's classic study, see now Michael A. Meyer, *Response to Modernity: A History of the Reform Movement in Judaism* (New York and Oxford: Oxford University Press, 1988).

[45] Paul Mendes-Flohr and Jehuda Reinharz, *The Jew in the Modern World: A Documentary History*, 2nd ed. (New York and Oxford: Oxford University Press, 1995), 125-35.

[46] Biale, 104.

[47] Alexander Altmann, *Moses Mendelssohn: A Biographical Study* (Philadelphia: Jewish Publication Society of America, 1973), 523. Altmann, 514-52, has an excellent study of Mendelssohn's political views as they were expressed in his *Jerusalem*.

that "the law of the land is the law" severely limited any rabbi's power to enforce his form of Judaism, for not only did the state have authority in areas such as marriage, divorce, and the transfer of property which previously had been solely the domain of rabbinic Halakhah, but also the state was the only entity which could exercise coercive power over individuals. The dangers inherent in the move of the state into areas formally controlled by the rabbis are found in the situation in Germany where in the early nineteenth century the various states sought to mandate what the rabbis should learn and the nature of their various functions inside and outside the Jewish community. As early as 1823 the government of Baden was willing to raise the status of rabbis to that of Christian clergy if the former would "instead of concentrating their attention principally on deciding matters of dietary law" raise "the spiritual level of their flock, visiting the sick, and presiding over the purified ritual of the synagogue." Some states attempted to regulate rabbinic garb, and in Württemberg and Bernburg rabbis even received financial support from state funds.[48] Clearly the other side of Samuel's dictum that the Jewish community should have control over its own affairs which did not affect the interests of the state was no longer in force. And, the ability of the Jewish community to exercise political power over its members was a thing of the past.

The theories of the German and French Enlightenment formed the basis for American society, and Reform Judaism prospered here as it did in Germany. But here, the situation of Judaism within the political context is more complex.[49] Within America's "enlightened" environment membership in the Jewish community and the practice of Judaism became truly voluntary. The American Jewish community is, in the words of Daniel J. Elazar, "best understood as a mosaic, a multidimensional matrix of institutions and organizations that interact with each other in their attempts to cover the range of communal concerns."[50] Within these organizations, "persuasion rather than

---

[48] Meyer, 103.
[49] Meyer, 225-63. Leon A. Jick, *The Americanization of the Synagogue, 1820-1870* (Hanover, NH: University Press of New England, 1976), 79-96. Jick argues that whereas Reform in Germany was designed to change the social order, Reform in America was created to maintain the social order. For an excellent discussion of the challenges the Jews faced in American society, see Naomi W. Cohen, *Jews in Christian America: The Pursuit of Religious Equality* (New York and Oxford: Oxford University Press, 1992).
[50] Daniel J. Elazar, *Community and Polity: The Organizational Dynamics of American Jewry* (Philadelphia: Jewish Publication Society of America, 1980), 7.

compulsion, influence rather than power are the tools available for making decisions and implementing policies."[51]

In America, the power of Judaism as a religion to exercise any political force or to develop a novel political theory is virtually impossible for at least two reasons. First, the American Jewish community is fragmented in many different ways, so that Judaism as a religious system affects only a fragment of the Jewish population. Interpreting the data from the National Survey of Religious Identification, Kosmin and Lachman write that "Jews by religion, who are 2.2% of the white population [of America], were split between those who identified with a national origin and those who self-reported as 'Jews' [as their ethic origin]. Among those who reported themselves as being of Jewish ethnic origin rather than of the nationality of the country from which their ancestors originated, only two thirds reported Judaism as their current religion. In fact, it appears that around 12% of Americans of Jewish descent are Christians. On the other hand, the Jewish ethnic group showed a large proportion, 22%, in the 'No Religion' or 'Miscellaneous' columns."[52] Thus, even if American Judaism could expound a political theory, a large number of self-proclaimed Jews would not adhere to it or be affected by it. Second, that portion of the Jewish community which claims to be followers of Judaism is sharply divided among Reform, Conservative, Reconstructionist, Humanistic, and several varieties of Orthodox, so that Judaism as one religion in America has no single meaning,[53] and its thoughts and ideas are hardly consistent or coherent.

Thus, the realities of the American Jewish community with its many divisions, its high level of secularization, and its Enlightenment heritage mediate against its having a theory which allows any coercive power to reside with its religious authorities outside of particular sectors of the Orthodox community. But even among the Orthodox Jews, the rabbi's authority often depends on nonreligious realities, such as the economic opportunities available to his followers.[54] We should also note the

---

[51] Elazar, 8.

[52] Barry A. Kosmin and Seymour P. Lachman, *One Nation under God: Religion in Contemporary American Society* (New York: Crown Trade Paperbacks, 1993), 121.

[53] Jacob Neusner, *Understanding American Judaism*, vol. 2, *Sectors of American Judaism: Reform, Orthodoxy, Conservatism, and Reconstructionism* (New York: KTAV, 1975). Gilbert S. Rosenthal, *Contemporary Judaism: Patterns of Survival*, 2nd ed. (New York: Human Sciences Press, 1986).

[54] At the end of his study of the Hasidic community in Williamsburg, Poll notes the problems facing this community and the breakdown of the *rebbe's* control as it expanded its economic activities to outside the limited confines of the neighborhood. Solomon Poll, *The Hasidic Community of Williamsburg: A Study in the Sociology of Religion* (New York: Schocken Books, 1969), 248-78.

growing rift between the "right" and "left" wings of the Orthodox community which makes even more unlikely that Orthodox Judaism in America will be able to formulate a coherent Jewish stand on almost anything.[55] Evidence of American Judaism's lack of concern with a political theory, as we have defined the term above, can be demonstrated by reviewing the most recent "platforms" of Reform and Conservative Judaism.

In truth, American Reform Judaism has never expounded a clear political theory. The Pittsburgh Platform of 1885 rejected most of the rabbinic tradition and accepted "as binding only the moral laws, and...only such ceremonies as elevate and sanctify our lives." The assembly specifically stated that they were "a religious community," not a nation, "and therefore, expect neither a return to Palestine, nor a sacrificial worship under the sons of Aaron, nor the restoration of any of the laws concerning the Jewish state." It did, however, express a broad social agenda: "We deem it our duty to participate in the great task of modern times, to solve, on the basis of justice and righteousness, the problems presented by the contrasts and evils of the present organization of society."[56] Although the 1937 Columbus Platform, the "Guiding Principles of Reform Judaism," differs markedly from the earlier document, again we find no attempt to explicate a political or social theory which does more than merely "applies" the principle of "progressive development" to "spiritual as well as to cultural and social life." While "affirm[ing] the obligation of all Jewry to aid in its [Palestine's] upbuilding as a Jewish homeland," the document also notes that "in all lands where our people live, they assume and seek to share loyally the full duties and responsibilities of citizenship." Further, the authors claimed that "justice to all...is the inalienable right and the inescapable obligation of all. The state and organized government exist in order to further these ends."[57] The 1937 statement on social justice is elegant, but does not clearly indicate which segments of society or what procedures should be followed to attain its goals:

> Judaism seeks the attainment of a just society by the application of its teachings to the economic order, to industry and commerce, and to national and international affairs. It aims at the elimination of man-made misery and suffering, of poverty and degradation, of tyranny and slavery, of social inequality and prejudice, of ill-will and strife. It advocates the promotion of harmonious relations between warring classes on the basis of equity and justice, and the creation of conditions under which human personality may flourish. It pleads for the

---

[55] Rosenthal, 311-26.
[56] Meyer, 387-88.
[57] Meyer, 388-91.

safeguarding of childhood against exploitation. It champions the cause
of all who work and of their right to an adequate standard of living, as
prior to the rights of property. Judaism emphasizes the duty of charity,
and strives for a social order which will protect men against the material
disabilities of old age, sickness, and unemployment.[58]

Note that the government, the *malkhuta*, has no role to play in
reaching these goals. The Central Conference of American Rabbis
Meeting in San Francisco in 1976 adopted "Reform Judaism: A Centenary
Perspective," a "platform" composed by a committee headed by Eugene
Borowitz. With regard to the State of Israel the document proclaims,
"We have both a stake and a responsibility in building the State of Israel,
in assuring its security and defining its Jewish character."[59] The decided
emphasis on the Jewish People as a collection of individuals precluded
those in San Francisco from expressing their collective views on the
social agenda found in both the Pittsburgh and Columbus documents, so
that there is no hint of any political or social agenda in Reform's last
institutional formulation of its principles and values.

While the Reform movement has expressed itself institutionally at
least three times, the Conservative movement has done so only once,
with the publication of *Emet ve-Emunah: A Statement of Principles of
Conservative Judaism* in 1988,[60] the work of a commission headed by
Rabbi Robert Gordis. However, in his foreword, Ismar Schorsch,
chancellor of the Jewish Theological Seminary, writes that the document
should be seen "as a point of departure and not a definitive resolution."
However, this is the first time that the leaders of the various elements of
the formally recognized institutions of Conservative Judaism have
promulgated an official document which expresses the "movement's"
views.[61]

In general, the document does not see Judaism as a political
phenomenon, and it uses the word "nation" to refer both to political
entities and large religious groups. The fear of political activism
becomes clear in the subsection "From Dream to Reality" under the
section entitled "Eschatology: Our Vision of the Future." Here, the
committee rejects the "revolutionary messianists" who "are impatient"
and "become militant activists and resort to aggressive political activity
and even, in the extreme, military action and violence." The authors

---

[58] Meyer, 390.

[59] Meyer, 383.

[60] (New York: The Jewish Theological Seminary of America, The Rabbinic
Assembly, The United Synagogues of America, 1988).

[61]The commission contained a representative from each of the various segments
of the Conservative movement, such as the rabbis, the cantors, the sisterhoods,
etc.

behind the document favor a "gradualist or evolutionary eschatological approach" which is much vaguer and which does not even hint that political activity may be a means through which human beings may play their role in bringing about the redemption of humankind.[62] Similarly, in discussing "relations with other faiths," we read, "What we have created, in the realms of religion, philosophy, law, social institutions, the arts, and science, has been freely appropriated by the rest of the world," a list which either consciously or not, excludes the terms politics or political thought.[63]

Like the Reform movement, the Conservative movement also has a sense of the importance of social justice, and again similar to the Reform movement, the political agenda is vague and unspecified. While the biblical prophets "fought vigorously against any attempt to limit Jewish faith to the sacral or cultic domain," there is no explicit reference to their political activities.[64] This is an important omission given what we know of Amos, Isaiah, and Jeremiah. Although the document states that "the Conservative movement has a long and honorable history of concern for social justice," and we find unspecified references to the activity of Abraham Joshua Heschel and "numerous Conservative rabbis," the activity is "social" and decided nonpolitical or in the realm of a political agenda.[65] However, unlike the Reform statement of principles, the Conservative agenda does refer to political action, as a last resort: "It is of the highest importance that both as a movement and as individuals we take actions to fulfill the call of our tradition to advance the cause of justice, freedom and peace....[We must] speak out on the dangers of nuclear annihilation, racism, hunger and poverty throughout the world, as well as the threats to our environment. We must work together with our fellow citizens of all faiths and *take political action if necessary* to achieve these goals."[66] Clearly the document envisions a means to achieve these goals without political action; it views political activity as independent of religious goals and its social agenda, for it views political action as a last resort.

We have seen that Samuel's dictum that "the law of the land is the law" forms the basis of Jewish political thought from the second century of the common era onward. In the medieval and premodern periods the Jewish communities applied the doctrine much as Samuel had intended, for the Jewish communities controlled their inner lives while the non-

---

[62] *Emet ve-Emunah*, 30-31.
[63] *Emet ve-Emunah*, 42.
[64] *Emet ve-Emunah*, 44.
[65] *Emet ve-Emuah*, 45.
[66] *Emet ve-Emunah*, 46, emphasis added.

Jewish powers pretty much left them alone except for purposes of taxation. During the Enlightenment the situation changed drastically because the ruling powers adopted some tasks which were formally performed by the religious authorities, and the non-Jewish governments began to regulate closely the internal religious life of the Jews, among others. However, the Jews willingly accepted the delimited scope of the areas under their control, for the liberal agenda was more important to them than controlling the fine points of their religious lives, which had also been severely limited in their minds.

In contemporary America it appears that the non-Orthodox Jewish communities have consciously attempted to separate themselves from presenting political ideas. While the Reform movement has a long history of expressing itself on matters of social justice, it has done so without any mention of the political powers needed to accomplish their goals. Similarly, the Conservative movement seems to view politics as a dangerous last resort for achieving its social agenda. The situation in American Judaism reflects first the Enlightenment's separation of church and state and its belief that religion should be a voluntary activity, a reality which exists in its fullest form in contemporary America. American Judaism's reluctance to formulate a political theory also reflects the diversity in American Judaism and the fact that many American "Jews" reject Judaism as a religion or as a meaningful phenomenon. American Jews wish to be a religion, free from the political arena and free of political ideas. While not always conscious of the classical sources of Judaism, the American Jews are fully aware of the Enlightenment's liberal agenda and what that means for their supporting a political agenda within the context of their or anyone else's religious system. While this reluctance to become involved in the political arena may be a common trait of religious groups in America, it does not detract from the ease with which American Judaism accepted the common American mythology of the separation of church and state. Our argument is that American Judaism's ability to fit into the common framework develops naturally out of the public transcript of its classic texts.

For American Judaism, politics, as "governance and statecraft, the power to tax, to wage war, to produce money, to enforce public order, and the ability to make the institutions of that power work for your own ends," is their domain, not ours as Jews qua Jews. However, as "Jewish" Americans we understand both the need and the danger of becoming involved in their political arena. The public transcript is "the law of the land is the law"; the hidden transcript reflects the danger and ambiguity we perceive in that situation.

Part III

CHRISTIANITY

10

Inclusion and Noninclusion: The Practice of the Kingdom in Formative Christianity

Bruce D. Chilton
Bard College

Preface

Politics as usually defined in our period involves the legitimate use of force, whether as sanctioned violence or as categorical influence. Violence as sanctioned might include war, punishment, and the limitation of physical conditions (such as nutrition, shelter, and clothing) below the possibility of survival. Categorical influence might include the loss of employment, preferment, or the possibility of marriage for failing to maintain the line taken by the political authority. Then, of course, sanctioned violence and categorical influence each has its obverse: there are livings to be made in purveying legitimate violence and accepting categorical influence. In his perceptive account of *Political Theory and Modernity*, William E. Connolly comments that, to understand ourselves politically, it is time to listen to the nihilists.[1]

Whether violent or influential, both these forces represent the coordinates of what is called power. So defined, secular power is a two-dimensional entity. Its vertical axis is the degree of violence it can deliver; its horizontal axis is the degree of influence it can exert. The presidency in the United States is a good example of the concentration of both vertical violence and horizontal influence. A successful president will use the one to bolster the other, but neither can be absent for him to wield power.

---

[1] (London: Blackwell, 1988), 15.

The fixation of politics with power has been detailed by a variety of theorists, including Connolly. He conceives of the state as the projection of power (in a Nietzschean sense), and sets out the current dilemma:

> Late-modernity is the era in which it is possible to understand both that the late-modern state cannot legitimize itself to the rest of the world unless its form is universalizable, and that the very form assumed by this state today makes it unsusceptible to universalization. (173)

To put the same thought less theoretically: I have never come to know a European well who has not expressed the views (however politely) that the United States is a bully and that the United Nations is a wimp.

The famous position of Carl von Clausewitz, that war is a continuation of political activity by other means, is spelled out in a way which precisely articulates a view of power with which Nietzsche could easily have agreed:

> If the state is thought of as a person, and policy as the product of its brain, then among the contingencies for which the state must be prepared is a war in which every element calls for policy to be eclipsed by violence.[2]

So conceived, power becomes its own legitimacy. During the siege of Mainz in 1792, in which Clausewitz took part as a young soldier, barely twelve years old, Johann Wolfgang von Goethe looked on the bombardment and commented on the beauty of the incendiary bombs in the night sky.[3] Violence as sanctioned by the modern state eclipses not only policy, but reason itself. Modernity gives us too many examples of that proposition for it to be reasonably questioned.

It is possible to be very clear about what is conventionally called "the politics of power" in the modern period, for the simple reason that the modern state has made politics into power and power into politics. But if the language of legitimate force is helpful for understanding what has been happening in the relations among modern states, that is largely because those states have shared that notion of political power. How shall we understand politics in other periods?

As soon as that question is posed, one naturally thinks of the ancient period. Notions of legitimated violence do not seem to comport well with the classic definition of Aristotle in the *Politics* 1:

> Every state is a community of some kind, and every community is established with a view to some good; for humanity always acts in order to obtain that which they think good. But if all communities aim at some good, the state or political community, which is the highest of all, and

---

[2] Quoted from "What is War?" in Peter Paret, *Clausewitz and the State* (Princeton: Princeton University Press), 394.
[3] So Paret, 29.

which embraces all the rest, aims at good in a greater degree than any
other, and at the highest good.

The definition of the state teleologically, in terms of its aims, became
routine within the Roman Empire, and comes to popular expression in
the Stoicism of the emperor Marcus Aurelius at the close of the second
century of the common era. One consequence of his conviction that the
empire reflected the rule of natural reason was that those opposed to the
empire could be subjected to pogroms, as occurred in Lyons in 177 C.E.
Marcus's chief complaint about the offending group (who were
Christians) was that they were obstinate people (see *The Meditations of
Marcus Aurelius* 11.3). Obstinacy impedes the greater good: one should
not wait for it to deteriorate into rebellion before dealing with it. Where
Clausewitz speaks of the legitimacy of violence, Marcus Aurelius
focused inexorably on the precise opposite: the violence of legitimacy.

Our particular concern is with the Christian politics reflected in the
documents of its classical period. But before we turn to that, it is worth
reflecting that the limitations of the modern definition of politics are not
only evident when we turn to the past. A famous article on what the
author called "the end of history" has understandably attracted
considerable criticism since its appearance.[4] But Francis Fukuyama there
developed a thesis which is more telling in political terms than in
historical terms. As "states" as usually defined in the "postmodern" era
cease to exist, so will their politics.

The twin axes of violence and influence are steadily being eroded for
most countries. The vertical axis of legitimate violence is curtailed by
agreements of arms control and limitation; the horizontal axis of
legitimate influence is curtailed by the growing power of "multinational
corporations," which is to say nonnational commerce. History has not
come to an end, but no nation today can seriously consider that
unqualified autonomy is a realistic strategy of survival and prosperity.
So as we consider the nonnational politics of the past, we may be
encountering elements of the postnational politics of the future.

Before we can take up that issue (at the very close of our paper), we
need to address our principal concern: the strange case of Christian
politics within its classical documents. *Classical,* for the present purpose,
means the period from the New Testament until Augustine, who is
commonly agreed to be the greatest political theorist of the Church in
late antiquity. What is strange about Christianity's politics is that, for

---

[4] See "Are We at the End of History?" *Fortune* 121 (1990): 75f., and *The End of
History and the Last Man* (New York: Free Press, 1992); and the reviews by
Michael Cornfield in *Journal of Communication* 44 (1994): 106-16; Lynne V. Cheney
in *The Historian* 57 (1995): 454-56.

most of the period which concerns us, Christianity had no power in the modern definition of politics. Moreover, it had no commonly agreed definition of "the good" which commended Christians to others in the empire. As far as Marcus Aurelius could see, conscientious Stoic though he was, Christians lacked any trace of the Aristotelian moderation which might have made them tolerable. Whether in a modern understanding or in an ancient understanding, then, Christians had no politics, and they could have had no politics. They were disempowered in the modern view, illegitimate in the ancient view. But by the fourth century their nonpolitics turned out to have been a politics of some sort all along, because they inherited the Roman Imperium from the time of Constantine.

The strange case of classical Christianity, then, is this: What seems to be a nonpolitics can overwhelm and restructure what seem to be unassailable fortresses (whether from the point of view of modern power or ancient legitimacy). But that can only mean that there really is a politics in this nonpolitics, that a political movement grounded in neither the legitimacy of force nor the force of legitimacy might be – and in late antiquity actually was – a viable force.

Because our task here is to understand that strange politics, we will begin with the ground change which the settlement under Constantine involved (see "Introduction: The Eusebean Revolution" below). Eusebius is used as the lens of the change, because he is the chronicler and first theorist of events. His perspective is thoroughly apocalyptic. Constantine in his vision is the image of Christ himself on earth, and recent events attest God's ultimate intervention in the world.

Eusebius's apocalyptic perspective was by no means original. He was reaching back to a common conviction among Christians that ultimate power was to be exercised by God. In his correspondence with churches in Corinth, Paul represents that consensus (see "Roots of Power: Non-inclusion and Its Consequences in Paul" below). Grounded in an apocalyptic anticipation of divine judgment, the terms of reference of communal discipline are taken to be beyond this world. If one is excluded from the community, the consequence is that one will be given over to Satan in eschatological judgment.

Paul's representation of Christian discipline in the primitive period does not reflect his originality in the matter. Throughout his apostolate, Paul was in a minority within Christianity as a whole, and reflects a keen awareness of that fact. But in conceiving of noninclusion as the foundation of communal discipline, Paul reached back to the practice and the theory of community which Jesus himself initiated.

That practice and theory is best reflected in Jesus' conception of "the kingdom of God" (see "Deeper Roots: Jesus' Practice of Transcendent

Power" below). Here is where a distinctively Christian understanding of power is first articulated, and that articulation is (as we should have expected) thoroughly Judaic. What distinguished Jesus among many of his rabbinic contemporaries was his practice of fellowship at meals, both personally and by means of disciples who were sent by him for the purpose of engaging in such fellowship. A precise motivation is reflected in the sources: the meal of the group delineated the circle of those received by God into his kingdom. Entering that circle involved accepting the generic purity of those of Israel who were present, and extending whatever forgiveness was necessary for that circle to function in fellowship.

Implicitly and explicitly, those who did not enter into that circle of practice were included out of the kingdom, or rather: they had included themselves out. Jesus' language of what noninclusion involved, "the weeping and gnashing of teeth," intimates the finality of refusing to be involved. Feasting in the kingdom implies a terrible counterpart. That is the source of power to which Jesus referred.

The reference does not involve the exercise of force (violence or influence), nor is the metaphysics of the common good invoked (as in Aristotle and in Marcus Aurelius). Rather, power is identified by Jesus as God's inclusion or noninclusion of people in his kingdom, and the choice between those alternatives is a function of what those people do or do not do. The implicit conception of power in Jesus' teaching of the kingdom of God involves not only eschatology, but transcendence.[5] In its emphasis upon the extension of the circle of purity and forgiveness, Jesus' program of fellowship may be compared and contrasted with the Mishnaic emphasis upon transcendence as static, unchanging sanctification.[6] In both cases, transcendence is at issue, but the quality of transcendence as it impinges upon the world as experience is differently understood. As eschatological, the kingdom proceeds from the future and reorders the present. As transcendent, the kingdom promises to create anew within its created universe whatever is in its image. So to be left out of the kingdom is to be left out of the future and left out of existence, out of time and out of place.

Within Jesus' conception of power, choices made in the present bear ultimate consequences. The extent of his conviction in that regard may be gauged by his attitude toward the authorities in the Temple. When they

---

[5] For a full discussion of the dimensions of power involved in Jesus' conception of the kingdom, see Chilton, *Pure Kingdom: Jesus' Vision of God* (Grand Rapids: Eerdmans, 1996).

[6] See Jacob Neusner, *Max Weber Revisited: Religion and Society in Ancient Judaism. With Special Reference to the Late First and Second Centuries* (Oxford: Oxford Centre for Postgraduate Hebrew Studies, 1981), 16-22.

refused to accept that the offerings of Israel could not be sold in the outer court of the Temple, his response was to occupy that court, and expel the animals that were sold and their vendors. In addition, he presented meals in his fellowship as a replacement of the altar as delineating what was acceptable to God in his kingdom (see "Spreading Roots: Broadening Exclusions in Primitive Christianity" below). Here is the source of the characteristically Christian understanding of discipline – excommunication. To be in the meal is to be in the kingdom, to be out of the meal is to be included out of the kingdom.

Once, then, the dynamic of noninclusion was consciously employed, Jesus defined the authorities in the Temple as engaged in unacceptable sacrifice, as compared to the acceptable sacrifice which his own meals represented. Other principal teachers within primitive Christianity deployed the dynamic of noninclusion within their own conceptions of what God found acceptable. For James, only Israel as usually understood, focused on worship in the Temple according to the Torah, could be regarded as guaranteeing the identity of the Jesus movement. Peter, on the other hand, tolerated suspensions of rules of purity on an occasional basis, in order to include non-Jews in the meals of fellowship. Paul, the most radical thinker represented in the New Testament, conceived of the definition of Israel as completely overtaken by the definition of who is included in meals of fellowship: participating in eucharist by belief in Jesus made believers into sons of Abraham, the true Israel of God.

At each stage in this progression, people were included out of the movement. The authorities loyal to Caiaphas the high priest were included out by Jesus. The people "outside" of Israel were portrayed as dense by the circle of James. (The Jacobean formulation, "those outside," is not only a social description, as in the Greek text of Mark 4:11 [*hoi exo*]; in Aramaic, '*inun behutza*' may mean both "those without" and "those who are thick.") Peter is portrayed by Paul as deliberately separating from a group which consistently refused to accept the practice of purity (Gal. 2:11-13), while Paul himself imposed the ban of refusing to eat with anyone who refused to accept the norms of the community (1 Cor. 5:9-13).

What becomes clear by now is that the practice of power in the circles of Jesus and his successors did not involve either the functional definition of power (as legitimated force) or the static, metaphysical definition of power (as forceful legitimacy). Nonetheless, it is much closer to the metaphysical definition than to the functional definition. That is because the locus of power is genuinely eschatological: it involves the conviction that the judgment of God is moving from its definitive moment in the future, toward the present. Fellowship at meals, which may conveniently be called eucharist, as within Christianity from this period, is the locus in the present of that vindication and that judgment which is coming. Inclusion in the eucharist is the locus in the present of the transcendent reality which is coming. That is both its promise, and the threat of noninclusion.

The New Testament reflects the attempt to meet the potentially disastrous problem that Christian practices of eucharist might become mutually exclusive. The contrast between James and Paul comes to open expression, but the willingness within the practice of Peter to countenance different sorts of practice, and therefore different standards of purity, could and did cause confusion. The first three Gospels represent the attempt, through the stories of the feedings of the five thousand and the four thousand, to establish commensurate but separate celebrations among Jews and non-Jews. The Fourth Gospel takes a daring turn, by insisting, for the first time within the literature of the New Testament, that in eucharist Jesus provides his own, personal body and blood. That made eucharist a religion of Mystery, in the Hellenistic sense of a ritual participation in the death and rebirth of a god. It also – and immediately – implied the exclusion from eucharist of all those who would not accept that meaning ("the Jews," in the vocabulary of John).

The danger of pluralism within early Christian practice, then, had been that a James could include a Paul out, a Paul include a James out, a Peter include them both out, and both of them include a Peter out, and so on. The resolution was to insist – in the manner of the synoptic Gospels – upon ecumenical recognition of diverse practice, but also to insist – in the Johannine manner – that eucharist was a personal Mystery which excluded those who would not accept that Jesus personally gave himself, body and blood.

By now, noninclusion had been transformed into exclusion, if only implicitly, and that transformation is amply instanced in the Fathers of the Church selected for discussion (see "Irenaeus, Cyprian, and Augustine" below). Irenaeus's conception unfolded from John's: in giving his body and blood, Jesus provided his followers with miraculous food, comparable to the manna given Israel in the wilderness at the time of the Exodus. As Irenaeus develops that theme, the very flesh of those who partake of eucharist is transformed by Jesus' "flesh." That is a pointed development of the Johannine Mystery, because Gnostics during the second century had insisted that spirit alone, without flesh, was susceptible of salvation. Irenaeus reads the Johannine eucharist in such a way that a Gnostic who believed that flesh was irredeemable could not participate in it.

Cyprian of Carthage, the most powerful Christian leader of his time, confronted the particular problem of how to reconcile those Christians who had acceded to Roman persecution after that persecution was over. He resisted the point of view that only those who had endured torment could extend forgiveness to "lapsed" Christians, but he also rejected the immediate incorporation of the "lapsed" into the continued practice of eucharist. His mediating position included the emergence of the Catholic teaching of eucharist in its classic form: the sacrifice of Jesus is offered all over again, preparing believers to become acceptable sacrifices themselves.

Augustine maintained that "if you receive well, you are what is received," that is, that believers become an acceptable sacrifice in the act of eucharist. His theology is in the lineage of Cyprian's, but there is a difference. Augustine writes in what he himself calls the "Christian epoch" (*Christiana tempora*), well after the time of Eusebius. Constantine has been and gone, and Goths have been to Rome; the Vandals will take Augustine's own city of Hippo shortly after his own death. The issue of acceptability before God here therefore intrudes to insist once again that the state cannot be equated directly with what Augustine calls the city of God in Heaven.

Nonetheless, the change under Constantine had been fundamental. The secular realm, within the terms and conditions of this world, had been subsumed within the city of God. All along, from the time of Jesus and his followers, through the conscious exclusions of John's Gospel, Irenaeus, and Cyprian, the dynamic of noninclusion in the kingdom had been implicit within eucharistic practice. But by the time of Eusebius and Constantine and those who came after, the power of the state, both functional and metaphysical, could be brought to bear to insist upon the discipline of the Church (see "In the Shadow of the Tree" below).

No place is the difficulty of this predicament clearer than in Augustine's attitude toward the Donatists. The problem itself was typically North African, but it illustrates a systemic feature in the Christianity of the period. Donatists had taken up the old hard line about martyrdom and forgiveness: only clergy who had not lapsed during persecutions could rightly exercise their authority. The result was that Donatist churches grew up as the doubles of Catholic churches, and frequently overtook them in size, influence, and fervor. At first, Augustine's view was that those who wished to separate from the Church at large would have only themselves to blame in the judgment to come. In that, he took up the classic stance from at least the time of Paul. But Augustine had a fateful change of heart. Since the power of this world had been given to Christ, and one lived in the millennial rule of the saints, a new world order applied. In the parable of the wedding feast, the king orders his servants to bring in those in the highways and byways, saying, "Compel them to come in" (see Luke 14:23). Christ authorized compulsion in order to maintain eucharistic discipline. This world had been invaded by the next, just as flesh had been invaded by spirit, so that the power of this world, this flesh, was rightly to serve as an enacted parable of the kingdom of God.

What sort of politics, neither of ultimate force nor of static legitimacy, are we dealing with in the case of Christianity in its classical sources? I think it is apparent from the sources than no single ideology will serve to answer that question. The pattern we are dealing with links the practice of eucharist with a dynamic of noninclusion, and the extent of what might be done to exclude people varies with the social conditions of the movement.

But while the means of inclusion and noninclusion vary, the pattern is consistent. The kingdom of God is understood to be coming from the future as eschatological and, as transcendent, to be transforming the world as we know it. The power envisaged is even more unqualified than the violence with which modern politics is obsessed. The power of the kingdom is to begin things and to end things, to do and to undo. Paul may be permitted the last word, again from 1 Corinthians (7:29-31):

> This is what I say, brothers: time is shortened. For the rest, let those who have wives be as those who have none, and those who weep as though they did not, and those who rejoice as though they did not, and those who buy as without possessions, and those who inherit the world as without rights. Because the form of this world is passing.

Marcus Aurelius was right. Christians are obstinate. They are so systemically, not merely as a matter of temperament. And the reason is that the power of their nonpolitics is not of this world; the power envisaged by their faith is rather what makes and unmakes this world.

Introduction: The Eusebean Revolution

Jesus was remembered to have said that it was not worth losing one's soul in order to gain the world (Matt. 16:26; Mark 8:36; Luke 9:25). Three hundred years later, Eusebius rejoiced with apocalyptic fervor at the vision of a Christian emperor who in imitation of the Son of God in Heaven "directs the course of all things upon earth" (*Praise of Constantine* 1.6, cited more fully below). The rejection of the world at one end of the period, and the attempt to embrace and control that same world at the other end of the period, punctuate the development of classical Christianity.

The history of the empire had prepared politically for Constantine's famous decision to permit the cross among his insignia at the battle of Milvian Bridge in 312. But Christian theology had just passed through the period of its most enthusiastic embrace of neo-Platonism; the events of this world had long been portrayed as remote from any sort of divine significance. A new sort of explanation was necessary, in order to account for revolutionary change. That explanation, and the beginning of Christian history, started with Eusebius (260-340), bishop of Caesarea. Through Pamphilus, his teacher and predecessor, Eusebius had been deeply influenced by the thought of Origen. So before there was a consciously Christian history, there was an irony of history: from the least historical perspective came the first comprehensive historical account of how the Church came to claim the world in the name of Christ. His prominence in the ecumenical Church at various councils from Nicea onward, as well as his friendship with Constantine, go a long way toward explaining why Eusebius should have made the contribution which makes him the Herodotus of ecclesiastical history.

Eusebius's Apocalypse in Reverse

As he attempted to express the startling breakthrough under Constantine, Eusebius portrayed the new emperor as chosen by God himself. The most famous result of his mediation of the significance of the new order is his *History of the Church,* a vitally important document which takes up the Christian story from the time of Christ. The settlement under Constantine is his goal, however, and his portrayal of the emperor is perhaps most vividly conveyed in his *Praise of Constantine.* After speaking of Christ as the word of God which holds dominion over the whole world, Eusebius goes on to make a comparison with Constantine (*Praise of Constantine* 1.6):

> ...our Emperor, beloved of God, bearing a kind of image of the supreme rule as it were in imitation of the greater, directs the course of all things upon earth.

Here the old Stoic idea of the rule of the emperor as commensurate with the divine rule is provided with a new substance: the emperor who obeys Christ himself imitates Christ's glory. Eusebius was inclined to describe himself as moderately capable,[7] and that may be an accurate assessment of him as a theologian and historian. But as a political theorist, he is one of the most influential thinkers in the West. He provided the basis upon which the Roman Empire could be presented as the Holy Roman Empire, and articulated the grounds for claiming the divine rights of rulers. At the same time, his reference to the conditional nature of those rights, as dependent upon the imitation of Christ, has

---

[7] See Williamson's comment in *The History of the Church,* trans. G. A. Williamson (Minneapolis: Augsburg, 1975), 8, and *History of the Church* 1.1; 10.4.1.

provided a basis upon which political revolution may be encouraged on religious grounds.

Part of Eusebius's argument was that Constantine restored the united form of the empire which had been the ideal of Augustus.[8] After a preface which sets out Christ's divine and human natures, Eusebius carefully places Christ's birth during Augustus's reign, after the subjugation of Egypt (*History of the Church* 1.5). The pairing of Augustus and Christ, Christ and Constantine is therefore symmetrical, and defines the scope of the work. The result is to present a theologically structured political history.

The extent of that history is determined by its political horizon, much as in the case of Eusebius's predecessors in classical history. Whether we think of Herodotus in his explanation of the Persian War, or of Thucydides in the case of the Peloponnesian War, the impetus of writing history seems to be the experience of political change and dislocation. The scope of such work would be extended by such writers as Polybius (the apologist for Rome) and Josephus (the apologist for Judaism), but the desire to learn from the past in the effort to construct a more politically viable present is evident throughout.

No reader of Eusebius can fail to feel uncomfortable at his apology for Constantine. Although the form is political history, the substance seems embarrassingly like flattery. How could Eusebius so thoroughly fail to be critical, whether as historian or as theologian? As an historian, he knew that kings and their flatterers were transient; as a theologian in the line of Origen, he knew that perfection eluded human flesh. The key to this riddle lies in Eusebius's conviction that Christ was at work in Constantine's triumph (*History of the Church* 10.1.8):

> From that time on a day bright and radiant, with no cloud overshadowing it, shone down with shafts of heavenly light on the churches of Christ throughout the world, nor was there any reluctance to grant even those outside our community the enjoyment, if not of equal blessings, at least of an effluence from and a share in the things that God had bestowed on us.

The sharp change from persecution and all it involved was as disorienting for Eusebius as the Peloponnesian War had been to Thucydides, and an explanation was demanded. In that explanation, ecclesiastical history was born: that is, not simply the anecdotes of experience, but a rational account of God's activity within human events.

Dramatic intervention for good in the case of Constantine and his colleague Licinius (who at first reigned with Constantine) was nothing

---

[8] See his *History of the Church* 10.9.6-9 and Lloyd G. Patterson, *God and History in Early Christian Thought: Studies in Patristic Thought* (New York: Seabury, 1967), 84.

less than the appointed plan of God within a definite sequence of events. Eusebius reminds the reader of the terrible tortures Christians had experienced, and then proceeds (*History of the Church* 10.4.14-15):

> But once again the Angel of the great counsel, God's great Commander-in-Chief, after the thoroughgoing training of which the greatest soldiers in his kingdom gave proof by their patience and endurance in all trials, appeared suddenly and thereby swept all that was hostile and inimical into oblivion and nothingness, so that its very existence was forgotten. But all that was near and dear to Him He advanced beyond glory in the sight of all, not men only but the heavenly powers as well – sun, moon, and stars, and the entire heaven and earth.

Only the language of apocalypse, of the sequenced revelation of God himself in Christ, can explain to Eusebius's satisfaction how the former agony can so quickly have been transformed into festivity. In Constantine, the promised future had begun, and there was no room for a return to the past.

The picture which Eusebius draws of the contemporary scene might have been drawn from an apocalyptic work in Hellenistic dress (10.9, after the narrative of the removal of Licinius):

> Men had now lost all fear of their former oppressors; day after day they kept dazzling festival; light was everywhere, and men who once dared not look up greeted each other with smiling faces and shining eyes. They danced and sang in city and country alike, giving honor first to God our Sovereign Lord, as they had been instructed, and then to the pious emperor with his sons, so dear to God.

History for Eusebius was not just an account of the past, it was an apocalypse in reverse. His account was designed to set out the sequence of events which brought about the dawn of a new age.

The Revolution of "Power"

Long before Eusebius, Origen had written that Rome would prosper better by worshiping the true God than even the children of Israel had (*Against Celsus* 8.69). For Origen, the argument was hypothetical; for Eusebius, it had become a reality. The new unity of the empire, under God, in Christ, and through the piety of the emperor himself, constituted for Eusebius a divine polity (*politeia* or *politeuma*), literally a breath away from paradise.

Politics in the usual understanding involves power: the ability to reward, cajole, coerce, and punish in order to achieve one's social ends. Conscious reflection on the use of that power is politics itself, whether in the theoretical key of an Aristotle and a Machiavelli on the one hand, or in the pragmatic key of a Constantine and a Napoleon on the other hand. By that definition, Christianity had no politics until Eusebius realized that there was real power at the disposal of the Church, and that it required a theological theory in order to be used effectively.

But the power and the politics which came Christianity's way during the fourth century were not the direct consequence of any will to exercise such power. As we have just seen, Christians were best prepared for a stance of alienation from the conventional sources of power, and precisely that stance was revolutionized by events. In order to understand how Christians during the fourth century and later reacted to the revolution of power which implicated them, we should turn to consider the roots of their politics. For if it was necessary to Eusebius to invent a politics, he was nothing if not a traditionalist, and the elements of a Christian politics were already well developed and at his disposal by the time he wrote.

Roots of Power: Noninclusion and Its Consequences in Paul

Paul provides an extraordinarily vivid account of how Christians, precisely at their most powerless, attempted to articulate a theory and an instrument of power. Paul wrote to a church (or churches) in Corinth around the year 55, a few years after he himself had been received as a Jewish sectarian by the governor Gallio in that same city.[9] His attitude reflects his alienation, and Christian alienation generally, from the conventional instruments of power. It is therefore not surprising that he refers to the ignorance of "the rulers of this age" (1 Cor. 2:6, 8) and rejoices that "the form of this world is passing away" (1 Cor. 7:31). Here, some twenty-five years after the death of Jesus, we observe the pointing of Jesus' own eschatology of God's kingdom into the keen apocalyptic expectation which was to become a trademark of early Christianity.

That stance of alienation from the world occasioned Paul's nearest approximation to political advice in 1 Corinthians. Confronted by the particular case of a man who married his father's wife, Paul instructs the congregation to gather in the presence of his own spirit and in the power of the Lord Jesus, and to "hand over such a one to Satan for destruction of the flesh, so that the spirit might be saved in the day of the Lord" (1 Cor. 5:1-5). The reference is so laconic, so much is taken for granted, that Paul's meaning has been a matter of dispute. But the apocalyptic framework within which Paul is operating provides the key for understanding what he says.[10] Those who gather "in the power of the Lord Jesus" invoke the authority of the one who is to judge the living and the dead. Judgment now of a member of the community permits the

---

[9] See Robert Jewett, *Dating Paul's Life* (London: SCM, 1979).
[10] See D. E. H. Whiteley, *The Theology of St. Paul* (Philadelphia: Fortress, 1964), 272-73.

hope of divine mercy later, but only because "God judges those outside" (1 Cor. 5:13). It is for God to show the compassion; the community is to "cleanse out the old leaven" by shunning those who practice the sins Paul believes are egregious (1 Cor. 5:6-12).

This shunning, a refusal to "mix socially" (*sunanamignusthai*, 1 Cor. 5:9, 11), for Paul and for Christianity generally, referred to exclusion from fellowship at meals. Paul does not need, here or elsewhere, to explain what is meant, because his assumption is that the dynamics of excommunication are clearly understood. Within the practice of Judaism, noninclusion in meals had been a characteristic among those who undertook to be faithful, the *haverim*. The most famous examples come from the Mishnaic tractate Demai (discussed below), which restricts and controls how one might offer hospitality to a person, and accept hospitality from a person, who may not have paid tithe on produce. Christian practice within its own understanding had involved widening the circle of those who might join in the fellowship of the kingdom, both within Israel and beyond Israel. Paul, however, is representative in the understanding that noninclusion in celebrations of the kingdom represents the direct sanction of a power beyond the terms of reference of this world.

Deeper Roots: Jesus' Practice of Metaphysical Power

Jesus' position focused on the transforming reality of the "kingdom of God," an Aramaic phrase he was familiar with from the prayers and the translations of the Hebrew Bible which were current in his time.[11] The practices Jesus engaged in on the basis of the kingdom, and what he had his disciples do, are a direct indication of his notion of the ultimate ground of power.

Sources for Understanding Jesus

Recent discussion of the source known as Q has brought about a remarkable consensus that at least some of the sayings within it were circulated a few years after the crucifixion, around the year 35 C.E. A recent study includes in the earliest version of Q a charge to Jesus' disciples (Luke 10:3-6, 9-11, 16), a strategy to cope with resistance to their message (Luke 6:27-35), examples of how to speak of the kingdom (Luke 6:20b-21; 11:2-4, 14-20; 13:18-21), curses to lay on those who reject those sent in the name of the kingdom (Luke 11:39-48, 52), and a section

---

[11] See Chilton, *A Galilean Rabbi and His Bible* (Wilmington: Glazier, 1984).

relating John the Baptist and Jesus as principal emissaries of the kingdom (Luke 7:24b-26, 28a, 33-34).[12]

The reconstruction proposed by Leif Vaage follows in the wake of the recent fashion of proposing multiple versions of Q prior to the composition of Matthew and Luke. He cites John Kloppenborg's hypothesis of three redactions of Q prior to the Gospels, but in his own analysis his concern is to distinguish the formative stage from the redaction more generally. In that approach, Vaage's work is comparable to the more conservative contribution of David Catchpole, which appeared in the previous year.[13]

Catchpole isolates the formative material of the charge to Jesus' disciples much as Vaage does (Luke 10:3, 4, 5-7, 9, 10a, 11a, 12). He sees that as "an integrated whole stemming from Jesus himself," which has been layered over with additional material (Luke 10:2, 13-15, 16). The additional material represents the especial concerns of Q: Christology, eschatology, and the final mission to Israel on Jesus' behalf.[14]

The agreement between Vaage and Catchpole in regard to the formative stage of Q makes their profound disagreement in regard to the cultural milieu of Q all the more striking. Two statements, placed side by side, will illustrate their dissonance:

> Like the Cynics, the "Galilean upstarts" whom Q's formative stratum represents conducted in word and deed a form of "popular" resistance to the official truths and virtues of their day. (Vaage, 106)

> ...there is a preoccupation with a mission to Israel, which needs to be expanded by means of yet more charismatically endowed missionaries sent out by a settled but charismatic community with the authority of God himself. (Catchpole, 188)

The opposition of these positions is even greater than may appear at first reading; for while Vaage is characterizing the formative stage of Q, Catchpole is speaking of the redactional product.

Both these perspectives are too rigid, and distort a critical reading of Q. Vaage relies extensively and unreflectively on John Dominic Crossan's work, which is based on a direct comparison between Jesus

---

[12] See Leif E. Vaage, *Galilean Upstarts: Jesus' First Followers according to Q* (Valley Forge: Trinity Press International, 1994). He defends his choice of the material at the formative shape of Q in agreement with the recent work of John S. Kloppenborg, 107-20. Since the time of Adolf von Harnack, there has been a lively discussion of whether Matthew or Luke more accurately represents Q. He sided with Matthew; see *The Sayings of Jesus*, trans. J. R. Wilkinson (New York: Putnam, 1908), 172-82. Vaage follows the current fashion in preferring Luke, and in citing Q according to chapter and verse in Luke.

[13] *The Quest for Q* (Edinburgh: Clark, 1993).

[14] *The Quest for Q*, 188.

and Cynic philosophers which has been found implausible. Catchpole understands the "confrontational sense"[15] of such statements as John the Baptist's claim that God could raise up children for Abraham from stones in order to replace those of Israel who refused to repent (Luke 3:8); but he does not adequately allow for the distance from Israel such a threat implies.

Q is better seen as evolving in two distinct stages. In the first, Jesus' teaching was arranged in the form of a mishnah by his disciples. They took up a ministry in Jesus' name which was addressed to Israel at large after the resurrection. The mishnaic form of Q was preserved orally in Aramaic, and explained how the twelve were to discharge their mission. It included just the materials which have already been specified, instructions to Jesus' disciples, a strategy of love to overcome resistance, paradigms to illustrate the kingdom, threats directed toward enemies, and a reference to John the Baptist which would serve as a transition to baptism in the name of Jesus.[16] As specified, that is probably the original, mishnaic order of Q. It is the order that accords with Q's purpose within the mission to Israel.

At the final stage, Q's order was changed to become quasi-biographical, in accordance with the order of teaching in the name of Peter (see Acts 10:34-43). At that stage, for example, material concerning John the Baptist was moved to the beginning, and the story of Jesus' temptations (Luke 4:1-13) was added, in order to make the transition to an unequivocal focus upon Jesus rather than John. The final redaction of Q probably took place a decade after the mishnaic stage of Q was composed, probably in Syria, an environment in which both Aramaic and Greek were spoken.[17]

The Kingdom and the Mission of the Disciples

Catchpole and Vaage are both competent guides in the attempt to understand Luke 10:1-12, the commission of the seventy or seventy-two disciples (the number varying with the manuscripts which are followed).

---

[15] *The Quest for Q*, 77. On p. 248, the passage is classed with John's prophetic preaching.
[16] It seems likely to me, in addition, that Q also preserved at least one saying in reference to eucharist (Luke 22:15). See Chilton, *A Feast of Meanings: Eucharistic Theologies from Jesus through Johannine Circles*, Supplements to Novum Testamentum (Leiden: E. J. Brill, 1994), 72-74, 94-96.
[17] See Siegfried Schulz, *Q. Die Spruchquelle der Evangelisten* (Zürich: Theologischer Verlag, 1972). It should be mentioned that there is an extensive bibliography on Q, reaching back over two centuries (and much of it in German). The appearance is sometimes given in North America that the hypothesis is new: in fact, it is an old and well-founded theory.

The former adduces much rabbinic material to elucidate the text, while the latter cites a range of Cynic sources. Both sorts of analogy are helpful in understanding the literary shape of the commission, but the focus here is different. Our purpose is to understand the commission of the disciples in terms of the kingdom, and the kingdom in terms of the commission. If, as seems to be the case, Q in its mishnaic phase represents Jesus' charge to his disciples as he sent them out to be his representatives, it should reflect his own programmatic activity more lucidly than any inference which we might draw regarding his intentions. Jesus' commission is the closest thing there is to his own commentary on his actions.

What the disciples are told to do seems strange, unless the image of the harvest at the beginning of the charge (Luke 10:2) is taken seriously.[18] Because they are going out as to rich fields, they do not require what would normally be required on a journey: purse, bag, and sandals are dispensed with (Luke 10:4). Their charge is to treat Israel as a field in which one works, not as an itinerary of travel; greeting people along the way (which would only lead to diversions from the task) is even proscribed in Luke 10:4.

In addition, staffs are also prohibited, although they were normally used on journeys for support and protection. That is a detail which we actually know from Luke 9:3, the commission of the twelve (rather than the seventy). Luke 9:3 also prohibits carrying a bag, a provision of bread, money, or a change of clothing. Matt. 10:9-10 agrees in regard to money, a bag, clothing, sandals, and staff, but nothing prohibits bread. Mark 6:8-9 prohibits bread, bag, and money, but both a staff and sandals are positively *prescribed!*

All those additional privations comport with the command to go without sandals, and were a part of the original charge. Each Gospel softens the stringent requirements somewhat. Matthew omits the prohibition of bread; Luke divides the prohibitions between the twelve (9:1-6) and the seventy (10:1-12). In a more radical way, Mark 6:9 turns the prohibition of sandals into a command to wear them. By the same transformation, Mark 6:8 specifies that a staff "alone" *should* be carried, so that the imagery of discipleship shifts, from treating all Israel as one's household, to passing through territory which might prove hostile. Such variations reflect differences in primitive Christian practice and in conceptions of discipleship. Similarly, the number of disciples in Luke 10:1, seventy or seventy-two, accommodates the traditional number of

---

[18] In this regard, I agree with Kloppenborg against Vaage; see Vaage, 107-8. The metaphor of harvesting is also applied to discipleship by Rabbi Tarfon in Avoth 2:15.

the nations of the world, while the earlier figure of twelve in Matt. 10:5 and Mark 6:7 represents both the intention of Jesus to address all Israel and the mishnaic stage of Q. The image of Israel as a field ripe for harvest dominates the details of the charge to the disciples in the earliest form of the commission, Jesus' mishnah.

Another, powerful analogy is at work with the commission. The Mishnah reflects the common practice in Jerusalem of prohibiting pilgrims to enter the Temple with the bags and staffs and purses which they had traveled with (Berakhoth 9:5).[19] All such items were to be deposited prior to worship, so that one was present simply as a representative of Israel. Part of worship was that one was to appear in one's simple purity. The issue of purity also features prominently in the charge to the disciples (although it is overlooked far too often).

The very next injunction (Luke 10:5-8) instructs the disciples to enter into any house of a village they enter, and to offer their peace. They are to accept hospitality in that house, eating what is set before them. The emphasis upon eating what is provided is repeated (Luke 10:7, 8), so that it does not appear to be a later, marginal elaboration.[20] Within Pharisaic constructions of purity, such as are reflected in the Mishnah, the foods one ate and the hospitality one offered and accepted were carefully regulated. In the tractate Demai (2:2), which concerns tithing, one who undertakes to be faithful must tithe what he eats, what he sells, and what he buys, *and not accept hospitality from a "person of the land."* ("Person of the land" ['*am ha-aretz*] is a phrase which had been used since the time of Zech. 7:5 to refer to people whose practices could not be trusted.) Demai (2:3) further specifies that a faithful person must not sell a person of the land wet or dry produce, and must not buy wet produce from him. (Wet produce was held to be susceptible to uncleanness.) The passage goes on to make the rule against hospitality more reciprocal, insofar as he cannot have a person of land as a guest when that person is wearing his own (probably impure) garments: he must first change his clothing. These strictures clearly reflect a construction of purity among the "faithful" (*haverim*) which sets them apart from other Jews by impinging upon the foods one might eat and trade, and the commerce and fellowship one might enjoy.[21]

---

[19] See Chilton, *The Temple of Jesus: His Sacrificial Program within a Cultural History of Sacrifice* (University Park: Penn State Press, 1992), 100-111.

[20] Catchpole may be correct in stating that the form of 10:8 is redactional, from the time of the composition of the Gospel (176-78). But he is also correct in assigning 10:7 to Q (184-85), and that is where the motif first appears, within the ministry of Jesus.

[21] For a discussion of the passage as a reflection of practice in the first century, see *A Feast of Meanings*, 165-66.

Jesus' insistence that his disciples accept hospitality in whatever house would accept him is fully consonant with his reputation as a "glutton and a drunkard" (see Matt. 11:19 and Luke 7:34). There is a deliberate carelessness involved, in the precise sense that the disciples are not to have a care in regard to the practices of purity of those who offer hospitality to them. They are true Israelites. When they join in the meals of the kingdom which Jesus' disciples have arrived to celebrate, when they accept and grant forgiveness to one another in the manner of the Lord's Prayer, what they set upon the table of fellowship from their own effort is by definition pure, and should be gratefully consumed. The twelve disciples define and create the true Israel to which they are sent, and they tread that territory as on holy ground, shoeless, without staff or purse.

The activities of the disciples in the fellowship of Israel are essentially to be the activities of Jesus. As Luke presents Q, they are to heal the sick and preach that the kingdom has drawn near (Luke 10:9); as Matthew presents Q, they are to preach that the kingdom has drawn near and heal, raise the dead, cleanse lepers, caste out demons, all the while taking and giving freely (Matt. 10:7-8). As Catchpole observes, the wording of Matthew correlates the disciples' activities with Jesus' activities, and he thinks the correlation was introduced when the Gospel was composed.[22] But the correlation involved is with material in Q: it agrees with Jesus' statement of what John the Baptist should be told he is doing (Matt. 11:5 and Luke 7:22). For that reason, Matthew at this point may be held to represent the more primitive wording. In any case, the coordination of the disciples' activity with Jesus' is manifestly an organic aspect of the charge in Q.

The extent of the identity between what Jesus does and what the disciples do is clearly represented at the close of the charge, when the disciples are instructed to shake the dust off their feet from any place that does not receive them (Luke 10:11). That gesture is, of course, vivid on any reading. But with the understanding of the charge which we have developed here, the symbolism is particularly acute. Towns which do not receive the disciples have cut themselves off from the kingdom of God, and can expect worse than what is in store for Sodom (Luke 10:11-12).[23]

---

[22] Catchpole, 167.

[23] The explicit reference to the kingdom in Luke 10:11 is attributed by Catchpole (185) to the stage of the redaction of the Gospel, although he admits that the actual form of words is nearer to Q's than is Luke 10:9 (164). That is a rare case of self-contradiction, and in this case his judgment should not be accepted. Vaage, on the other hand, would excise 10:12 from Q's formative stage (108): his Cynic Jesus can have simply nothing to do with judgment.

Taken as a whole, Jesus' charge of the disciples at the mishnaic stage of Q is an enacted parable of the kingdom of God. The disciples are to perform the reality of which Jesus speaks, and which he himself enacts. The meal of the group with Jesus constituted a circle of purity, whose acceptability to the divine was asserted by associating that social meal with the kingdom of God. Jesus accepted that others called him a glutton and a drunkard, a friend of those whom many Pharisees despised, because he ate and drank as a characteristic activity (see Matt. 11:19; Luke 7:34). He also commissioned some of his disciples to engage in such a program (see Matt. 10:11-14; Mark 6:10; Luke 9:4). The practice of social eating was an activity commissioned by Jesus, with the result that a conscious view of purity was involved as a coordinate of the kingdom.

The Gathering of the Kingdom

A prominent image employed by Jesus, attested in varying forms in the source called Q (Matt. 8:11-12; Luke 13:28-29), pictures people being gathered from east and west in order to feast with Abraham, Isaac, and Jacob in the kingdom of God. It has been argued that the reference to east and west implies that people beyond the boundaries of Israel are to be included in the eschatological banquet. So understood, the image is a promise of "the Gentiles' share in the salvation of the Messianic age."[24] That reading identifies how the saying could have been understood among those in the Church who later faced the issue of how Jews and non-Jews are to be related, but Jesus' saying was distinct from that concern of the Church in the Greco-Roman world.

Jesus' movement centered in Galilee, and was characterized by fellowship at meals involving various people with different practices of purity. His circle needed to cope with the issue of defilement as one member of Israel (with a certain set of practices) met with another member of Israel (with another set of practices). To deal with that question, a single aphorism of Jesus was precisely designed:

> Nothing that is outside a person entering one defiles one, except that things coming from a person, these defile one.[25]

As Jesus saw the matter, once one is identified with Israel, it is not that which is without which defiles, but those things which come from oneself.

---

[24] So Joachim Jeremias, *Jesus' Promise to the Nations: The Franz Delitzsch Lectures for 1953*, trans. S.H. Hooke, Studies in Biblical Theology 24 (London: SCM, 1958), 62.
[25] The rendering is of the Aramaic *mashal* which I have identified behind the Greek text of Mark 7:14-15. See "A Generative Exegesis of Mark 7:1-23," *The Journal of Higher Criticism* (forthcoming).

The second line of the aphorism makes it clear that originally its meaning was not limited to food, since many things proceed from a person which have nothing to do with his alimentary canal. The limitation to food is accomplished by the packaging of the saying within the Hellenistic concerns of the Gospels, where the controlling issue is whether or not hands are to be washed (see Matt. 15:1-2; Mark 7:1-5). Jesus' point was rather that contagion from impurity was a matter of what one did, not one's contacts. Separation from that which is outside one does not therefore assure purity, and non-Jews in the mixed environment of Galilee pose no particular danger to Israel.

The circle of Jesus frames its rhetoric for its specific, social circumstance, of Galilee: Israel in the midst of the nations.[26] Defilement here is a matter of failing to recognize the others of Israel, refusing to share with the pure Israel which those others represent. Jesus' concern with Israel in the midst of non-Jews led to his conviction that their non-Jewish environment did not compromise the identity of Israel.

That conviction was transmuted at a later stage into the equally firm insistence – by Paul and those like him – that in Christian gatherings the distinction between Jew and Greek no longer matters (Gal. 3:28). That stance of Hellenistic Christianity could only be developed in the Greco-Roman world once non-Jewish constituents of the movement were so significant that they could challenge the assumption that ordinary, Judaic practices of purity were to be honored. Jesus' position was worked out at too early a stage to be a simple matter of universalism. He at no point challenged the identity of Israel as the people of God, and he assumed that purity and sacrifice in the Temple would be matters of concern for those who listened to him.

His focus upon Israel in the midst of nations explains the force of Jesus' promise that peoples will come from east and west in order to feast with the patriarchs. The imagery was inspired by the Book of Zechariah, which also pictures God as gathering his people from east and west (Zech. 8:7). The purpose of the gathering is to bring them to Jerusalem, to know their God in that place (Zech. 8:8) and to join in feasting (Zech. 8:19). Zechariah sees the exemplary value of the feast as so strong that even non-Jews will seek to join themselves to the presence of God (so Zech. 8:20-23).

Jesus shared the Zecharian vision, that Israel's gathering would draw in those beyond Israel. His development of motifs and language from the

---

[26] See Seán Freyne, "The Geography, Politics, and Economics of Galilee and the Quest for the Historical Jesus," *Studying the Historical Jesus: Evaluations of the State of Current Research,* ed. Chilton and C.A. Evans, New Testament Tools and Studies 19 (Leiden: E. J. Brill, 1994), 75-121.

Book of Zechariah, by means of his statements and his activities, has been amply discussed.[27] But he did not articulate that vision by claiming – in the Pauline manner – that the distinction between Israel and the nations no longer existed. His entire approach was to focus on the assembly of Israel as the hope of all.

Neither Zechariah nor Jesus represents a theology of uncritical inclusion within the kingdom of God. As Zech. 13:8-9 depicts matters, two-thirds in all the land are to perish, and the final third is to pass through fire. The issue of who does and does not turn to the new opportunity for cleansing (see Zech. 13:1, with its reference to a fountain opened for the house of David and the inhabitants of Jerusalem) is made crucial by the strong eschatology of the book. In Jesus' case, as well, not heeding the invitation to the feast of the kingdom involves one's ultimate punishment (see Matt. 8:12; Luke 13:28-29). Jesus' articulated and adhered to a vision of how ultimately people could be included within the kingdom of God. Not to accept his practice was to exclude oneself from that kingdom: that is the inexorable logic of excommunication, the only power (from outside this world) which Christianity could ever exercise on the basis of Jesus' teaching.

Spreading Roots: Broadening Exclusions in Primitive Christianity

Jesus' Dispute in the Temple

To speak of God as king, and to preach that kingdom on God's behalf, involved Jesus in disputes regarding the grounds of his authority. The acknowledged cultic authorities in Jerusalem held that his teaching subverted the authority of the Temple. When Jesus occupied that Temple, and expelled those who were trading in animals, he directly opposed the unusual arrangement which Caiaphas (the high priest) had sanctioned, which provided for trade within the great court of the Temple.[28]

Jesus acted as he did, not to prevent sacrifice as such, but to insist that what was offered in the Temple should belong to Israel, and not be a matter of simply paying for the property of priests. Jesus' vision was of the accessibility of sacrificial worship, such that one would have no need of commercialism. His statement in Mark 11:17 puts the matter starkly: Trade in the house of God is theft. But Jesus' stance is no less radical than the Book of Zechariah (14:20-21), which predicts that the goods in Jerusalem will be ready for sacrifice, without commercial transaction.

---

[27] See *The Temple of Jesus*, 135-36.
[28] The particulars of the dispute are detailed in *The Temple of Jesus*, 91-111.

In Jesus' radical theology, the kingdom of God was restructuring the principal institution of Israel in his time: the Temple. It was natural that the authorities there would resist him. Given that Jesus' activity extended to the use of physical force, it was also inevitable that the full power of the high priest would be brought to bear against him. But did his position make him a blasphemer, or a prophet of God's ultimate aim for his people? One's answer to that question, around the year 30 C.E. in Jerusalem, told the difference between those whose loyalty was to the Temple as sanctioned by God and those who shared Jesus' vision of the kingdom. Jesus himself, however, did not finally locate himself as outside Judaism, and the authorities who sympathized with Caiaphas were only able to dispatch with him through the intermediary of Pilate, the Roman governor.

Jesus' occupation of the Temple did not result in the definitive expulsion of traders at the time. Caiaphas was able to restore order, along with his own preferred arrangements. The true resolution of the dispute, in his mind, would involve the execution of Jesus, which he achieved by means of Pilate (whose likely role in the proceedings is described below). The teaching of Jesus after his occupation of the Temple, and specifically his reference to his meals of fellowship as a replacement of sacrifice in the Temple, played into Caiaphas's hands. However they learned of Jesus' new interpretation of his meals of fellowship, the authorities arrested him just after the supper we call last.

Jesus continued to celebrate fellowship at table as a foretaste of the kingdom, just as he had before. As before, the promise of drinking new wine in the kingdom of God joined his followers in an anticipatory celebration of that kingdom (see Matt. 26:29; Mark 14:25; Luke 22:18). But he also added a new and scandalous dimension of meaning. His occupation of the Temple having failed, Jesus said over the wine, "This is my blood," and over the bread, "This is my flesh" (Matt. 26:26, 28; Mark 14:22, 24; Luke 22:19-20; 1 Cor. 11:24-25; Justin, *Apology* I.66.3)

In Jesus' context, the context of his confrontation with the authorities of the Temple, his words can have had only one meaning. He cannot have meant, "Here are my personal body and blood"; that is an interpretation which only makes sense at a later stage in the development of Christianity.[29] Jesus' point was rather that, in the absence of a Temple which permitted his view of purity to be practiced, wine was his blood of sacrifice, and bread was his flesh of sacrifice. In

---

[29] For a scholarly discussion of that development as reflected within the texts of the New Testament, see Chilton, *A Feast of Meanings*. In a popular way, the question is also treated in Chilton, "The Eucharist: Exploring Its Origins," *Bible Review* 10, no. 6 (1994): 36-43.

Aramaic, "blood" (*d^ema*) and "flesh" (*bisra*, which may also be rendered as "body") can carry such a sacrificial meaning, and in Jesus' context, that is the most natural meaning.

The meaning of the "last supper," then, actually evolved over a series of meals after Jesus' occupation of the Temple. During that period, Jesus claimed that wine and bread were a better sacrifice than what was offered in the Temple, a foretaste of new wine in the kingdom of God. At least wine and bread were Israel's own, not tokens of priestly dominance. No wonder the opposition to him, even among the Twelve (in the shape of Judas, according to the Gospels) became deadly. In essence, Jesus made his meals into a rival altar.

That final gesture of protest gave Caiaphas what he needed. Jesus could be charged with blasphemy before those with an interest in the Temple. The issue now was not simply Jesus' opposition to the siting of vendors of animals, but his creation of an alternative sacrifice. He blasphemed the law of Moses. The accusation concerned the Temple, in which Rome also had a vested interested.

Pilate had no regard for issues of purity; Acts 18:14-16 reflects the attitude of an official in a similar position, and Josephus shows that Pilate was without sympathy for Judaism. But the Temple in Jerusalem had come to symbolize Roman power, as well as the devotion of Israel. Imperial funds actually paid for some sacrifices in Jerusalem, so that the empire would become part of the prosperity which was prayed for in the Temple. Rome guarded jealously the sacrifices which the emperor financed in Jerusalem; when they were spurned in the year 66, the act was taken as a declaration of war.[30] The Romans were engaged in the cult because they wished for political reasons to protect the operation of the Temple. They saw sacrifice there as a symbol of their tolerant acceptance of Jews as loyal subjects, and on that basis they arranged to pay for some of the offerings.[31] The same Temple which was for the priestly class a divine privilege was for the Romans the seal of imperial hegemony. Jesus stood accused of creating a disturbance in that Temple (during his occupation) and of fomenting disloyalty to it and (therefore) to Caesar. Pilate did what he had to do. Jesus' persistent reference to a "kingdom" which Caesar did not rule, and his repute among some as messiah or prophet only made Pilate's order more likely. It all was probably done without a hearing; Jesus was not a Roman citizen. He was a nuisance, dispensed with under a military jurisdiction.

---

[30] See Josephus, *Jewish War* II @ 409.
[31] See Josephus, *Jewish War* II @ 197 and 409; *Against Apion* II @ 77; Philo, *Embassy to Gaius* 157, 317.

We have focused on the dispute at the end of Jesus' life in order to set the stage for the developments which followed. None of them can be understood unless and until it is appreciated what a radical and contentious figure Jesus was. His perspective was so thoroughly determined by his understanding of the kingdom of God, there was no room for the consideration of another authority. His terms of reference were given by the Judaism of his time, yet he offered no compromise with the institutions of Judaism. That provided the occasion for competing definitions of Christianity among Jesus' most prominent followers.

James, Peter, and Paul

James, the brother of Jesus, practiced devotion to the Temple as well as to Jesus' teaching. A reintegration with the sacrificial cult had become possible for Jesus' followers generally, because the vendors of animals were restored to their usual position: not in the Temple, but on the Mount of Olives opposite. James shared this reintegration into the ordinary worship of Israel with Peter, Jesus' most famous disciple. But James's devotion to the Temple was such that he claimed that Jesus' purpose was the restoration of the house of David, and insisted that non-Jews who wished to follow his brother's teaching should keep certain elementary laws of purity (see Acts 15:15-21). Still, his requirements were less stringent than those who insisted that any male who sought baptism should first be circumcised (see Acts 15:1). Baptism for James could be offered to those outside the usual definition of "Israel," but there was still a position of privilege for those who accepted the law of Moses. It was within his circle that Jesus' "last supper" was strictly associated with Passover (see Matt. 26:17-19; Mark 14:12-16; Luke 22:7-13). Because only those who were circumcised were to eat of Passover (see Exod. 12:48), the limiting implications of such a presentation – for liturgy and for the leadership of Jesus' movement – are evident.

In that same Temple, Peter and those of his circle were also sometimes to be found. Unlike James, however, Peter associated with non-Jews for the purpose of baptizing them (which took him far from Jerusalem). On his understanding, the same spirit which was active among Jesus' first followers was available to non-Jews who believed in him, so that ordinary requirements of purity could be suspended (see Acts 10:1-48). Peter did not deny the law of Moses, but he held that the same spirit which was active in the case of Moses was also available in the case of Jesus. Just as there were circumcisers to the right of James, there were what we might call socializers to the left of Peter. Paul is the most famous example of a radical application of Peter's approach: those who believed in Jesus were the true sons of Abraham, and the law of Moses was only a way station on the road to that realization (see Gal. 3).

The differences among the circumcisers, the followers of James, the followers of Peter, and Paulinists cannot be pursued here.[32] The present observation is simply that, given the radical, contentious perspective of Jesus, it was inevitable that his followers would develop disagreements over the fundamental question of their relationship to "Israel," as most people understood that term. Some would insist, with the circumcisers, that the movement was for Israel alone; others, with James, would see Israel at the center of the movement, supported by pious non-Jews; the Petrine vision involved an accommodation among Jews and non-Jews; and Paul envisaged old Israel virtually swallowed up in a new effulgence of faith. Those differences could and did lead to the most profound disputes, so that the very concept of a "Church," a unified body of faithful people, was itself the source of heated, sometimes violent, contention.

Trunk: Eucharist in the Synoptic Gospels and John

Diversity of Practice in Primitive Christianity

A generative exegesis maintains a particular focus in the midst of the many critical questions which might arise in the course of reading. The issue of generation is: In association with what practice and in which community did a text arise, so as to attest that practice and the meaning attributed to it? In the case of the eucharistic texts of the New Testament, the obvious diversity of extant witnesses alerts us to the possibility that a variety of practices and communities might be reflected. We have seen that six types of practice interacted sequentially to produce the texts we can read today. The types of practice may be briefly reviewed now, as a prelude to understanding the particular importance of the synoptic Gospels and John.

Jesus joined with his followers in Galilee and Judea, both disciples and sympathizers, in meals which were designed to anticipate the coming of God's kingdom. The meals were characterized by a readiness to accept the hospitality and the produce of Israel at large. A willingness to provide for the meals, to join in the fellowship, to forgive and to be forgiven, was seen by Jesus as a sufficient condition for eating in his company and for entry into the kingdom.

Jesus' view of purity was distinctive, and – no doubt – lax in the estimation of many contemporary rabbis. In one regard, however, he

---

[32] For a discussion, see Chilton and Neusner, *Judaism in the New Testament* (London: Routledge, 1995).

typifies the Judaism of his period: there was an evident fit between his practice of fellowship at meals and his theory of what was clean. Meals appear to have been a primary marker of social grouping within the first century in Palestine. Commensal institutions, formal or not, were plentiful. They included the hierarchical banquets of Qumran, but also occasions of local or national festivity throughout the country. Any patron who mounted a banquet would appropriately expect the meal to reflect his or her views of purity, and guests would not be in a good position to agitate in favor of other views. But meals need not be on a grand scale to be seen as important, and much more modest events might be subject to custom: a household might welcome a feast or Sabbath with a cup of sanctification (the *kiddush*), and bless bread as a prelude to a significant family affair (the *berakhah*). In addition, collegial meals shared within fellowships (*ḥaburoth*) at which like-minded fellows (*ḥaberim*) would share the foods and the company they considered pure would define distinct social groups.

Jesus' practice coincided to some extent with that of a *ḥaburah*, but his construal of purity was unusual. Given the prominence accorded wine in his meals, we might describe the first type of his meals – the practice of purity in anticipation of the kingdom – as a *kiddush* of the kingdom. But his meals were not limited to households. Any analogy with the meals of Qumran would seem to be strained, unless the feedings of the five thousand and the four thousand are held originally to have been staged as massive banquets designed to instance Jesus' theory of purity and his expectation of the kingdom.

Indeed, there is practically no meal of Judaism with which Jesus' meals do not offer some sort of analogy, because the meal was a seal and an occasion of purity, and Jesus was concerned with what was pure. But both the nature of his concern and the character of his meals were distinctive in their inclusiveness: Israel as forgiven and willing to provide of its own produce was for him the occasion of the kingdom. That was the first type in the development of the eucharist.

Jesus brought about the final crisis of his career. His teaching in regard to the kingdom and its purity, including his communal meals as enacted parables, might have been continued indefinitely (for all the controversy involved) outside of Jerusalem. But he sought to influence practice in the Temple, where the purity of Israel was supremely instanced and where the feast of all nations promised by the prophets was to occur. A dispute over the location of vendors of animals for sacrifice was the catalyst in a raging dispute over purity between Jesus (with his followers) and the authorities in the Temple.

The riot in the Temple which Jesus provoked may have been sufficient by itself to bring about his execution, given the importance of the Temple within both Judaism and the settlement with Rome. But he compounded his confrontation with the authorities by putting a new interpretation upon the meals people took with him in their expectation of the kingdom. As he shared wine, he referred to it as the equivalent of the blood of an animal, shed in sacrifice; when he shared bread, he claimed its value was as that of sacrificial flesh. Such offerings were purer, more readily accepted by God, than what was sacrificed in a Temple which had become corrupt. Here was a sacrifice of sharings which the authorities could not control, and which the nature of Jesus' movement made it impossible for them to ignore. Jesus' meals after his failed occupation of the Temple became a surrogate of sacrifice, the second type of eucharist.

The third type is that of Petrine Christianity, when the blessing or breaking of bread at home, the *berakhah* of Judaism, became a principal model of eucharist. A practical result of that development was that bread came to have precedence over wine. More profoundly, the circle of Peter conceived of Jesus as a new Moses, who gave commands concerning purity as Moses did on Sinai, and who also expected his followers to worship on Mount Zion. As compared to Jesus' practice (in its first and second stages), Petrine practice represents a double domestication. First, adherents of the movement congregated in the homes of their colleagues, rather than seeking the hospitality of others. Second, the validity of sacrifice in the Temple was acknowledged. Both forms of domestication grew out of the new circumstances of the movement in Jerusalem and fresh opportunities for worship in the Temple; they changed the nature of the meal and the memory of what Jesus had said at the "last supper."

The fourth type of eucharist, the contribution of the Jacobean circle, pursued the tendency of domestication further. The eucharist was seen as a seder, in terms of both its meaning and its chronology. So understood, only Jews in a state of purity could participate in eucharist, which could be truly recollected only once a year, at Passover in Jerusalem. The Quartodeciman controversy (concerning the timing of Easter) of a later period, fierce though it appears, was but a shadow cast by much a more serious contention concerning the nature of Christianity. The Jacobean program was to integrate Jesus' movement fully within the liturgical institutions of Judaism, to insist upon the Judaic identity of the movement and upon Jerusalem as its governing center.

Paul and the synoptic Gospels represent the fifth type of eucharist. Paul more vehemently resists Jacobean claims, by insisting Jesus' last meal occurred "on the night in which he was betrayed," not on Passover (1 Cor. 11:23-29). He emphasizes the link between Jesus' death and the eucharist, and he accepts the Hellenistic refinement of the Petrine type which presented the eucharist as a sacrifice for sin. That type is also embraced in the synoptic Gospels, where the heroism of Jesus is such that the meal is an occasion to join in the solidarity of martyrdom (Matt. 26:26-29; Mark 14:22-25; Luke 22:15-20).

Synoptic Ecumenis

The synoptic strategy is not to oppose the Jacobean program directly; in fact, its chronology is accepted (although not without internal contradiction). Instead, the synoptics insist by various wordings that Jesus' blood is shed in the interests of the communities for which those Gospels were composed, for the "many" in Damascus (Matthew) and Rome (Mark), on behalf of "you" in Antioch (Luke). The synoptic tradition also provided two stories of miraculous feeding which symbolized the inclusion of Jews and non-Jews within eucharist, understood as in the nature of a philosophical symposium.

In the first story (Matt. 14:13-21/Mark 6:32-44/Luke 9:10b-17), the eucharistic associations are plain:[33] Jesus blesses and breaks the bread prior to distribution (Matt. 14:19/Mark 6:41/Luke 9:16). That emphasis so consumes the story, the fish – characteristic among Christian eucharistic symbols[34] – are of subsidiary significance by the end of the story (compare Mark 6:43 with Matt. 14:20 and Luke 9:17). Whatever the pericope represented originally, it becomes a eucharistic narrative in the synoptic transformation of meaning. Jesus gathers people in orderly way (see Matt. 14:18/Mark 6:39, 40/Luke 9:14, 15), by "symposia" as Mark literally has it (6:39); without that order, they might be described as sheep without a shepherd (Mark 6:34).

The authority of the Twelve, the number which corresponds to the primordial tribes of Israel, is a marked concern within the story. Their return in Matt. 14:12b, 13/Mark 6:30, 31/Luke 9:10a after their commission (see Matt. 10:1-42/Mark 6:7-13/Luke 9:1-6) is what occasions the feeding, and their function in the proceedings is definite:

---

[33] See Alan Hugh McNeile, *The Gospel according to St. Matthew* (London: Macmillan, 1957), 216 and C. E. B. Cranfield, *The Gospel according to St. Mark,* The Cambridge Greek Testament Commentary (Cambridge: Cambridge University Press, 1963), 222, 223. Cranfield also notes the associations between the feeding stories, eucharistic celebration, and the motif of the manna in the wilderness. Moreover, he picks up the sense of συμπόσια συμπόσια in Mark 10:39 (218). See also W. D. Davies and Dale C. Allison, *A Critical and Exegetical Commentary on the Gospel according to Saint Matthew,* The International Critical Commentary (Edinburgh: Clark, 1991), 2:481, 493, 494.

[34] Cf. C. H. Dodd, *Historical Tradition in the Fourth Gospel* (Cambridge: Cambridge University Press, 1965), 200, 201. W. D. Davies and Dale C. Allison, 481, refer to 2 Baruch 29:3-8 and 4 Ezra 6:52 to support their suggestion that "both bread (or manna) and fish (or Leviathan) are associated with the messianic feast in many Jewish texts."

Jesus gives them the bread, to give it to others (Matt. 14:19/Mark 6:41/Luke 9:16). Their place here is cognate with their position within another pericope (from the Jacobean cycle) which features the Twelve, the parable of the sower, its interpretation, and the assertion that only the Twelve possess the mystery of the kingdom (Matt. 13:1-17/Mark 4:1-12/Luke 8:4-10).[35] Such a mystery is also conveyed here, in the assertion that twelve baskets of fragments were gathered after the five thousand ate. The lesson is evident: The Twelve will always have enough to feed the Church.

The story of the feeding of the four thousand (Matt. 15:32-39/Mark 8:1-10) follows so exactly that of the five thousand, its omission by Luke – perhaps as a redundant doublet – may seem understandable. The four thousand are a multiple of the four points of the compass, the story follows that of the Canaanite or Syrophoenician woman (Matt. 15:21-28/Mark 7:24-30), and concerns a throng from a number of different areas and backgrounds (see Matt. 15:21, 29/Mark 7:24, 31). Likewise, the number seven, the number of bushels of fragments here collected, corresponds to the deacons of the Hellenists in the church of Jerusalem (cf. Acts 6:1-6), and is related to the traditional number of the seventy nations within Judaism.[36] Moreover, the reference to Jesus as giving thanks (εὐ𝔁αριστήσας) over the bread in Matt. 15:36/Mark 8:6 better corresponds to the Hellenistic version of the Petrine eucharist in Luke 22:17, 19; 1 Cor. 11:24 then does the reference to his blessing the bread (εὐλόγησεν) in Matt. 14:19/Mark 6:39, which better corresponds to the earlier Petrine formula in Matt. 26:26/Mark 14:22.[37]

The Lukan omission of such stories, in fact of the whole of what corresponds to Mark 6:45-8:26 (conventionally designated as "the great omission" of Mark by Luke) seems natural, once their meaning is appreciated: they concern the sense of Jesus in an environment characterized by a mixture of Jews and Gentiles.[38] Luke takes up that theme in Acts, and regards its reversion into the ministry of Jesus as anachronism.

---

[35] Cf. *A Galilean Rabbi*, 95, 96.

[36] Cf. Jöram Friberg, "Numbers and Counting," *Anchor Bible Dictionary*, (ed. D. N. Freedman (New York: Doubleday, 1992), 4:1139-46, 1145.

[37] See Davies and Allison, 562-65, for a discussion of the features here adduced. Their conclusion that the story does not concern only Gentiles, but (in the Matthean formulation) "the lost sheep of the house of Israel" (564), seems justified. Nonetheless, the geographical references which precede the second feeding make it apparent that the four thousand were not simply Jews in a conventionally recognizable sense.

[38] That the feeding of the four thousand relates particularly to Gentiles is argued, for example, in John W. Bowman, *The Gospel of Mark: The New Christian Passover Haggadah*, Studia Post-Biblica (Leiden: E. J. Brill, 1965), 176-78.

After the second feeding, Jesus rebukes his disciples for a failure to understand when he warns them about the leaven of the Pharisees and Sadducees, and asks whether they truly grasp the relationship between the number twelve and the five thousand and the number seven and the four thousand (Matt. 16:5-12/Mark 8:14-21). In the mind of the Hellenistic catechesis, the meaning is clear, and its implications for eucharistic discipline are evident.[39] Celebration is neither to be limited to Jews at Passover, as the Jacobean program would have it, nor forced upon communities in a way which would require Jews to accept reduced standards of purify, as the Pauline program would have it. There is for the Hellenistic catechesis of which the synoptic transformation is a monument, an ongoing apostolate for Jews and Gentiles, prepared to feed as many of the Church that gather.

The synoptic catechesis was a paradigm which was then developed and published in Rome (Mark, c. A.D. 71), Damascus (Matthew, c. A.D. 80), and Antioch itself (Luke, c. A.D. 90). The spine of each Gospel is the narrative catechesis of the Petrine cycle, supplemented by Jacobean revision of that catechesis, the apocalyptic addendum of Joseph Barsabbas and Silas (Mark 13 and parallels), and the instruction of the Twelve with its addenda (Q). Their similarities and differences are best understood as functions of the particular sort of catechesis (preparation of catechumens) which was current in each community. No Gospel is simply a copy of another; rather, each represents the choices among varying traditions, written and/or oral, and the development of those traditions which had taken place in a given locality.[40]

Johannine Separation from Judaism and the Master Types of Eucharist

The feeding of the five thousand – understood as occurring at Passover – is taken up in John 6 in a fully paschal sense. Jesus himself is identified as the manna, miraculous food bestowed by God upon his people. The motif was already articulated by Paul, but John develops it to construe the eucharist as a Mystery, in which Jesus offers his own flesh and blood. Any crude misunderstanding is avoided, because Jesus defines himself as the true bread of life which is given by God, the surety of eternal life and of resurrection on the last day (6:32-40). Johannine Gospel associates the synoptic *haggadah* of the feeding of the five

---

[39] See Paul J. Achtemeier, *Mark*, Proclamation Commentaries (Philadelphia: Fortress, 1986), 29, who rightly observes that the statement attributed to Jesus "presupposes not only the present order of events in Mark, but also the present form of the Greek prose." His conclusion of particularly Markan authorship, however, is not warranted.

[40] For a further elaboration, see *Profiles of a Rabbi: Synoptic Opportunities in Reading about Jesus*, Brown Judaic Studies 177 (Atlanta: Scholars Press, 1989).

thousand with Passover (6:4) and then fully develops the quasi-magical exposition of the eucharistic bread as manna which Paul in 1 Cor. 10 only tentatively indulged (John 6:26-59). That autobiographical reading of Jesus' words – as giving his personal body and blood in eucharist – had probably already occurred to Hellenistic Christians who followed synoptic practice. The Johannine practice made that meaning as explicit as the break with Judaism is in the fourth Gospel. The sixth type of eucharist can only be understood as a consciously non-Judaic and Hellenistic development. The Johannine "last supper" is swallowed up in a heroic symposium in chapter 13, because for John it is truer to say that Jesus is the bread of eucharist than to say that he instituted eucharist.

From the roots of the practice of Jesus, Peter, James, and Paul, there emerged two master types of eucharist. They constitute a twin trunk arising from the ground of the Gospels: the heroic martyr of the synoptic liturgy, and the self-giving bread of the Johannine homily. Those two master types were developed within subsequent generations of patristic theology.

Irenaeus, Cyprian, and Augustine

The three Fathers cited have been chosen for discussion because they are the most creative thinkers, and at the same time the most representative theologians, of three distinct periods in the history of the Church. Irenaeus was bishop of Lyons, a position to which he was elected after the deadly persecution of 177 which had been unleashed there under Marcus Aurelius. Cyprian was bishop of Carthage, and arguably the most influential ecclesiastic of his day. The systematic persecution under Decius, which lasted one vicious year (250-51), forced Cyprian into hiding, and then confronted him with the most difficult question for the Church during the third century: how to deal with lapsed Christians. Augustine (354-450) was bishop of Hippo during a much more settled period from the point of view of the Roman recognition of Christianity, but he had to face the dissolution of the empire itself, which was amply attested by the sack of Rome itself in 410 by Alaric the Goth. Each of these great thinkers has a distinct teaching of what the eucharist means, and each relates himself to the great master types conveyed in the synoptic Gospels and John.

Irenaeus

A great patrist, Richard A. Norris, once summed up Irenaeus's doctrine of the eucharist in the following terms: the bread is magical, and you eat it.[41] That succinct statement needs to be unpacked to be understood, but it is accurate. Irenaeus's appreciation of the eucharist is essentially of the Johannine type, based upon the miraculous provision of bread in chapter 6 (see *Against Heresies* 2.22.3; 3.9.5): here is a blessing for the last times which compares with the miraculous sustenance of Israel. But where eating the bread of life in John results in having eternal life in oneself, for Irenaeus the result is a transformation of one's own flesh.

Irenaeus's insistence upon this notion is inexorable. He is keen to point out that Jesus took bread which had been produced from the earth in order to give thanks in John 6:11 (*Against Heresies* 3.9.5); the same God who creates also redeems, and what he redeems is the flesh of which the bread is a symbol. When Irenaeus speaks of the eucharist itself, he returns to the same theme. Jesus says, "This is my body," of bread which had been created in the ordinary way, and its offering is "the new oblation of the new covenant" (*Against Heresies* 4.17.5). The theological significance of this sacrifice is explicated powerfully and simply (*Against Heresies* 4.18.5):

> For as the bread, which is produced from the earth, when it receives the invocation from God, is no longer common bread, but the eucharist, consisting of two realities, earthly and heavenly, so also our bodies, when they receive the eucharist, are no longer corruptible, having the hope of resurrection to eternity.

Explicitly and deliberately, Irenaeus makes resurrection into a transformation of human flesh, and eucharist announces "consistently the fellowship and union of the flesh and spirit."

That transformation occurred within what Irenaeus described as a "recapitulation" of humanity in Christ. The description offered by Henry Chadwick can scarcely be improved upon:

> The divine plan for the new covenant was a "recapitulation" of the original creation. In Christ the divine Word assumed a humanity such as Adam possessed before he fell. Adam was made in the image and likeness of God. By sin the likeness became lost, though the image remained untouched. By faith in Christ mankind may recover the lost likeness. Because Irenaeus regarded salvation as a restoration of the condition prevailing in paradise before the Fall, it was easy for him to accept Justin's terrestrial hopes for the millennium. Because he believed that in the Fall only the moral likeness to God was lost, not the basic

---

[41] Private tutorial in the spring of 1971 at the General Theological Seminary. By way of general introduction, see John Lawson, *The Biblical Theology of Saint Irenaeus* (London: Epworth, 1948).

image, he was able to regard the Fall in a way very different from the deep pessimism of the Gnostics.[42]

For all his stress upon the authority of apostolic tradition, Irenaeus here shows himself to be one of the great, synthetic philosophers of early Christianity.

In a single theory he elevated the flesh to the realm of what may be saved, set out a general approach to the relationship between the Testaments of the Scriptures, and articulated a symmetrical theology of primordial sin and eschatological hope. The whole was expressed with his incomparable simplicity, focused on the Word who became "the son of man for this purpose, that man might even become the son of God" (*Against Heresies* 3.10.2; see also 3.19.1; 4.33.4, 11). Although there were more creative thinkers in the history of classical Christianity (such as Origen), and more accomplished theologians (such as Augustine), none was more influential than Irenaeus in his theory of recapitulation. It was a masterful advance alone lines already laid down earlier,[43] and Christianity ever since (consciously and not) has been exploring its implications. Norris once explained the relevance of studying Irenaeus by saying, "He invented Christianity, you know." What he did invent, without much question, was an account of humanity as a whole which was grounded in Christ, and – at the same time – a doctrine of eucharist which presented it as the completing step in humanity's appropriation of what Christ recapitulated.

Cyprian

Just as Irenaeus proceeded on a Johannine basis, Cyprian grounded his theology of the eucharist in the synoptic Gospels. The theme of solidarity with Jesus the martyr reaches its classic expression in Cyprian, along martial lines (*Letter* 58:1):

> ...the end of the world and the time of the Antichrist draw near, so that we must all stand prepared for the battle. Do not consider anything but the glory of life eternal, and the crown of the confession of the Lord; and do not regard those things which are coming as being such as were those which have passed away. Now a more serious and ferocious battle threatens, for which the soldiers of Christ ought to prepare themselves with uncorrupted faith and sturdy courage.[44]

---

[42] *The Early Church* (London: Penguin, 1993), 80.

[43] For a discussion of that issue, see M. Widman, "Irenaüs und seine theologischen Väter," *Zeitschrift für Theologie und Kirche* 54 (1957) 155-66 and Jean Daniélou and Henri Marrou, *The Christian Centuries* (New York: McGraw-Hill, 1964), vol. I, *The First Six Hundred Years*, 112.

[44] For this translation, and for his analysis of Cyprian, I am indebted to Bernhard Lang, *Christian Worship: A Cultural and Historical Study* (New Haven: Yale

Martyrdom here finds its power in the imitation of Christ, in struggling as he struggled, and it exerts an impact within the final travail of the world as a whole.

In his study of the eucharist, Bernhard Lang has identified Cyprian as the founder of the classical, Catholic theology:

> For the bishop of Carthage, the eucharist is a ritual repetition and imitation of the Last Supper of Jesus. Since the subsequent of the Lord's Supper follows Cyprian's conception, this statement may appear as a banality. However, the novelty of Cyprian's understanding deserves to be highlighted. Before Cyprian, the eucharist was not so much a repetition of the Last Supper of Jesus as it was a ritual producing and consuming of sacred food. With Cyprian, the biblical context of the Last Supper and the connection with Jesus' death are given prominence. Like the original Last Supper, the eucharist was now celebrated in an atmosphere of "tribulation," the foes' assault upon Christ and his followers.[45]

In precisely this sense, Cyprian would routinize the use of the verb *sacrificare* in order to refer to the celebration of the eucharist: it was after all *oblatio et sacrificium nostrum* (see, for example, *Letter* 63.9):

> Whence it appears that the blood of Christ is not offered if wine is lacking in the chalice and that the sacrifice of the Lord is not celebrated with lawful sanctification unless the oblation and our sacrifice correspond to the passion.

In the eucharist, believers offered the sacrifice of Jesus, so that they also might be an acceptable sacrifice.

Augustine

Cyprian's theology was developed by one his successors in North Africa, Augustine of Hippo. A thorough neo-Platonist, Augustine dwelled more on the significance of eucharist than on what was offered. The point of sacrifice is to be "united to God in holy fellowship" (*City of God* 10:6; for what follows, see 19:23.5):

> Now we ourselves who are his City are his most splendid and best sacrifice; such is the mystery that we celebrate in our offerings, which are known to the faithful.[46]

University Press, forthcoming). See Rose Bernard Donna, *Saint Cyprian: Letters (1-81)*, The Fathers of the Church (Washington: Catholic University of America Press, 1964). The epistle is numbered 55 in A. Roberts and James Donaldson, *Ante-Nicene Christian Library* (Edinburgh: Clark, 1868), vol. 8, *The Writings of Cyprian*.

[45] Lang, 62.

[46] Quoted in Lang, 69-70.

"If you receive well, you are what is received," was Augustine's motto (*Sermon* 227),[47] and it sums up his theology of God and his "city" by eucharistic means. The emphasis upon being received in eucharist in fact antedates Augustine; it is already evident in Eusebius's work, where the eucharist becomes a civic affair, and therefore one's incorporation becomes a public benefit of Christianity.[48] Augustine's theology, however, is far more precise, in that it concerns, not the empire as such, but "the city of God."

If Christian history was born under the pressure of success, its baptism of fire was the experience of an unimaginable failure. In 410 C.E., Alaric sacked the city of Rome itself. That event was a stunning blow to the empire generally, but it was a double blow to Latin Christianity. First, the pillage occurred while the empire was Christian; two centuries before, Tertullian had argued that idolatry brought about disaster (see *Apologeticus* 41.1), and now Christianity could be said to do so. Second, Latin Christianity – especially in North Africa – had been particularly attracted to a millenarian eschatology. How could one explain that the triumphant end of history, announced by Eusebius and his followers, seemed to be reversed by the Goths?

The explanation of that dilemma occupied Augustine in his *City of God*, a tremendous work of twenty-three books, written between 413 and 426. From the outset, he sounds his theme, that the city of God is an eternal city which exists in the midst of the cities of men; those two cities are both mixed and at odds in this world, but they are to be separated by the final judgment (*City of God* 1.1). That essentially simple thesis is sustained through an account of Roman religion and Hellenistic philosophy, including Augustine's critical appreciation of Plato (books 1-10).[49]

In the central section of his work, Augustine sets out his case within a discussion of truly global history, from the story of the creation in Genesis. From the fall of the angels, which Augustine associates with the separation of light and darkness in Gen. 1:4, he speaks of the striving between good and evil. But the distinction between those two is involved with the will of certain angels, not with any intrinsic wickedness (*City of God* 11.33). People, too, are disordered in their desire, rather than in their creation by God (*City of God* 12.8).

---

[47] For other references, and discussion, see Joseph B. Bernardin, "Augustine as Pastor," in *A Companion to the Study of St. Augustine,* ed. R. W. Battenhouse (New York: Oxford University Press, 1969), 57-89.

[48] On this theme, see Lang, 76-82. As he shows, the motif is a development of Cyprian's theology.

[49] For a brief discussion of *City of God,* see E. R. Hardy, "The City of God," in *A Companion to the Study of St. Augustine,* 257-83.

The difference between the will God intends for his creatures and the will they actually evince attests the freedom involved in divine creation. But the effect of perverted will, whether angelic or human, is to establish two antithetical regimes (*City of God* 14.28):

> So two loves have constituted two cities – the earthly is formed by love of self even to contempt of God, the heavenly by love of God even to contempt of self. For the one glories in herself, the other in the Lord. The one seeks glory from man; for the other God, the witness of the conscience, is the greatest glory....In the one the lust for power prevails, both in her own rulers and in the nations she subdues; in the other all serve each other in charity, governors by taking thought for all and subjects by obeying.

By book 18, Augustine arrives at his own time, and repeats that the two cities "alike enjoy temporal goods or suffer temporal ills, but differ in faith, in hope, in love, until they be separated by the final judgment and each receive its end, of which there is no end" (*City of God* 18.54).

That perspective commits Augustine to speak of eschatological issues, which he does until the end of the work as a whole. It is in his discussion of eschatology that Augustine frames classic and orthodox responses to some of the most persistent questions of the Christian theology of his time. He adheres to the expectation of the resurrection of the flesh, not simply of the body (as had been the manner of Origen). In so doing, he refutes the Manichaean philosophy which he accepted prior to his conversion to Christianity. In Manichaeanism, named after a Persian teacher of the third century named Mani, light and darkness are two eternal substances which struggle against one another, and they war over the creation they have both participated in.[50] As in the case of Gnosticism, on which it was dependent, Manichaeanism counseled a denial of the flesh. By his insistence on the resurrection of the flesh, Augustine revives the strong assertion of the extent of God's embrace of his own creation in the tradition of Irenaeus.

At the same time, Augustine sets a limit on the extent to which one might have recourse to Plato. Augustine had insisted with Plato against the Manichaeans that God was not a material substance, but transcendent. Similarly, evil became in his mind the denial of what proceeds from God (see *Confessions* 5.10.20). When it came to the creation of people, however, Augustine insisted against Platonic thought that no division between soul and flesh could be made (so *City of God* 22.12). Enfleshed humanity was the only genuine humanity, and God in Christ was engaged to raised those who were of the city of God. Moreover, Augustine specifically refuted the contention of Porphyry (and Origen) that cycles of creation could be included

---

[50] See Stanley Romaine Hopper, "The Anti-Manichean Writings," in *A Companion to the Study of St. Augustine*, 148-74.

within the entire scheme of salvation. For Augustine, the power of the resurrection was already confirmed by the miracles wrought by Christ and his martyrs. He gives the example of the healings connected with the relics of St. Stephen, recently transferred to Hippo (*City of God* 22.8).

Even now, in the power of the Catholic Church, God is represented on earth, and the present, Christian epoch (*Christiana tempora*) corresponds to the millennium promised in Rev. 20 (*City of God* 20.9). This age of dawning power, released in flesh by Jesus and conveyed by the Church, simply awaits the full transition into the city of God, complete with flesh itself. The metaphysical power of the kingdom was being exerted in physical terms within the understanding of Augustine.

In the Shadow of the Tree

Each type of eucharist which we have considered conveys a promise of participation, but also the threat which is implicit in noninclusion. Those who do not join in the feast are consigned to a place of "weeping and gnashing of teeth" in the famous idiom of Jesus (Matt. 8:12; Luke 13:28), repeated from the Galilean phase of his ministry, and again and again from that time. In Jerusalem, the authorities who oppose him are condemned as thieves. For Peter, accepting Jesus' fellowship in meals involves joining the covenant mediated by Moses and Elijah; shunning the former means rejecting the latter. James's position made being circumcised a formal requirement of fully celebrating eucharist, with marginal status for others, while Paul reserved excommunication as a discipline the local church might impose as a power derived from the Lord.

The master types of eucharist, supplied by the synoptic and Johannine Gospels, represent two great resolutions of the earlier theologies. The synoptic type presents a catechetical indoctrination of martyrdom, in which Jesus is principal and best in the solidarity of witness. The Johannine type invites reflection on the homiletic theme on Jesus as the true manna supplied by God to his people. Not to be part of the synoptic eucharist is to join the opposition who killed Jesus; to be scandalized by the flesh which Jesus offers in John is to join "the Jews" who refused him in their literalism.

Similarly, Irenaeus is explicit that God will judge "all those who are beyond the pale of the truth, that is, who are outside the Church" (*Against Heresies* 4.33.7). From that point it is a short step to Cyprian's dictum that "he cannot have God for his Father who has not the Church for his mother" (*On the Unity of the Church*).[51] And if the Church is that apart from which salvation is impossible, and secular force is at the disposal of a bishop, then

---

[51] Cited and discussed in Henry Chadwick, *The Early Church* (London: Penguin, 1993), 118-20.

we understand why Augustine should have taken the words "Compel them to come in" (Luke 14:23) to justify military campaigns against the Donatists who opposed him (*Letter* 185, to *Boniface* 7).[52]

The metaphysical power invoked by Jesus against a refusal to be included in the kingdom finds itself articulated along distinctly physical lines by the time of Augustine. The fact that an overtly Christian politics had only been practiced for a century did not prevent the eucharistic definitions of inclusion and exclusion to be plumbed in a new sense, to characterize what Augustine famously called the *res publica Christiana*.

The Absorption of Politics in Eucharistic Sacrifice

The Christian meal itself, especially as it constituted a distinctively sacrificial act, combined typical pragmatics (things and people gathered to conduct a specific ritual), typical emotions, and typical ideologies which explained the proceeding as a whole and its results. As we move through our types (of Jesus' practice in Galilee and Jerusalem, Petrine practice, Jacobean practice, Pauline practice, then the synoptic and Johannine master types, and on to the types set out by Irenaeus, Cyprian, and Augustine), it becomes plain that no single definition of the sacrifice of eucharist will cover all of its variations. Definitions might convey the substance of ideologies, but eucharist is a characteristic activity, rather than an idea. For that reason, it is better approached along the lines of typology. As students of ancient Christian practice, we can characterize eucharist at any point according to its pragmatic, affective, and ideological dimensions. We cannot reduce the typology to a single definition, but we can map the activity along those lines.

The form the typology will take cannot be predicted, but it does regularly involve taking the people who accept forgiveness into an experience of sharing with gratitude, to the end that they should be transformed into an image of Christ. And the social dimension of their fellowship is to some extent expressed by the people they take to be excluded from – because they have included themselves out of – that fellowship.

The typology of saving eucharist, is accompanied by a typology of those who are not included, the shadow of that tree into which all the peoples are to be gathered (see Ps. 104:16-17, and its reflection in Jesus' parable of the mustard seed, Matt. 13:31-32; Mark 4:30-32; Luke 13:18-19). Like eucharist itself, the typology of noninclusion may not be reduced to a definition, but emerges from the confluence of pragmatics, emotions,

---

[52] Cited and discussed in Frederick W. Dillistone, "The Anti-Donatist Writings," in *A Companion to the Study of St. Augustine*, 191. In the same volume, see Thomas J. Bigham and Albert T. Mollegen, "The Christian Ethic," 389-95.

and often conflicting ideologies. When the pragmatics of eucharist absorb political power, the result (as Augustine consciously shows us) is that coercion becomes a branch of theology.

11

The Development of
Christian Political Theory

John Morreall
University of South Florida

I. Did the Apostles Have a Political Theory?

Standard history books say that Christians started developing political theories in the fourth century, when, thanks to Constantine, they were no longer persecuted. Professor Chilton challenges this account, and says that Christian political theory actually goes back to the Apostles. He admits that "whether in a modern understanding or in an ancient understanding,...Christians had no politics and they could have had no politics." But he argues that they *must have had* "a politics of some sort" – a "strange politics," he calls it. Chilton analyzes this politics as being based on the ways Peter, Paul, James, John, and other early Christians counted some people in, and excluded others from, their religious communities.

I am always willing to listen to new interpretations of history, but I find unconvincing both Chilton's argument that early Christians must have had a political theory, and his analysis of what that theory was. Let me consider his argument and his analysis separately.

First, Chilton argues that the early Christians must have had a political theory, because without one they could not have risen to power in the Roman Empire. In his words, "By the fourth century their nonpolitics turned out to have been a politics of some sort all along, because they inherited the Roman Imperium from the time of Constantine." "What seems to be a nonpolitics," he says, could "overwhelm and restructure what seem to be unassailable fortresses....But that can only mean that there really is a politics in this nonpolitics."

This argument is shaky both logically and historically. From the fact that a group gained political power, it does not follow that they had a political theory. It does not even follow that they had political skills. They might simply have been *given* power. Consider the kindergartner from Seattle who recently left for Tibet to take over as the reincarnated Dalai Lama. This boy is coming into political power, but has neither a political theory nor political skill. Rather, the leaders of Tibetan Buddhism decided that he is their leader, and so they are giving him power.

Similarly, the early Christians needed no political theory or political skill to come to power in the Roman Empire. If they had been politically savvy, indeed, they would have stopped the persecutions inflicted on them by the emperors Decius, Valerian, and Diocletian. When the fortunes of the Christians changed under Constantine, it was not through any political maneuvering on their part. They did not overwhelm unassailable fortresses, as Chilton claims. They simply got lucky.

In the year 311, the deputy emperor Galerius, who had been one of the most violent persecutors of Christians, issued an edict tolerating them, probably at the prompting of his Christian wife. In 312 the co-emperor Constantine, struggling with his rival, Maxentius, had a dream or vision in which he saw his own victory under a Christian banner. When he then won a decisive battle at the Milvian Bridge, the triumphal arch he had built in Rome ascribed his victory to the "inspiration of the Divinity," that is, the Christian God. He also had a statue of himself erected holding up a cross. The legend read, "By this saving sign I have delivered your city from the tyrant and restored liberty to the senate and people of Rome."

Constantine's promotion of Christianity went hand in hand with his political self-promotion. Inside the monumental basilica he built near the Roman Forum was a statue of himself nearly forty feet tall. To keep his good political ratings with the majority of Romans who were still pagan, he maintained the pagan state religion, and put off being baptized until the very end of his life. He also maintained the cult of the emperor.

His Edict of Milan extended toleration to Christians and restored their property confiscated during the persecutions. Constantine also gave them land for new churches, exempted their clergy from paying taxes, and granted judicial authority to their ecclesiastical courts. He even called a council at Nicea to tackle a doctrinal issue dividing Western and Eastern churches – the relation of Jesus to God the Father. He opened the council personally, telling the participants that while they were bishops for the internal matters of the church, like the sacraments, he was the bishop for external matters, that is, the church's legal and administrative affairs.

Through the rest of the fourth century, as the Roman Empire declined, most of Constantine's successors also treated the Christians well. Near the end of the century, the emperor Theodosius banned celebration of the pagan cults and made Christianity the official religion of the empire.

Historians have different explanations of why different emperors treated the Christians well, but nowhere do these explanations require attributing a political theory to the Christians themselves, as Chilton does. The Christians were simply lucky beneficiaries of Roman politics in the waning years of the empire.

I said earlier that I found two things unconvincing in Professor Chilton's presentation. The first I have covered – his argument that Christians before Constantine must have had a political theory. The second is his analysis of the political theory he thinks early Christians had. Let me explain what I find lacking on this second score.

Political theory is an account of certain kinds of power, and according to Chilton, the power involved in early Christian politics was that of counting some people in, and others out of, the meal of fellowship, and therefore the religious community. Chilton admits that there was no uniform ideology or practice here. James limited these meals to Jews who worshipped in the Temple and lived according to Torah. Paul accepted non-Jews and did not require the rules of purity. Peter was in between, with no consistent criteria. John required that participants in the meal believe that it was the body and blood of Jesus that they were consuming.

What I do not understand in Chilton's treatment of all these conflicting ideologies and practices, is where the political theory is supposed to be. What the various groups had in common was that they included some people or other, and excluded some people or other. That is not a theory – it is just a number of practices, and not even political practices at that. All social groups admit some people and exclude others – every scout troop and bridge tournament does that. So even if the early Christians had constituted a single group with a single ideology and set of membership requirements, I still do not see where there would have been any political theory or even political activity.

Politics is *an* exercise of power, but it is not just *any* exercise of power. Not even all exercises of social power are political acts. If I force my nine-year-old to stay home tonight to practice piano, that is hardly a political act. If I exercise my privilege as a member of the National Geographic Society to recommend you for membership, that is not political either. What makes an exercise of power political is that the power is of a legislative body, an emperor, or some other governmental entity.

Let me summarize my critique of Chilton. The various ways early Christians included and excluded people were not even political activities, much less political theories or the bases for political theories. And even if there had been one consistent set of practices, that would not yield a political theory, any more than a set of immigration laws would yield a national constitution. Chilton's analysis, then, is not an analysis of politics, not even strange politics.

II. Christians before Constantine:
Politics as Irrelevant to Christian Life

So far I have been mostly negative, arguing that we have not been given good reason to think that Christian political theory began before the fourth century. Now I would like to offer something positive – an explanation of Christian political theory in the fourth century and its development up to the time of Thomas Aquinas, who was in many ways the classical political theorist of Christianity.

To understand how Christian political theory developed, we need to explain why it took three centuries to get started. Why did the earliest Christians not think politically? The standard answer is that they were powerless. But why was that? Why did they not even care about politics? My answer here is that their founder did not care about politics. Jesus spoke of the "kingdom of God" and the "kingdom of Heaven," of course, but he made it clear that he was not speaking of a political institution. His kingdom, as he told Pontius Pilate, was not of this world.

Why did Jesus not care about politics? There are at least three reasons. First, he thought that the end of this world was at hand, so that getting involved in the politics of this world would be wasting valuable time. Secondly, because he saw politics as based on violence and coercion, and he was opposed to violence and coercion. His apolitical philosophy of life is clear in the Sermon on the Mount (Matt. 5-7). There he presents a two-fold approach to violence: do not engage in violence yourself – not in retribution, not even in self-defense; and endure the violence of others.

> How blest you are, when you suffer insults and persecution and every kind of calumny for my sake. Accept it with gladness and exultation....
>
> Do not set yourself against the man who wrongs you. If someone slaps you on the right cheek, turn and offer him your left. If a man wants to sue you for your shirt, let him have your coat as well. If a man in authority makes you go one mile, go with him two. Give what you are asked to give; and do not turn your back on a man who wants to borrow.

The third reason Jesus was apolitical is that he was antilegalistic. The life he advocated was not based on following a set of laws. When asked what the law was, Jesus said to love God and love your neighbor. Obviously, these are not laws in the usual sense of enforceable statues which fit into a political framework; they are simply principles for how to live.

After Jesus, Paul promoted and extended his simple ethic of love, and many early Christian communities took it to heart. This ethic seemed radical at the time, as it should today. If practiced, it eliminates the need for violence and coercion, and so for government.

Jesus' advice to work out disagreements on the basis of love, to settle out of court, can be generalized to all political institutions. Conventions such as obligations, rights, duties, property, crime, punishment, and the whole legal system set up to manage them, should give way to a life of supererogatory actions, that is, doing more than was asked. The Kingdom of Heaven that was to come offered the ideal to strive for here. Heaven, of course, would be without violence or coercion, and so without laws, rulers, courts, police, armies, and all the rest of politics.

But if the early Christians' ideal was to live apolitically, how could they live in the Roman Empire? The same way anyone opposed to a government lives under it – they put up with it. They paid their taxes, as Jesus had advised, and obeyed the laws that did not violate their religious principles. But they stayed out of politics. What about when governmental violence turned against them, as in the persecutions of the third century? Jesus had already covered that question in the Sermon on the Mount.

III. Constantine and Eusebius: The Emperor as God's Agent

In the Roman Empire, Christians were sometimes considered odd for their pacifism and their refusal to worship the state gods. But for two centuries they were generally tolerated. As economic and political conditions declined in the middle of the third century, however, they became scapegoats for problems of all kinds, even natural disasters. Around 250 the emperor Decius called on the state gods to help the imperial army defeat the Goths. All citizens were required to worship the state gods publicly. When Christians refused, he persecuted them. His successor Valerian found the persecutions useful for confiscating the property of Christians. The persecutions died down after a decade, but then in 303 the emperor Diocletian instituted the worst persecutions yet, creating laws like those Hitler would use against the Jews. Over the next several years, thousands of Christians were enslaved, tortured, and killed. The persecutions were so bad, in fact, that many pagan Romans felt sympathetic toward the Christians. In 311, as I said earlier, the deputy emperor Galerius issued an edict tolerating Christian worship, and then in 313 the co-emperor Constantine began several programs reversing the persecution and favoring the Christians.

To the Christians this quick reversal seemed like a miracle. Indeed, as Eusebius of Caesarea, bishop and apologist for Constantine, explained it, it was the action of God. All of history, he said, was the working out of God's plan, and Constantine's coming to power, followed by his favoring of Christianity, was the high point of that plan.

It was a short step from that view to the idea that Constantine, in carrying out God's plan, was ruling in the place of God. The idea that the emperor received his power from divinity was already official Roman ideology, and Christians readily understood it. Their Bible told of God's conferring kingship on men like David, and Paul had said, "There is no power but of God." And so many Christians, grateful to the emperor who had reversed their fortunes, accepted Eusebius's theocratic account of the emperor.

Other actions of Constantine were also seen as God's acting in history, especially his reunification of the empire and his elimination of the co-emperor to become sole emperor. The empire accepting the one Christian God was itself becoming one. One God, one emperor, one church – they all went together.

Constantine promoted theocratic ideas, of course, for they meant that his decrees were God's decrees, and thus beyond criticism. With the senate powerless, he ruled the empire with absolute authority anyway, and the Eusebian story gave his rule the extra legitimacy of divine authority. Under the Byzantine emperors following Constantine, indeed, it became impossible to distinguish political from sacred. In the Palm Sunday procession, the emperor took the role of Christ entering Jerusalem. On Holy Thursday he washed the feet of those representing the Apostles. Imperial banquets mimicked Christian rituals, with hymns and genuflections. The emperor promulgated dogmatic decisions about theological doctrine, and ecclesiastical institutions such as councils had no standing unless he summoned and approved them. Ecclesiastical officers were civil servants, appointed and dismissed by the emperor.

Constantine and Eusebius, then, mark the beginning of Christian politics. Before them, Christians had neither political power nor political theory. After them, Christians were on the political map, and they had at least one idea about government: that imperial power was God's power. This idea prepared Christians for later ideas like the Holy Roman Empire and the divine right of kings. It became the standard way of understanding the papacy, from Pope Leo I in the mid-fifth century to

Pope John Paul II, who still holds that *Papa a nemine judicatur*, the pope is judged by no one.

IV. Augustine: The Reversion to Politics as Irrelevant, and the Beginning of Christian Natural Law Theory

If the Roman Empire and the Church had continued to prosper together, perhaps theocracy would have become the single Christian political theory. But after Constantine and his sons came the emperor Julian, "the Apostate," who turned against the Christians, withdrawing the privileges of the Church and planning new forms of pagan worship. Whatever the relation between Constantine and God, clearly not all emperors were acting on God's behalf.

The empire continued to weaken militarily and politically, too. Constantine himself saw the Western part of his empire declining, and so he moved east to the site of ancient Byzantium on the Bosporus, renaming it Constantinople. The Vandals, Goths, Franks, and other barbarians grew stronger in the West, and then in 410 the Visigoths sacked Rome itself. Could the empire really be God's instrument, some asked, if He let it be destroyed by the barbarians?

One Christian who answered this question in the negative was Augustine. He rejected the idea that the emperors were ruling as God's agents. Indeed, he said that no political institution was a necessary part of God's plan in history. The whole of politics was not natural to human beings, nor part of their spiritual destiny. Before the Fall of Adam, there was no politics; after the Fall, God merely permitted politics as a way of minimizing social discord among the now degenerate humans. For Augustine, *all* political institutions, including the Christianized Roman Empire, were part of the "city of Man," not the "city of God." What Christians should concentrate on is the city of God, that is, the kingdom of Heaven, which, as the early Christians had said, was not a political kingdom at all. With Augustine, then, Christians could once again treat politics as irrelevant to the Christian life.

If Augustine's political thinking had stopped here, it would hardly have been noteworthy. But he had other ideas which would eventually contribute to Christian political theory. The major one was natural law.

Augustine was not the first to talk of natural law. Roman jurists distinguished between law established by a particular people for their state, civil law, *ius civile*, and law dictated by reason throughout all human communities, the law of nations, *ius gentium*. But Augustine Christianized this concept by linking it with God the Creator.

Law, Augustine said, is a pattern with which human activity must conform. Our human laws cover only certain aspects of life and vary from society to society. But there is a higher kind of law which covers all of human life and is the same everywhere and at all times. Augustine called it eternal law or divine law. It exists, first of all, in God's mind as the idea of human nature from which he created us. For Augustine, eternal law and eternal truth are aspects of the same reality in the divine mind. Eternal law is just eternal truth as it regulates our behavior.

Made in God's image, we have minds, too, and can come to understand our human nature, what makes it flourish, and what frustrates it. The eternal law for human beings, as it is found in all human minds, is natural law.

Now Augustine's belief that politics is unnatural to human beings and not part of the city of God, kept him from developing a Christian political theory. But some of his ideas about law would survive to be worked into a political theory anyway, eight centuries later, by Thomas Aquinas.

V. Thomas Aquinas: Toward Modern Political Theory

The political ideas presented so far might be interesting historically, but do any of them match the ideas about government of contemporary Christians? If most Christians today were asked about the political power Bill Clinton has, I doubt that they would say either that Clinton has absolute power given directly by God, or that the government is irrelevant to their life. They may sometimes feel frustrated with the government, but that is probably because they think that the government is *supposed to* exist for their benefit. Most Christians in the United States, that is, have democratic beliefs about government. They hold some version of what has been called the ascending theory of government.

In the ascending theory, the original power resides in the community who are governed. The ancient Athenians had that idea; Aristotle discussed it in his *Politics*. The Roman historian Tacitus described the Germanic tribes as understanding government this way. They chose their leaders and conferred certain limited powers on them. If those leaders failed to govern for their benefit, they could be ousted. Our own national constitution has provisions for impeachment; the constitution of New Hampshire spells out a right to revolution.

Constantine's understanding of his power as God's power, on the other hand, is a version of the descending theory of government. In this account, the original power is found not in the community but in divinity – God for Christians, and the gods for the pagan Romans. Political power is that divine power, exercised through the ruler. The people did not choose the ruler and his power came from divinity, so they have no right to oust him or even criticize him. Indeed, they have no rights at all. Some of the ruler's decrees will undoubtedly benefit them, but that is not anything they deserve. Whatever good comes their way is a manifestation of divine favor, divine grace. It is a *beneficium*, a good deed.

What happened to Christian political thought between Constantine and the American Revolution, between the imperial, theocratic model of government and modern democracy? How did Christians change from either regarding politics as irrelevant, or holding a descending theory of government, to holding an ascending theory?

To trace every step of this transformation would require a book in itself, but let me present one important position along the way, that of Thomas Aquinas in the thirteenth century. I regard Aquinas as the classical Christian political theorist, because his position nicely explains political power in both the monarchies of his time and the democracies of ours.

Aquinas's account of politics, like the rest of his philosophy, puts God at the center, but does not make God the whole story. God created human beings as rational creatures, who can think for themselves and guide their own actions. Government is our rationality applied to guiding ourselves in society. Aquinas even used the term *political science* for this rationality. It is because government is as natural to humans as their rationality that all cultures, theistic and nontheistic, have government. Politics is not, then, as Augustine claimed, unnatural or irrelevant to our lives.

The key notion in Aquinas's political theory is law.[1] In this respect, he is in a venerable tradition extending from ancient Judaism to modern democracy. For Aquinas, law and rationality go hand in hand. Laws are how we think and guide our actions. They can be descriptive, as in science, or prescriptive, as in morality and government. The most basic form of laws might be schematized: If A, then B. A *descriptive* law of gravitation, for example, says that if an object is falling, then it accelerates at thirty-two feet per second, per second. Many city traffic codes have a *prescriptive* law like: "If you are driving on a city street, then you should not exceed thirty miles per hour. In both kinds of law, Aquinas said, our God-given rationality is at work. In the first, we grasp some general pattern in the world, and in the second we are controlling our behavior to create some general pattern, such as safe traffic conditions.

As the way intelligent beings understand and guide action, law is also found in God. Indeed, in our framing of laws, we show that we are

---

[1] Thomas Aquinas, *Summa Theologiae*, I-II, qq. 90-95.

made in God's image. The four kinds of law Aquinas discusses reveal
deep connections between God and government.

The first kind he calls the *eternal law*. Here, as in Augustine, law is
the exemplar ideas in God's mind of his creatures and how they are
supposed to operate. It is part of the eternal law, for example, that all
living things endeavor to remain alive.

Humans come to understand parts of the eternal law in
understanding the many things in the world around them. But the most
important part of this law for them is, of course, the part about how they
are supposed to live. The eternal law for humans, as it is found in our
minds, Aquinas calls the *natural law*. Some of the natural law we have in
common with other animals – such as our natural inclination to
reproduce and raise our children. Other aspects of natural law pertain to
us as rational beings, such as our desire to know God and to live in
society.

Now if we were very simple creatures living in very simple groups,
our natural inclinations found in the natural law might be enough to
regulate our behavior. But in fact, human society is complex – we each
have many competing desires, and the desires of individuals often
conflict. So in addition to the general precepts of natural law, which are
the same for all humans, societies create detailed laws to cover their
individual situations. Aquinas calls these *human laws*. It is part of
natural law that we should live in peace with our neighbors, for example,
but not that we should refrain from playing loud music after 10 PM.
Human governments had to create laws like that.

Sometimes, too, God himself has thought it necessary to reveal to
humans directly how we should live, either because of the difficulty of
figuring it out for ourselves, or because he wanted to announce loud and
clear crucial parts of the eternal law. Aquinas calls this *divine law*. The
primary example is the Ten Commandments given to Moses. Divine law
Aquinas distinguishes into the Old Law found in the Hebrew Bible, and
the New Law found in the New Testament.

In his treatment of human law, Aquinas moves toward democratic
ideas. A law, he says, is directed toward the common good. That is,
laws should motivate human beings to do what will fulfill their natures.
A statute requiring everyone to undergo a lobotomy or to commit
suicide would of necessity be an invalid law.

Aquinas adds one more phrase to his definition of law, that it is
promulgated by someone who has care for the community. Laws cannot
be created by just anyone – an edict we followed just because the person
issuing it threatened us would be simple coercion and not law. The
lawgiver must be someone whose function it is to order society for the
common good. That function, Aquinas says, "belongs either to the

whole people or to a public personage who has care of the whole people."

In the thirteenth century, most people lived under lords and kings; today many live in representative democracies with legislatures to make laws and executive branches to enforce them. Aquinas's definition of law as "an ordinance of reason for the common good, promulgated by one who has the care of the community"[2] covers both arrangements, and others besides, and relates everything back to God. That is why it has endured for seven centuries to become, for many thinkers, the classical Christian political theory.

---

[2] *Summa Theologiae*, I-II, q. 90, art. 4.

12

Catholicism and Politics

Andrew Greeley
University of Arizona
University of Chicago

Introduction

The Catholic social ethic, founded on the work of the medieval scholastics and updated and clarified by the papal encyclicals of the last two centuries is no longer understood clearly by Catholics or by anyone else. Recent papal encyclicals, whatever their merit, are less focused than earlier ones; Catholic social activists have abandoned their commitment to the Catholic social ethic (if they ever knew there was one) in favor of the pop Marxism of "liberation theology"; the teachings of the American bishops have taken on the flavor of op-ed page redistributionist left-liberalism (usual when the teachings the bishops embrace have gone out of fashion); turncoat Catholics like Michael Novak and Richard John Neuhaus have equated Catholic social teaching with American capitalism. There is nonetheless a clear Catholic social and political perspective. It does not purport to provide answers to all the political questions which preoccupy Americans today. It does, however, provide orientations from which one may consider social and political problems.

This perspective can be articulated under five headings:

1. The individual and society
2. The state and society
3. Decentralization of power
4. The nature of politics
5. The Church and politics

The Individual and Society

The American paradigm for considering the relationship between the individual and society, based on what David Tracy calls the dialectical imagination of the country's Protestant founders, places individual freedom and social structure in opposition to one another. Moreover, since individual freedom is taken to be an essential good, social structure is viewed as, at best, a necessary evil. This paradigm is so deep and so powerful in American culture that it is difficult to challenge it, even to bring it to the surface as a subject for discussion. Of course society and the individual are opposed to one another: what is the point of talking about that opposition?

It is not an exaggeration to say that much of the so-called revolution which Newt Gingrich and his allies are trying to accomplish these days takes that assumption for granted. It is an attempt to free the individual from the constraints on his (pronoun used advisedly in this context) freedom which society has imposed on him since 1933.

In this perspective every regulation diminishes freedom. Environmental rules, for example, constrain individual freedom. To suggest that such rules may in fact enhance freedom by making the country and the world a better place in which to live appears to be speaking nonsense.

The Catholic heritage on the other hand does not view society as a necessary evil but as a positive good; in line with what David Tracy calls the analogical imagination Catholicism sees an ordered society as a sacrament, a revelation, however flawed, of God. Humankind in this perspective is a social animal which can achieve its growth toward perfection only through intense and ordered social activity. Society exists to serve that growth toward perfection of the human person. Humans are not lonely animals in a jungle who enter a social contract so that they may fend off the forces and energies which might destroy. Rather they are born into a network of social relationships which sustain and enhance them through their lives. Like all human networks society can become oppressive but such abuse is neither inevitable nor immutable. Person and society are not opposites but complementaries. Parents, spouse, children, neighborhood, friends, co-workers all impose certain restraints on unmitigated selfishness, but it is through interaction with such role opposites that the human person finds fulfillment and happiness. We are not Shane or the cowboy with no name who at the end of the film rides off by himself over the mountains. Rather we have powerful (but not irresistible) propensities to stay and settle down.

The obligations which emerge in human relationships (such as the obligation of the employer to his workers and not merely to his stockholders) are not so much constraints on the freedom of isolated individuals but the glue which holds together the social network without which the human person cannot be free because she cannot survive.

Loyalty is therefore an important virtue in the Catholic social and political ethic. If you are not loyal to your family and your friends, the Catholic asks, to whom will you be loyal? In the absence of loyalty, the social structure cannot survive. That structure is not a formal organizational chart pinned to someone's wall; it is rather a pattern of ordered (though not always logical) relationships created by ties of mutual loyalty.

This perspective of the Catholic social ethic would incline one to view with profound dismay some of the current behaviors of American business people, from "downsizing" or "outplacing" by large corporations (especially when combined with exorbitant executive salaries) to wandering professional athletic franchises and traveling athletes. (What, one asks, would be the fate of the Chicago Cubs if the Tribune Company had been loyal to four-time Cy Young-winner Greg Maddeux?)

It will be argued that the constraints of loyalty do not make economic sense and that they deprive individuals of freedom of choice. To this two replies might be made: (a) there are more important concerns in the human condition than economic rationality, and (b) it is not clear that in the long run loyalty is not an economically rational choice.

What about the right of the individual male of the species, should he become successful even to the extent of becoming a presidential candidate, to abandon his loyalty to his family and seek a trophy wife (and continue to proclaim his belief in "family values" and to decry the lack of stable family life in certain impoverished groups)?

This, the Catholic theory might argue, is the freedom of the baboon or the chimpanzee.

Does the individual have the right to drive at whatever speed he wishes and thus to endanger his own life and the life of others? Does he have the right to refuse to wear a seat belt or on his bike a crash helmet? Does he have the right to do to his body whatever he wants, such as ingesting a narcotic of one sort or another, before he turns on the ignition of his car? Is it a violation of his freedom to prevent him from spewing nicotine smoke into the atmosphere when others are present? Or do these constraints rather enhance his freedom by granting him and others an opportunity for a longer life?

I merely suggest that that the Catholic social ethic creates a propensity to a certain kind of answer to all of those questions.

The State and Society

The Catholic tradition also distinguishes sharply between the state and society. Contrary to the Napoleonic and Marxist theories which tend to equate the state (and its government) with society, the Catholic ethic insists that the state is an agent of society and is subservient to it. Here the Catholic ethic and the American Constitution are in fundamental agreement – the government possesses only those powers which are explicitly delegated to it and all other powers remain with the people (or the political subunits which have constituted a higher order government). The omni-competent bureaucratic state which assumes all power to itself unless specific powers are denied it, is therefore a monster, a Leviathan which destroys personal freedom precisely because it attempts to substitute itself for the bonds of loyalty which hold together human relationships. The bureaucratic state which controls everything (even, as in Germany, the names given to children) is in principle totalitarian even if the ideology which motivates its behavior is benign, as it often is in the welfare state, though not in the Communist or Fascist regime.

In the Catholic paradigm, government exists to serve and protect society and society exists to serve and protect and enhance the person. In the totalitarian model the person exists to serve society and society exists to serve the state (which means government bureaucrats). While the more extreme forms of the bureaucratic state disappeared with the collapse of Eastern European socialism, the temptation of the bureaucratic state persists and will always persist in complex, modern, urban industrial societies.

Do we have such a state in this country? If you don't believe that certain bureaucracies believe that they are an end in themselves and that the rest of us exist to serve them, you haven't had any recent dealings with clerks of the United States Postal Service or with the administrations of public school systems.

On the other hand, if you think that the American government has too much power, you must explain the pathetic inability of the federal government to enforce existing antitrust laws in the face of the dangerous and foolish amalgamation of power in the current merger mania. Or you must account for the criminal folly of the nation's inadequate air-safety measures.

Governments, even bureaucratic governments, are essential. They are not in themselves necessary evils, but rather positive goods. However, they must also be kept in line and bureaucratic procedure must be subject to constant supervision and review. Two questions must be asked of any government office: Is it necessary? Is it efficient?

Unfortunately, it would seem that the process by which the people supervise government agencies in this country is rarely able to prevent the agencies from turning themselves into ends instead of means. In a freely operating economy, competition sorts out the inefficient and incompetent. But in governmental monopolies (or quasi-monopolies) there is rarely such competition. The failures of the postal service have produced United Parcel and Federal Express and thus mail delivery has been at least partially privatized. But there is yet no meaningful competition in primary and secondary education, and until there is, the public school monopoly will continue to be incompetent and inefficient.

It will seem to some that this canon of the Catholic social ethic is inconsistent. On the one hand it is skeptical about the bureaucratic state and on the other, at least as I express it, the Catholic ethic wants the state to do more and to do what it does better. However, in the view of my ethical heritage the state is the servant. It should be an efficient and effective servant, but never more than a servant.

As a footnote, since Catholicism does not believe in enforced virtue (virtue is acquire by a repetition of FREE acts), it does not in principle believe that the state should enforce morality when immoral acts are not an obvious social harm. The ethic I am describing hardly approved of the "noble experiment" of Prohibition and could live with a legalization of other narcotics if sufficient reasons were advanced for such a policy. On the other hand it would oppose – I hope vigorously – the notion that the government has the right to demand the bodies of young men and young women for its service save in times of the gravest emergencies. Hence it would tend to be suspicious of a peace-time draft (which usually leads to war) and of compulsory "volunteer" service – of the sort which Father Hesburgh and other doers of good would impose on young people.

What about the Church's efforts in this and other countries to impose through political pressure its own vision of virtue on others in society who do not accept that vision of virtue?

That behavior, I would contend, represents the Inquisition temptation which the Church has yet to completely relinquish and a violation of its own political ethic.

Moreover, as should be patent, attempts to impose virtue on others don't work anymore because the Church can no longer deliver the votes of its own people. Nonetheless Church leaders, following the dictum that when in doubt, instead of doing good things you do the things you do well, will continue to try to throw their political weight around.

Decentralization and Pluralism

The central insight of the Catholic social and political ethic is subsumed under the difficult word *subsidiarity* – by which label it is, incidentally, explicitly enshrined in the philosophy of the European Union. It asserts, in the words of Pius XI's encyclical *Quadragesimo Anno*, that nothing should be done by a larger and higher authority which can be done just as well by a smaller and lower authority. Social institutions should be no bigger than is necessary that their tasks be accomplished efficiently. Nothing should be done by the federal government which can be done equally well by the state government. Nothing should be done at the state level which can be done equally well by the local municipality. Nothing should be done by the city which can be done equally well by the neighborhood.

This is a profoundly radical principle, far more radical than anything that communists or socialists or liberation theologians have devised. It runs contrary to the propensities of all bureaucratic states whether they be of the Right or the Left. It argues in effect for a multiplication of efficiently functioning social structures which are permitted to do their work without interference so long as they do not violate anyone's fundamental rights. The government oversees, encourages, facilitates, sustains, but it does not dominate. Subsidiarity protects both the person from society and society from the state.

It is such a radical principle that Catholic social theorists and activists have abandoned it, apparently on the grounds that it "would never work." Thus in the bishops much-praised redistributionist pastoral on poverty ten years ago, it is mentioned only once and then only to justify government intervention to support redistributionist policies.

While Catholics remain silent about the principle of subsidiarity – or pretend that it never existed – the rich get richer and the big get bigger, usually without protest from social critics who are more interested in affirmative action than they are in the manic amassing of power by ever-larger corporations. The media celebrate the size of the mergers and the stock market is generally enthusiastic. Only *Business Week* in its recent careful study of the mega-mergers of the last decade dares to say that these mergers do not work and that, outside of the drug industry, stockholders suffer a loss of wealth in the mergers. Top executives make lots of money, employees lose their jobs, and stockholders eventually lose money. The antitrust laws are moribund and no one protests. Not even the Catholic theorists and activists who ought to be shouting louder than anyone else.

I will tell you a story of a bank. It was a small, neighborhood bank in a prosperous suburb. Its staff knew most of the customers – depositors and loan recipients – personally. The bank was popular in the suburb because it was efficient and supportive. More to the point perhaps, it made lots of money and its profit rate was one of the highest in its metropolitan region. It was so successful that it was merged into a holding company with other successful local banks. That merger impeded its freedom somewhat but it continued to be successful. Then the holding company, itself very profitable, was sold to a larger banking corporation with national reach. The local bank was reduced to a facility. Many of its employees were phased out. Most of its loan officers were dismissed. Still the bank was profitable for its new owners because the depositors still liked the friendly personal service they received at the bank. Finally, however, the owner corporation was bought out by an even larger corporation and the local bank was closed on the grounds that it unnecessarily duplicated the work of other banks in this mega-corporation. Its employees were "phased out."

A perfectly good and extremely successful bank was eliminated despite its success, indeed in great part because it was a success. Its employees were fired not because they had done poor jobs, but because they had performed too well. Eventually it was proven that the various mergers had merely made top executives richer and gave them more apparent power. The worth of the stock of the merged corporations was not as great as had been the stock of the unmerged banks. By that time it was too late to revive the local bank. It had become a supermarket.

Piedmont and Pacific Southwest were relatively small and highly profitable airlines. They were gobbled up by USAir, a notoriously unprofitable line (which has been plagued with troubles since the days when it was Allegany). Since then USAir has abandoned many of the routes which Piedmont flew and almost all that PSA flew. Big is beautiful, it turns out, even when it is ugly.

The Catholic bishops favor redistribution of wealth, which is not a component of their tradition (and which doesn't have a chance politically), and they ignore blatant violations of the principle of subsidiarity which is at the center of their theory. This failure is especially ironic because it is precisely these foolish mergers which lead to greater concentration of wealth in the hands of the corporate executives who engineer the mergers.

The Nature of Politics

Politics is a dirty word in the United States at the present time and "politician" is about the nastiest thing you can say about someone. A large proportion of Americans want a third political party which isn't political. A similar large proportion was enthusiastic recently about the possible candidacy of a military officer who was avowedly not a politician. In neither case do they seem to realize that once a new political party came into existence, it would have to take stands for and against certain policies and would have to win support of voters for those stands. It would, upon arrival, have to engage in politics. Moreover once a nonpolitician decided to run for office and was faced with the degrading necessity of seeking votes, he would become a politician.

Given the attitude of the Catholic social and political ethic toward the person, the state, and society, it has a very different view of politics and politicians. It agrees with Aristotle that politics – the art of governing – is an honorable art, second only to poetry in its dignity. A political leader cannot govern without a broad consensus behind his program. To do that he must fashion coalitions and work out compromises. He has to provide something for almost everyone or something with which almost everyone can live. He must strive to keep if not everyone happy, at least a solid majority happy. His efforts to do so are not contemptible but admirable, even if they are dismissed with contempt by the Washington press corps and the editorial writers of the *New York Times*.

If this is what government is supposed to be about, then one must be profoundly skeptical of the candidate who announces that he has been a successful businessman and, if elected to office, will run the country/state/county/city like it is a business. It should be patent that consensus, coalition, and compromise are not required to be a successful business person and that indeed they would probably destroy a business firm.

It may be that a business executive also has the skills of a politician – so too may a professor or a clergy person – but there is no guarantee of this and one should be profoundly suspicious of the man who thinks that the United States of America is nothing more than a large corporation.

In Arizona we have a governor who was elected twice on the successful-businessman image. Now it turns out that he is bankrupt and is twenty million dollars in debt. Arizona is such a crazy place politically that he will probably be reelected with a sympathy vote.

There is nothing wrong with being a bankrupt. Moreover such a person may very well have the requisite skills for politics. But there is some irony in such a person having been elected on the successful-businessman plank.

Some politicians are doubtless corrupt. So too are some corporation executives, some journalists, and some clergy. The media nonetheless set out to destroy politicians who are only slightly and technically corrupt and tolerate flagrant ethical violations in other sectors of society including their own. Thus in my city an editorial-page editor who was caught in flagrant plagiarism continues to work for the paper, though not in a journalistic capacity. This was the same paper that did all it could to destroy Congressman Rostenkowski because of what were at worst technical violations.

Just as the Catholic social and political ethic is woefully out of sync with the rest of American culture on the decentralization of political and economic power, it is clearly out of sync in its attitude toward politics and politicians. However, if one depended on what is taught in Catholic schools or is written in episcopal pastorals (which are drafted by "new-left" staff members) one would not know that there was this sympathy and indeed admiration for men who chose the high and difficult art of politics for their vocation. Those few folks who study Catholic political philosophy are aware of this component of the Catholic social and political ethic. But hardly anyone knows that they exist.

Catholics still go into politics and apparently in disproportionate numbers, especially if they are Irish. But no one in the Church is apparently ready to praise this vocational choice, to sympathize with the difficulties of the political art, and to challenge the constant assault on their lives and their persons in which the media vultures engage.

The Church and Politics

There is an emergent consensus in Catholic political thought that, with rare exceptions, the political world belongs to the laity – at least when specific social policies and programs are at issue. The clergy and the hierarchy may and should speak out on general issues, but the concrete daily battles of the political game should be left to the laity. The institutional Church is of two minds about this matter. Priests may become involved in politics in Poland but not in Latin America. Bishops should not engage in political campaigns unless the issues are really important – like abortion and divorce and religious instruction in public schools.

Bishops should not try to dictate to politicians except when they (the bishops) think they should. I have never been able to understand how men like the cardinal archbishop of New York can denounce abortion as another holocaust and still maintain the semblance of public friendship with Catholic politicians who think that in a pluralistic society one must be careful about trying to impose one's own convictions on others. However, consistency is not a virtue that is usually demanded or expected of an archbishop, to say nothing of a cardinal.

Note that the position that the Church should not interfere directly in the political game is not the same as that proposed by the "culture of unbelief," as Professor Carter calls it. The Catholic principle does not say that religion should be excluded from public life (neither does the

Constitution, by the way), much less that secularism should become the established religion of America. It merely says that generally such under-appreciated virtues as discretion and prudence suggest that the institutional Church should leave the daily political conflicts to the laity.

In the old days of the immigrant church, when many pastors felt obliged to tell their parishioners how to vote on the Sunday before the election (often for anyone who was running against Franklin D. Roosevelt), the people of the parish would listen very closely and then treat the pastor's recommendation as though it were an endorsement of the other candidate. Your typical priest or bishop would have a hard time delivering a pack of starving vampires to a blood bank.

In recent years the Church in other countries (Ireland, Italy, and Poland, for example) has consistently involved itself in elections and referenda and has just as consistently lost. It has always had a ready excuse – the people are materialists, and consumerists, and secularists, and pleasure-mad hedonists. It does not seem to occur to such leaders that their authoritarian political style and their scapegoating of their own laity might just possibly be a counterproductive strategy.

The status of this fifth and last principle of the Catholic social and political ethic is still in doubt, approved in theory, violated in practice. However, the recent trends seem to be in its favor. In the recent presidential election in Poland and referendum in Ireland about legalizing divorce, the organized hierarchies elected to play a low-key role because some of them had begun (finally) to comprehend that their high-profile involvement was winning votes for the other side. Individual bishops and archbishops, however, could not keep their mouths shut. The old temptation to use the civil society to impose and enforce rules on one's own laity remains hard to resist.

Conclusion

To be candid, I believe that the notion of a distinctive Catholic political and social ethic is moribund. When I was growing up, the theory I have presented here was routinely taught in Catholic high schools and colleges. Today one hears nothing about it. The elites who ought to have preserved and developed and passed on this theory seem unaware of its existence. Rather they have reduced everything to the slogans of "liberation theology" and the "fundamental option for the poor" – unless the poor happen to be those who work for the Church. I don't know when and where we lost this awareness of our traditional political and social perspectives, and especially the principle of subsidiarity. We seemed to know about it in the early sixties and to have lost it in the late sixties, perhaps in the enthusiasm of the elites for

Berriganism, for simple solutions to complex problems, and for "concern" as a substitute for intelligence.

I've often thought that the last real Marxist in the world will be a Jesuit with a tenured faculty position at a Catholic university – and a pop Marxist at that.

However, I suspect that eventually this political and social ethic will be rediscovered. It has too many insights into what human society should be like to be ignored indefinitely.

13

A Reflection on the Catholic Political and Social Ethic

Allyson M. Schneider
University of South Florida

In his insightful paper, Dr. Andrew Greeley presents a model for the Catholic political and social ethic. The Catholic social ethic in the United States has evolved to become an intricate tapestry of dependence: a crafted web of relationships in which a person is complemented by those around him/her. From this interdependence arises the virtue of loyalty that can be found in the Roman Catholic community, and with this loyalty comes the political ethic that Greeley addresses in his paper: an ethic of subsidiarity. Greeley goes on to discuss his theory under five headings, yet the ideas that compose his theory are scattered throughout so I will begin with society.

Society is a complex entity. On one hand, it provides a forum for the growth and evolution of the individual to a "higher" state of being. On the other, it can inhibit individualism. As stated by Greeley, this second effect is the view that most Americans take on society, the idea that "social structure is viewed as, at best, a necessary evil." Conversely, Catholics view society "not...as a necessary evil but as a positive good." With this, I agree. Catholics are born into sin. With baptism comes not only the cleansing of this original sin, but also the initiation into the Catholic society, a society with a sense of loyalty. To add to Greeley's list of questions with respect to the freedom of a "baboon" as opposed to the freedom of a man is a question posed to me in a catechism class: Is it a violation of individual freedom to prevent a man from walking down the street brandishing a fully automated assault weapon? Following Greeley's model, one would draw the conclusion that it is indeed not a violation of personal freedom. Rather, it is the responsibility of this individual, this man, to preserve the feeling of safety in his community, a feeling that would be destroyed by his doing such an act as carrying around a loaded weapon.

Another entity Greeley discusses is the state. He proposes that the Catholic ethic views the state as " an agent of society and is subservient to it [society]." Thus, in a government such as one exacted by the Constitution of the United States, this ethic becomes a reality. In addressing the point that the canon of the Catholic social ethic is inconsistent with respect to the bureaucratic state, Greeley refers to the principle of the role of the state with respect to society. In his model, government exists to serve and protect society. This is a valid point; the desire for the state to do more and to do better is not in contradiction with the ethic when looked upon in the totality of the theory. The state should protect society and can do so by doing "more, better". This isn't "wrong," providing that the state retains the role of a servant of society. The one glaring incongruency that I found under the discussion of state is the idea of enforced virtue, the idea that Catholics do not believe that the state should enforce morality. It seemed a bit confusing, and led me to wonder if it would confuse even a minimally read non-Christian taken into account, say, Catholic pro-life activism. Greeley states that this issue can be written off as merely an "Inquisition temptation" which the Church has yet to completely relinquish. I don't see it that simply. It is a part of the Catholic ethic to become a part of society because in such a situation the media serves to enhance the mind and spirit. Catholics enhance mind and spirit through the interactions with those around them. Catholics, as do most other religious persons, bring their religious morals into this larger social network. I don't believe that this "carrying in" will be lost in the near future. Sadly, while bringing these beliefs into society, Catholics have yet to do what the Jewish community in this country has done so well: establish a strong enough consensus among themselves to have a significant voting bloc.

Greeley also brings forth the principle of subsidiarity. He goes on to state that the Catholic bishops, theorists, and activists believe it won't work, and therefore do not follow it. Perhaps he is wrong in his assumption that it has been abandoned because the principle is ineffective in action. Greeley, later in the paper, speaks of bishops, priests, and clergy in general following a trend of silence, politically speaking, in the past few years. This reticence, according to Greeley, has resulted from some of the clergy who "had finally begun to comprehend that their high-profile involvement was winning votes for the other side." Perhaps this is the case with the principle of subsidiarity. A vocal argument would hinder the activation of such a principle; so, as Greeley summarizes, with the power of silence the idea will eventually be "rediscovered" because of its insights.

In his summary, Greeley states that the idea of a distinct Catholic political and social ethic is moribund, yet he has faith that it will be rediscovered because it "has too many insights into what human society should be like to be ignored indefinitely." This is a valid assumption. In theory, Greeley's interpretation of the Catholic political and social ethic is accurate. His model can be correlated to the behavior of the population as a whole and when studied sociologically, as Greeley has done, observed in the individual as well.

What this argument leaves, however, is the question of whether Greeley's document is, indeed, sanctioned as a Catholic ethic: a Catholic doctrine calling forth for this system of politics. Without documentation, the ethic presented in Dr. Greeley's paper can only be accepted as a single interpretation of an idea, however insightful an interpretation it may be. Given the time constraints of this conference, I do not feel that Andrew Greeley had adequate time to introduce documentation. In a future course of study, he could build a bridge from idea to authenticity through the introduction of new material. He could make a valid argument for his ethic as a Catholic ideology that indeed holds far too many insights to be abandoned or ignored.

14

Greeley's Insights

William Shea
St. Louis University

I find it odd to be responding to Andrew Greeley in the matter of Catholicism and politics, for I have only the expertise of the practitioner – I go to mass and I vote. But I do know that my Church does have interests, policies, diplomats, goals, and objectives which one can reasonably and not at all pejoratively call "political." It also has stories and myths that encompass and explain politics. What is all this paraphernalia? And what has it to do with politics and political theory?

Father Greeley's comment on the status of the Catholic position on politics is correct: it is not a theory. His comment recalls Mark Noll's about nineteenth- and twentieth-century evangelical political and social thought – it is not theoretic, it is homiletic, a direct jump from the gospel to political and social practice.[1] But the Catholic teachings cited by Father Greeley are not exactly homiletic. Nor are they dogmas. The Catholic teaching is a series of insights, as Bernard Lonergan might have put it, common sense insights picked up over centuries of Church life, insights rather than rules, a set of leanings and leadings observed nearly as much in their violation as in their observance.[2] The proper and full realization of them in intentional action is less than consistent, in fact perhaps even sporadic, and of its nature reliant on a set of practical insights into specific circumstances and goals. These teachings arise during centuries of experience and meditation on human nature and on the nature of human community. I suspect that the primary carriers of these

---

[1] Mark A. Noll, *The Scandal of the Evangelical Mind* (Wm. Eerdmans, 1994).
[2] See Bernard Lonergan, *Insight: A Study of Human Understanding* (New York: Philosophical Library, 1957), chapters 6 and 7 on common sense, its articulation and its uses, including politics.

unarticulated meanings are the liturgy, the sacraments, the local parish communities of Catholics even when presided over by a monarchical pastor, and the Catholic family caught in the cultural-religious crossfire.

The teaching often seems to be a lost wisdom, as Father Greeley paints it, but I have some faith in its being found again, at least on occasion. The wisdom is lost in the political dealings of Catholic leaders with surrounding social and political communities especially, but they are also lost in the inner life of the Church. There the loss appears in the comments of ecclesiastics who, confronted by sociological data and the demand for reinterpretation of the Church's life, respond, "But the Church doesn't teach by polls," and who, confronted by statements of the aspirations and suggestions of groups of Catholics, respond, "But the Church isn't a democracy," comments utterly true and utterly irrelevant to the issues at hand.

The Catholic Church has had a desperately hard history in the "modern world," much of it enshrined in the deadly antimodernism of some popes in the nineteenth and twentieth centuries. In the wake of the Reformation and its politics, the Enlightenment and its naive political and intellectual ideals and doctrines,[3] the age of revolution and fear-filled reactions to it, the secularization of society and concentration of power in the modern secular state, Catholic Church leaders found the world well on its way to hell in a handbasket. The more this newly "liberated" and antiecclesial world developed, the more a stranger the Catholic Church found itself, and the more it felt the modern world to be the final enemy. The official view, even the papal view, was often apocalyptic. Catholic monarchism in France and the mad romantic medievalism of British Catholics are two examples of losing strategies. But the most poignant example of all is the crushing of the few Catholic modernists at the beginning of the century by a mystified Pope Pius X.[4]

This, of course, is a simplification, unworthy of a scholar and a scholarly audience. But I will risk another simplification, an equally helpful one, in addressing the problem of the Church and politics. Joseph Komonchak of Catholic University has sketched the curious mirroring of the emerging secular, centralized, and bureaucratic state in

---

[3] See Jacob Neusner, "Organizing the Past," in W. Shea and P. Huff, eds., *Knowledge and Belief in America* (Cambridge University and Woodrow Wilson Center Presses, 1995), 165- 94.

[4] For discussions of Catholic modernism and Rome's reactions to it, see Lester B. Kurtz, *The Politics of Heresy: The Modernist Crisis in Roman Catholicism* (University of California Press, 1986); R. Scott Appleby, *"Church and Age Unite": The Modernist Impulse in American Catholicism* (University of Notre Dame Press, 1992); and Marvin R. O'Connell, *Critics on Trial: An Introduction to the Catholic Modernist Crisis* (Catholic University Press, 1994).

an emerging centralized and bureaucratic sacred Church.[5] The leaders of the Church thought to fight fire with fire, and subsidiarity was buried in an avalanche of authoritarian reaction to a world gone mad.

And so the Church, from the time of the French Revolution down to the middle of the twentieth century, with various pitches of fervor, denounced the -isms marking the modern world, and especially modern political arrangements. Paul Blanshard, who served New York as its water commissioner and the nation's Protestants as a carping and insufferable critic of Catholicism in the 1940s and 1950s, wrote a couple of anti-Catholic books which told an occasional truth.[6] The truth was that the leaders of the Church disapproved of the pomps and works of the emerging secular West and condemned most facets of its organized life – among them religious liberty, the separation of church and state, the disenfranchising of the Church, and various other liberal aberrations.

Blanshard's truth – that the Catholic religion is antidemocratic – was quite a surprise to my parents, New York Irish Catholics who had no particular resentment at all against the modern world and were trying with some small success to make their way in it. They never quite made it into the middle class, but they never missed a meal and that was a decided improvement over the lot of their immediate ancestors in Ireland. One son became a lawyer and one a priest, something which could not have happened in Ireland to people of their class. They thought that religious liberty and democracy were just what Catholics needed. As Father Greeley has pointed out so well and so often that even bishops believe him now, Catholics got on and get on swimmingly in the United States, that most modern of the modern societies during those decades in which Rome and the bishops constantly warned against a faithless modern world and yearned for a return to Christendom. These curious facts – official Roman distrust of modern political and social organization and popular American Catholic enthusiasm for republican and democratic forms of social organization, collided at the Second Vatican Council, and some of the most important changes effected by that council in 1961-65 were American contributions.

The point I want to make, if not too clearly as yet, is that the Catholic experience in American politics and culture has had profound effects on the Catholic Church. So, it is important to keep in mind that, as the Church has its subliminal and half-articulated insights arising from and

---

[5] Joseph A. Komonchak, "Modernity and the Construction of Roman Catholicism" lecture, Woodrow Wilson International Center for Scholars, 1985.

[6] Paul Blanshard, *Communism, Democracy, and Catholic Power* (Beacon Press, 1951). The outstanding evangelical broadside of the period was Loraine Boettner, *Roman Catholicism* (Presbyterian and Reformed Press, 1962), which combined typical political worries with a summary of the failings of Catholic religious life.

guiding its practice in some graced moments, so also the political
experience of Catholics, especially the Catholic laity, have corrected some
of the aberrations and mistakes in the hierarchy's instinctive suspicions
of the "modern world."

There remain continuities between the older and more recent official
Catholic evaluations of modernity.[7] The most obvious is that the
criticism of "unbridled capitalism" still flows over the papal letters on
social issues – Michael Novak and Richard Neuhaus to the contrary not
withstanding. Richard Neuhaus's constant cry that the secular should
never set the agenda for the Church (his Lutheranism is not entirely
washed away by his conversion to Rome) is simply wrong about the
most important Catholic event in the century. "Politics," then, shaped the
agenda at Vatican II. The "world" is not leaving the Catholic religion
behind and the Catholic religion will not turn back the clock of history.
In addition, many of the internal adjustments and arguments in
Catholicism since Vatican II are also political.

Let me give two examples of how Catholic experience in American
social and political life decisively influenced the Church's reevaluation of
its negative stance toward modernity and affected its politics. The two
are interrelated and, I believe, are the most important and consequential
changes made by the council. First, the ancient Catholic teaching on the
Jews and Judaism continued into the modern world and there
undergirded rabid anti-Judaism. That "teaching of contempt" has
undergone drastic change since 1965, especially noteworthy in Catholic
liturgical and catechetical practice. *Nostra Aetate* (1965) led to a
predictable conclusion, the Vatican recognition of the State of Israel, and
has transformed Catholic attitudes and practice toward other religions as
well. At Sunday mass in my parish church just a few weeks ago, in the
prayer of the faithful the Jews were prayed for as "the people God has
chosen for himself and the flower of humanity." Can you imagine how
this falls upon the ears of one who reached adulthood still praying on
Good Friday for the conversion of the "perfidious Jews"? Second, the
teaching on the rights of religious conscience in the political arena was
redefined by *Dignitatis Humanae*. The old European Catholic doctrines
that "the Jews" killed the Messiah and that only the true Church has
public rights vanished overnight.

To catch the momentousness of these documents which have
fundamentally altered the *practice* of the Church, we recall the story told
at this conference by Darrell Fasching of the University of South Florida.
The Roman emperor Theodosius wanted the Christians who burned a

---

[7] Patrick Carey, "American Catholicism and the Enlightenment Ethos," in Shea
and Huff, 125-64.

synagogue to pay for its reconstruction, and Ambrose, bishop of Milan, forbade it. The emperor then wished to pay for it out of the public treasury, and Ambrose forbade that, too. This moment, said Fasching, Christendom was born. Vatican II marked the end of Christendom for Catholics, in the very same symbolic sense – for there and then Catholics secured their existence in the modern world by accepting living dialogue with Jews and the religions, and by accepting the primacy of conscience in religious exercise. As William Scott Green pointed out, the Enlightenment took Judaism as the test case (a test it failed to a significant extent), and the Catholic Church took its place in our world by beginning its first dialogue with Judaism.

The historians of Vatican II tell us that in these two conciliar decisions American Catholic experience counted heavily. Cardinal Spellman, whose conservatism led him to a failed effort to keep the priests' prayer book in Latin and who forbade the all-too-"liberal" Hans Kung to speak in the archdiocese of New York, lobbied hard for *Nostra Aetate*. In addition, it was his own theological advisor, John Courtney Murray, S.J., who shaped the document on religious liberty. Thus American political experience bent the antimodernist spine of Roman Catholicism, showing once again that religion and politics have profound effects on one another. A second lesson is that sometimes, perhaps all-too-few times, subsidiarity actually works in the Catholic Church itself which, in its vigorous reaction to modernity, had forgotten it! With a bit of leeway provided by a pope, some of the things Catholics learned by way of real experience in the real modern world surfaced and triumphed. The child has taught the mother.

The struggle between official antimodernism and modern Catholic experience was not all that was going forward. At the very same time that the popes were condemning what they saw around them, and reacting to the earthshaking changes in Europe by hurling condemnatory lists of modern and modernist errors and by centralizing power in the Roman See, they were also developing and recording some of the basic insights (which Father Greeley lists in compressed fashion) in what seem at first sight a set of curious, obscure, and formal letters on society. But those letters, and even the sensibilities behind some of the condemnations, have left Catholics a significant legacy of social teaching which, I hope, is not as lost as Father Greeley fears. The Catholic Church is surely political, but it doesn't have a political theory or even a social theory. It has some insights and instincts born of its historical experience and of its poor attempts to live out its religion. For these letters and teachings I am grateful. I am also grateful for the work of Father Greeley, for his own faithful and loyal work building upon and extending the American Catholic achievement. He, more than any contemporary American, knows Catholicism in American culture. This hound sniping at the heels of the American church turns out to be its lover after all.

Father Greeley sees a complicated world and a complicated Church, and a complicated relationship between the Church and politics. Once the world was simpler, however. In the Bronx of my youth, Catholics voted Democratic with only one exception – Jake Javits, and he wasn't really an exception. To this day my anti-Republican bias remains healthy. I receive no Republicans at my table, with only two exceptions – my mother-in-law and Jacob Neusner. The local Catholic doctrine taught that there were two preeminent mortal sins: premarital sex and voting Republican. One could not vote Republican even if the priest told you to do so, proving once again that Catholics believed even then in the primacy of conscience. That doctrine was put to the test in the 1960 election when New York Catholics went overwhelmingly for Kennedy while its clergy voted for Nixon. I confess here publicly to a mortal sin – I voted for Nixon, an event which my father took to be a sure sign of a vocation to the priesthood. Though I never again voted Republican, I don't think my father ever forgave me for voting against an Irish-American Catholic Democrat. Professor Neusner once tried to fathom my nearly unblemished Democratic voting record. After listening to my simple-minded political babble for a few minutes he said, "Oh, I get it – its tribal!" He never brought it up again and he hasn't held it against me. So maybe even tribal Democratic voting isn't as bad as premarital sex; but I am as convinced as my father that voting Republican is far worse. Perhaps I am permitted the hope of the repentant sinner.

Part IV

ISLAM

15

The State and the Sacred in Classical Islamic Thought

Tamara Sonn
University of South Florida

Introduction

The purpose of this paper is to answer the question, What theory of politics as a medium for religious activity governs the political order of Islam in its classical theological formulation? Although there is no theology as such in Islam, there is a well-developed legal tradition which determines normative thought in Islam. According to this tradition, the purpose of Islamic society is to submit to the will of God, which has been clearly expressed through revelation as the desire that human beings create a just society. Since political activity is essential for the creation and maintenance of social justice, all political activity is essentially religious activity in Islam. In this paper, however, I will limit my discussion to the nature of government – the ideal Islamic state.

Among contemporary commentators on Islam, it has become popular to claim that there is no separation of religion and politics in Islam. This claim, combined with the rejection of secularism on the part of many contemporary Muslim activists, has led some observers to assume that Islam espouses a kind of theocracy. I will demonstrate, however, that this is not the case. The term *nomocracy* is more suitable to describe Islamic political theory. A theocracy is a state governed by God/gods or those who claim to act on divine authority. A nomocracy, by contrast, is a state governed by a codified system of laws. The ideal Islamic state is one governed by individuals or bodies bound by Islamic law.[1]

In this context, classical Islamic legal theory implicitly distinguished between those empowered to interpret the law (the legislative and judicial branches) and those empowered to make sure the law is being followed (the executive branch). The executive political power – with its coercive authority – would ideally concern itself with safeguarding Islamic law. But it was prone to abuse and therefore an unreliable repository of religious responsibility. Formulators of Islam's classical theory therefore placed the primary responsibility for influencing the life of the community in the hands of legal scholars: the legislative and judicial branch of Islamic authority.

I will therefore demonstrate that in classical Islamic thought the ideal Islamic state is one dominated by laws derived from divine revelation. Even the chief executive officer, whether king or caliph, is theoretically subject to Islamic law. Legal scholars comprise the legislative and judicial branches of the ideal Islamic state, logically prior in importance to the executive. I will introduce this discussion with some background on the centrality of legal theory to Islamic thought.

Introduction to Islamic Thought

As noted, there is no theology as such in Islam. Instead, there is *kalam* ("disputation" or "discussion"). Kalam developed in the early centuries of Islam as an effort to analyze rationally, using Greek philosophical principles, certain Qur'anic descriptions of God. This was done in response to the effort by some scholars to demystify the Qur'an, interpreting some of its statements about God figuratively. The preeminent formulator of kalam, al-Ash`ari (d. 935 C.E.), determined that God is beyond human comprehension. Only God's effects are knowable, but they are intelligible only *as* God's effects. He concluded, therefore, that there is no natural causality (there are only occasions for God to cause things, which God does with great regularity so that it looks, for example, like putting a flame to cotton makes the cotton burn when, in reality, it is God's direct action that makes the cotton burn). Nor is there any such thing as inherent good and evil (things are good or evil only because God declared them so, so that humans cannot figure out what is good and evil except through revelation). This strain of thought is severely criticized by

---

[1] I will confine this discussion to Sunni Islamic thought; Shi`i Muslims, some 12-15 percent of the world's Muslim population, maintain a different theory.

many contemporary Muslim reformers as having led to the decline in intellectual and spiritual vitality that paved the way for the colonial domination whose effects most of the Muslim world is still struggling to survive.

Whether or not Ash`ari kalam was the culprit in the decline of Islam, it never played the central role in Islamic thought that theology played in Christianity. Islam never accepted the classical Greek division of sciences into the practical and the speculative, upon which Christian theology is based. According to that division, the practical sciences are the lower sciences, having to do with material things and everyday life. They must be mastered before one can venture into the speculative or theoretical sciences. One effect of this division is the separation of ethics, a practical science, from theology, a speculative science. Such a separation is unworkable in the Islamic paradigm, wherein ethical behavior is a response to recognition of divinity – ideally, the inevitable response. In Islam, that is, ethics proceeds from thinking about God; it does not make sense the other way around.

There are other examples of this emphasis on ethical behavior as the response to God. One is Islam's insistence on "bearing witness" rather than simply "believing." By the time Prophet Muhammad was working in the Middle East, Christianity had already begun to develop its creedal system. According to the authoritative councils of the Church, one was identified as a true Christian on the basis of what s/he believed (her/his creed). The Nicene Creed, formulated at the Council of Nicea in 325 C.E. as the litmus test of Christian identity, is still recited daily in Catholic masses around the world. By contrast, the first pillar of Islam – the statement by which Muslims identify themselves – is called the *shahada*, which has no adequate translation in English but it comes from the verb meaning "to bear witness." It does not mean "to say" (give verbal assent) or "to believe" (give intellectual assent); declaring the shahada means (ideally) to vow to demonstrate in one's behavior that one recognizes that "there is no god but the God [in anglicized Arabic: Allah], and Muhammad is the messenger of God."

The emphasis on the inseparability of belief and action is also symbolized in the origin of the Islamic calendar in the year 622 C.E., the year of the emigration (in anglicized Arabic, hijra) of Prophet Muhammad and his followers from Mecca to Medina. In Mecca the Prophet was preaching and gaining followers, but they were being persecuted by the leaders of the city. In Medina they were welcomed and, in fact, the various tribes of the city agreed to abide by Prophet Muhammad's leadership. This event, therefore, signifies the transition of the Prophet's mission from that of simply preaching about the need for submission (in anglicized Arabic, Islam) to God's will that people create a just society, to actually creating social institutions designed to insure social justice. Had they remained in Mecca and been wiped out, the community's beliefs would have been correct, but they would not have been able to put them into effect. Many scholars, therefore, believe this event symbolizes the uniquely Islamic emphasis within the monotheistic tradition. Earlier prophets had taught the same truths confirmed in Prophet Muhammad's teaching; Muhammad was the "seal of the prophets" (meaning that no more prophets would be necessary) because he made it clear, once and for all, that correct belief is not enough to fulfill the covenant. True belief must be "witnessed" in social action, in ethical behavior.

What is important for this discussion is that Islam's emphasis on belief-in-action is reflected in the fact that the controlling and unifying role played by theology in Christianity is played by law in Islam. But law in Islam is not simply a list of rules and regulations. In fact, as Fazlur Rahman puts it, Islamic law "is not strictly speaking law [in the Western sense], since much of it embodies moral and quasi-moral precepts not enforceable in any court." "[O]n closer examination," he says, it is "a body of legal opinions or, as Santillana put it, 'an endless discussion of the duties of a Muslim,' rather than a neatly formulated code or codes."[2] That is why we must look to Islamic legal thought, rather than to theology, for ideas about politics as a medium for religious activity.

Development of Islamic Jurisprudence

Unlike Judaism and Christianity, Islam developed from the very beginning in the context of political power. Yet its founder left no detailed political theory nor institutions empowered to develop one.

---

[2] Fazlur Rahman, *Islam and Modernity* (Chicago and London: University of Chicago Press, 1982), 32. Historian of Islamic law N. J. Coulson puts it this way: "The ideal code of behavior which is the Shari`a has in fact a much wider scope and purpose than a simple legal system in the Western sense of the term. Jurisprudence (*fiqh*) not only regulates in meticulous detail the ritual practices of the faith and matters which could be classified as medical hygiene or social etiquette – legal treatises, indeed, invariably deal with these topics first; it is also a composite science of law and morality, whose exponents (*fuqaha'*, sing. *faqih*) are the guardians of the Islamic conscience." N. J. Coulson, *A History of Islamic Law* (Edinburgh: The University Press, 1964), 83.

Classical Islamic theory, therefore, developed only gradually and in dialogue with actual political developments.

The classical institution of Islamic leadership is the caliphate. From the death of Prophet Muhammad in 632 until 1924, there was – at least theoretically – a successor (in Arabic, *khalifa*) to the Prophet's political leadership. Muhammad's prophetic mantle was not inherited by his successors. Nor did the Prophet devise a specific political system or designate a successor (according to Sunni belief). The Prophet was himself considered a just arbiter and the source of divine revelation. Yet the two roles were not fused; even the Qur'an commanded that the Prophet make decisions on practical issues only in consultation (*shura*) with members of the community. In addition, the Prophet elicited periodically from the community an oath of allegiance to his leadership (*bay`a*). Beyond establishing these precedents and, of course, delivering the Qur'an, the Prophet apparently left it to the community to devise its own ways of governance.

The Prophet's successors were generally expected to behave according to the guidance left by the Prophet and to be personally pious as well, but there was no formal theory upon which to either determine leadership of the community or judge its legitimacy. The first successor, Abu Bakr (r. 632-34 C.E.), was chosen by consensus of the elders of the community in Medina. Abu Bakr appears to have suggested his successor to a council of community leaders who approved the choice (`Umar). The next two successors (`Uthman and `Ali) are also reported to have been chosen by such a council, the choice again presumably ratified by the oath of allegiance of the community. Yet it is unclear even what titles these leaders were accorded. Abu Bakr apparently used the title "successor to the messenger of God" (*khalifat* [caliph] *rasul Allah*), while `Umar seems to have preferred "leader of the faithful" (*amir al-mu'minin*). However, as W. Montgomery Watt points out, there is no evidence of clearly defined significance of either designation.[3] The Qur'an had simply commanded, "Obey God and the Messenger and those among you in authority" (4:62). We have no record that the early Muslim community believed it was doing anything more or less than that.

---

[3] Watt (*Islamic Political Thought* [Edinburgh: The University Press, 1968], 32ff) discusses the meanings of the term *khalifa* at the time Abu Bakr seems to have used it. His conclusion that the term had no more specific meaning than "one who comes after" is generally accepted among scholars, although the term is used in the Qur'an in a few places with the connotation of "deputy" or "vicegerent."

The caliphate only came to be institutionalized gradually and on an ad hoc basis, specifically as Muslim sovereignty began to spread and the office of caliphate came to be a coveted prize. In 661 C.E., following violent competition, the descendants of a leading Meccan family, the Umayyads, assumed control of the caliphate and established their headquarters in Damascus. Again, we see a distinction between executive and legislative-judicial religious authority: Damascus became effectively the political capital of the empire while Mecca remained the religious center. The Umayyads maintained control over the office until they were overthrown in another revolution by the `Abbasid family in 750 C.E. And still there was no theory upon which the institution was based.

On the other hand, the field of Islamic law was developing at the same time, and a great deal of theorizing was taking place there. In the early days of the Muslim community there had been no official organs of either law or the interpretation of scripture on which it was supposed to be based. During the lifetime of the Prophet and his first four immediate successors (his closest companions who are regarded by Sunni Muslims as having been of exemplary character and judgment and are therefore called the Rashidun or "rightly guided" caliphs), the model of governance was basically that of a revered tribal elder whose behavior becomes normative. As noted, Muhammad's prophetic role was explicitly distinguished from his practical leadership role. He is even reported to have told his community that they are the best judges in practical matters, except where the Qur'an directs otherwise. In a document believed to have been dictated by him when he established the community at Medina, the Constitution of Medina, he defined his political role as that of arbiter of disputes. After designating the rights and responsibilities of the community members toward one another, he said, "Wherever there is anything about which you differ, it is to be referred to God and to Muhammad for a decision." Elsewhere, "Whenever among the people of this document there occurs any disturbance or quarrel from which disaster is to be feared, it is to be referred to God and to Muhammad the Messenger of God."[4] Clearly, it was assumed that Muhammad's behavior was divinely guided and that his judgment was sound. The only monotheists referred to in the constitution were Jews and, although they were designated as part of the community of the Prophet, it was stipulated that they retain their own religious laws and

---

[4] Articles 23 and 42 of the Constitution of Medina, from Ibn Hisham's *Al-Sirah*, translated by Watt, in ibid., 132-33.

practice. Those who declared themselves Muslim, in lieu of a developed legal system, deferred to the Prophet's judgment, on a case-by-case basis. Apparently, the Rashidun followed this same model.

The assumption of power by the Umayyad family (661 C.E.), however, changed that model. The Umayyads oversaw the conquest of vast territories. Umayyad policy concerning their administration (particularly regarding matters of taxation) was generally to leave in place the extant system, which varied from region to region depending upon whether the area had previously been under Roman (Byzantine) or Persian administration, the means of acquisition (whether by conquest or treaty), etc.[5] Thus, huge chunks of policy

---

[5] The general pattern was for the Muslim conquerors to exact some sort of tribute to reflect their sovereignty while leaving it to the local authorities to collect the taxes according to their established customs. The degree of autonomy of the local officials was often affected by the nature of the conquest. When the lands were acquired by means of military conquest, the administrative system established generally reflected more the conqueror's discretion than those acquired by a treaty of capitulation. At times, however, a system of taxation was simply imposed regardless of means of conquest, or the amount of tribute expected may have been fixed in advance of the conquest and only the means of collection left to local officials. Iraq, for example, was conquered by military victory over the drained Sasanid forces and with the help of the Shayban bedouin. The native Arab subordinates were left in control of taxation and followed the Sasanid tradition. The Sasanid system included both a land tax and a poll tax which varied according to the degree of wealth among the populace, except for the aristocracy, who were exempt from the poll tax. In order to maintain this exemption, the aristocracy generally converted to Islam. In Syria, on the other hand, where Islamic dominance was achieved largely by treaty, the tax collection and tribute were left to the discretion of the native administrators. They followed in general outline the fiscal system of the previous Roman overlords. More complex than the Persian system, the Roman model included a personal tax only on colonists and non-Christians and a property tax which varied with the size of the estate A small parcel was apparently taxed according to the measure of its cultivation, while larger estates were taxed according to the number of people working the land. In Iran and the Transcaucasus/Central Asia, the Sasanid system of land tax and poll tax, regardless of conversion, seems to have remained intact. A tribute was simply fixed by the conquerors and the local chieftains were left to administer taxes as they saw fit. See al-Baladhuri, *Futuh al-Buldan*, ed. DeGoeje (Leiden: E. J. Brill, 1866), translated by Phillip K. Hitti as *The Origins of the Islamic State* (New York: Columbia University Press, 1916), 110-12; Ahmad G. Abi Ya`qub al-Ya`qubi, *Ta'rikh*, ed. Th. Houtsma (Leiden: E. J. Brill, 1883), 2:150-51; al-Tabari, *Tarikh al-Rusul wa'l-Muluk*, ed. M. deGoeje, et al. (Leiden: E. J. Brill, 1879-1901), 1:2111-13, 2121-24; Ibn `Asakir, *al-Ta'rikh al-Kabir*, ed. `Abd al-Qadir Badran and Ahmad `Ubayd (Damascus, 1329-51) 1:130; Ibn al-Athir, *al-Kamil fi'l-Ta'rikh*, ed. C. J. Thornberg (Leiden:

and legislation were incorporated into the Islamic administrative system with virtually no input from Islamic sources. Furthermore, it became apparent to some at least that Umayyad leadership no longer evinced the model of wisdom and piety that Islamic leadership ideally symbolized. This recognition fostered the growth of opposition groups. Among them were religious scholars whose objections to Umayyad policies were based on what they perceived to be Islamic principles. It was only in this context that the Islamic community began to develop the foundations upon which to build political theory: the scholars' articulation of the components of legal reasoning, which gave rise to the four schools of Sunni Islamic law.[6]

The Umayyads had introduced into their administration the office of judges (qadis). They were political appointees with varied administrative responsibilities, including police and treasury work, but generally charged with settling disputes in accordance with local custom. They were accorded a great deal of latitude, exercising their own discretion with regard to what was permissible in view of Islamic principles and administrative necessities. But by the mid-eighth century, there was a discernible body of religious scholars who were popularly regarded as having the authority to identify and interpret the sources of normative Islamic practice (Islamic law). They fell into schools of thought which generally developed according to regional practice. In Medina, for example, a school of Islamic law developed based on local practice and in view of the interpretations of scripture and hadith reports known locally. It was expressed in the work of Malik ibn Anas (d. 796), around which developed what is referred to as the Maliki school of law. Another center, with different local customs and different hadith reports, grew up in Kufa: the school of Abu Hanifa (d. 767), largely developed by Abu Yusuf (d. 798) and al-Shaybani (d. 804), and known as the Hanafi school. The development of these schools was essentially democratic; determination of what was normative in the Qur'an and Sunna was based on local consensus, *ijma*`. And in cases where there were no apparently applicable precedents in the Qur'an or Sunna, legal scholars were to use their discretion, as had the

---

E. J. Brill, 1867), 2:312-13. See also Daniel C. Dennet, Jr., *Conversion and the Poll Tax* (Cambridge, MA: Harvard University Press, 1950), 12ff; C. Cahen, "Djizya," *Encyclopedia of Islam*, 2nd ed., 2:559; H. Lammens, *Etudes sur le règne du Calife Omaiyade Mo`awia Ier* (Beirut: Imprimerie Catholique, 1930), 226.
[6] See N. J. Coulson, *A History of Islamic Law* (Edinburgh: The University Press, 1964), chaps. 2-3, upon which this account is based.

Umayyads' qadis, to determine the implications of what they did find in the Qur'an and Sunna with regard to the novel situation. They were to practice *ijtihad*, the name given to this interpretive work.

As members of the opposition, the legal scholars (*fuqaha'*) were naturally favored by the dynasty succeeding the Umayyads, the `Abbasids (750-1258 C.E.) and came to play an important role in their administration. But their incorporation into the imperial administration made the need apparent for greater rigor in legal thought, in the hopes of greater uniformity of practice throughout the empire. Thus a third school of Islamic law developed, that attributed to al-Shafi`i (d. 820 C.E.), who held that only the consensus of the entire Islamic community (not just the various regions) was considered authoritative. But that was virtually impossible to attain given the extent of the Islamic community by the time he was working. Therefore, it was preferable to follow precedent as much as possible. For al-Shafi`i, then, the third source of Islamic law was established consensus regarding the meaning of the Qur'an as interpreted in light of hadith reports. Ijtihad could be practiced only as a final resort, but it too was circumscribed: the intellectual effort to determine the implications of the Qur'an and Sunna was to be according to syllogistic reasoning, or reasoning by analogy (*qiyas*). A fourth school of Islamic law eventually developed which placed even greater emphasis on precedent as expressed in the Sunna.[7] To al-Shafi`i's student Ahmad ibn Hanbal (d. 855) was attributed the origin of what is now called the Hanbali school.

This articulation of the components of Islamic law would become the basis for a comprehensive theory of political sovereignty. As legal historian N. J. Coulson puts it, "The legal scholars were publicly recognized as the architects of an Islamic scheme of state and society which the `Abbasids had pledged themselves to build, and under this political sponsorship the schools of law developed rapidly."[8] But the need for a comprehensive political theory apparently did not present itself until the early eleventh century, by which time the `Abbasid caliphs were facing strong competition from regional usurpers, particularly in Egypt and even Baghdad, the

---

[7] See ibid., 70-71, and Wael B. Hallaq, "Was al-Shafi`i the Master Architect of Islamic Jurisprudence?" *International Journal of Middle East Studies* 25/4 (November 1993): 587-605.

[8] Coulson, op. cit., 37.

`Abbasids' capital. It was this challenge that finally gave rise to a theory of government, that of Shafi`i jurist al-Mawardi (d. 1058).[9]

Classical Theories of Islamic Government

According to al-Mawardi, the office of the caliphate was established in order to continue the work of the Prophet in his capacity as defender of Islam and in worldly governance.[10] Furthermore, it is obligatory upon the community that someone be placed in the position of caliph. He says scholars' opinions are divided as to whether that obligation is based on reason or revelation. Reason tells us that "it is in the nature of reasonable men to submit to a leader who will prevent them from injuring one another and who will settle quarrels and disputes, for without rulers men would live in anarchy and heedlessness like benighted savages." Revelation tells us, as noted above, that we must "obey God, the Messenger, and those in authority among you" (4:62). Furthermore, there is a hadith report that the Prophet said, "Other rulers after me will rule over you, the pious according to his piety, the wicked according to his wickedness. Hear them and obey in all that accords with the truth. If they do good, it will count for you and for them. If they do evil, it will count for you and against them." Either way – whether on the basis of common sense or revelation – there must be a caliph, says al-Mawardi. If no one is in the position of caliph, then the community must come up with a group of candidates eligible for the position and a group of electors to choose from among the

---

[9] In Marshall G. S. Hodgson's analysis, the dynastic families had seized control of the central political power of the Muslim empire (the army and the treasury that supported it) before there was any theory of political legitimacy in Islam. But by the tenth century, regional principalities had emerged and while they were generally content to pay nominal allegiance to the Baghdad caliphate, they posed a challenge to the central caliphate's real power. Hodgson says, "The caliphate itself was in question, in a world ruled by arbitrary amirs [princes], and the caliphate had proved willing to turn to Shar`i principles in its crisis. Hence the scholars set about developing the theory of a *sihasah shar`iyyah*, Shar`i political order." See *The Expansion of Islam in the Middle Periods*, vol. 2 of *The Venture of Islam*, (Chicago and London: University of Chicago Press, 1974), 55. It should be noted, however, that even in al-Mawardi's formulation, the term *imamate* is used, rather than *caliphate*. Scholars agree, however, that the terms are interchangeable in this context.
[10] The following account is taken from pp. 3-6, 14-15, and 19-20 of al-Mawardi's *Al-Ahkam al-Sultaniyya*, translated by Bernard Lewis in *Politics and War*, vol. 1 of *Islam*(New York, Hagerstown, Sna Francisco, London: Harper Torchbooks, 1974), 171-79.

candidates. The candidates must be of honorable character; be able to practice ijtihad; have sound hearing, vision, and speech; be "sound of limb;" have sound judgment; be courageous and vigorous; and be (male) members of the Quraysh tribe (the tribe of Prophet Muhammad). The electors must have integrity, enough intelligence to recognize the qualifications of the candidates, and the ability to choose wisely from among the candidates.

In al-Mawardi's words, the duties of the caliph are as follows:

1. To maintain the religion according to established principles and the consensus of the first generation of Muslims. If an innovator appears or if some dubious person deviates from it, the [caliph] must clarify the proofs of religion to him, expound that which is correct, and apply to him the proper rules and penalties so that religion may be protected from injury and the community safeguarded from error.

2. To execute judgments given between litigants and to settle disputes between contestants so that justice may prevail and so that none commit or suffer injustice.

3. To defend the lands of Islam and to protect them from intrusion so that people may earn their livelihood and travel at will without danger to life or property.

4. To enforce the legal penalties for the protection of God's commandments from violation and for the preservation of the rights of his servants from injury or destruction.

5. To maintain the frontier fortresses with adequate supplies and effective force for their defense so that the enemy may not take them by surprise, commit profanation there, or shed blood, either of a Muslim or an ally.

6. To wage holy war [*jihad*] against those who, after having been invited to accept Islam, persist in rejecting it, until they either become Muslims or enter the Pact [*dhimma*] so that God's truth may prevail over every religion.

7. To collect the booty and the alms in conformity with the prescriptions of the Holy Law, as defined by explicit texts and by ijtihad, and this without terror or oppression.

8. To determine the salaries and other sums due from the treasury, without extravagance and without pasimony, and to make payment at the proper time, neither in advance nor in arrears.

9. To employ capable and trustworthy men and appoint sincere men for the tasks which he delegates to them and for the

money which he entrusts to them so that the tasks may be
competently discharged and the money honestly safeguarded.

10.   To concern himself directly with the supervision of affairs and
        the scrutiny of conditions so that he may personally govern the
        community, safeguard the faith, and not resort to delegation in
        order to free himself either for pleasure or for worship, for
        even the trustworthy may betray and the sincere may deceive.[11]

Beyond the final article, which stipulates generally that the
caliph must pay attention to his work and not delegate it
irresponsibly, each of the duties of the caliph falls into one of three
categories: defense, treasury, or executive. He is to defend the
community from attack (article 3), maintain frontier defenses (article
5), and wage war against those who refuse to either become Muslims
or enter into treaty with Muslims (article 6); regarding fiduciary
responsibility, he is to collect both the alms payments required of all
Muslims to be spent on the needs of the community at large and the
legitimate spoils of wars (article 7), fairly determine and pay
salaries from the treasury (article 8), and make sure those he
appoints handle treasury moneys honestly (article 9); finally, he is
to make sure that the established principles of religion are
safeguarded (article 1), and that legal judgments and penalties are
enforced (articles 2 and 4). In no case is the caliph granted
legislative or judicial authority.

It should be noted that these are the qualifications set out by the
legists in the event the community is given the chance to determine
its own candidates. As al-Mawardi notes, that is only the case when

---

[11] Nevertheless, al-Mawardi notes that the caliph may delegate the
following four kinds of authority:

1.   Those who have unlimited authority of unlimited scope. These are
     the viziers [ministers], for they are entrusted with all public affairs
     without specific attribution.
2.   Those who have unlimited authority of limited scope. Such are the
     provincial and district governors, whose authority is unlimited within
     the specific areas assigned to them.
3.   Those who have limited authority of unlimited scope. Such are the
     chief qadi [judge], the commander of the armies, the commandant of
     the frontier fortresses, the intendant of the land tax, and the collector
     of the alms, each of whom has unlimited authority in the specific
     functions assigned to him.
4.   Those with limited authority of limited scope, such as the qadi of a
     town or district, the local intendant of the land tax, collector of tithes,
     the frontier commandant, or the army commander, every one of whom
     has limited authority of limited scope.

the previous caliph fails to designate his successor, and not surprisingly it was virtually unheard of that someone did not at least claim to have been designated by the previous caliph. It should also be pointed out that although al-Mawardi's treatment implies that a wayward ruler may be replaced by due process, in fact, none ever was. Indeed, given the fact that there were insurrectionary groups attacking the caliphate at the very time the legists were working out Islamic political theory, thinkers from al-Mawardi on insisted that even a ruler who fails to live up to the ideal standards must be obeyed.[12] As the saying usually attributed to Ibn Hanbal has it, sixty years under a tyrant is preferable to a single night of anarchy.

Furthermore, as the list of qualifications for the office stipulated, the caliph should be capable of ijtihad. Nevertheless, it was also quickly recognized that he rarely was. This seems to be the source of the idea that he could delegate his authority to the legal scholars, as well as to the idea, expressed by the Shafi'i scholar al-Juwayni (d. 1085), that the real authority in the community belongs to the legal scholars anyway. Therefore, the caliph could be a *muqallid* (follower of precedents or imitator, rather than an independent thinker), so long as he consulted the religious scholars.[13] This would become the defining paradigm of Islamic political thought: Islamic law is the ultimate source of political authority.

The classical theory of Islamic government received its fullest treatment in the work of thirteenth-century Hanbali jurist Ibn Taymiyya (d. 1328). In his best-known work, *al-Siyasah al-Shar'iyyah*, he explains that he is setting out the requirements of Islamic government. He begins by clarifying that the exercise of authority is one of the greatest religious duties, because "the children of Adam cannot insure the realization of their (common) interest except by meeting together, because every one of them is in need of every other one."[14] And their "common interest" is to live in justice: "To judge

---

[12] See Fazlur Rahman, "The Law of Rebellion in Islam" in *Islam in the Modern World*, 1983 Paine Lectures in Religion, ed. Jill Raitt (Columbia, MO: University of Missouri-Columbia Department of Religious Studies, 1983), 1-10.

[13] Muhammad al-Juwayni, *Ghiyath al-Umama* (Iskandariyya, 1979), 274-75: "If the sultan does not reach the degree of ijtihad, then the jurists are to be followed and the sultan will provide them with help, power, and protection." Quoted by Wael Hallaq, "Was the Gate of Ijtihad Closed?" *International Journal of Middle East Studies* 16 (1984): 13.

[14] Ibn Taymiyya quotes Prophet Muhammad in this regard: "If three of them were on a journey, they should choose one of them as a leader [qa'id]." Ibn Taymiyya, *al-Siyasah al-Shar'iyyah fi Islah al-Ra'i wa'l- Ra'iyyah*, ed. Muhammad al-Mubarak (Beirut: Dar al-Kutub al-'Arabiyyah, 1966). Except

according to justice, to render dues to those who have a claim on them, constitute the essential principles of just government and the very purpose of public life."[15]   Elsewhere: "On justice rests the preservation of both worlds; this world and the next do not prosper without it."[16]

To Ibn Taymiyya, it is both self-evident and confirmed by revelation ("according to religion and reason") that some people are leaders and most are followers. But he distinguishes real leadership ability from another ubiquitous human tendency, the desire to control. "[L]onging for exaltation over the people is (an aspect) of oppression, since all people are of the same kind."[17] The fact that we are social animals makes it necessary for us to establish some kind of government; the fact that many are prone to try to control others makes it necessary to establish righteous government. Taking his cue from the Qur'anic verse he once described as one third of the Qur'an (3:110), Ibn Taymiyya says, "The ruler is there to enjoin good and forbid evil – this is expected of him in his position."[18] However, it is not the leader who makes a community righteous, in Ibn Taymiyya's opinion. It is the guidance of the community by Islamic law. Thus the title of the work: *al-Siyasah al-Shar`iyyah* means "government by Shari`a." (*Shari`a* is the term generally used to designate the entire body of Islamic law but which more precisely means God's unchanging will for humanity; the practical codes of law developed by Islamic jurisprudents are called *fiqh*, which is human in origin and subject to revision. This distinction will be discussed in greater detail below.) A community guided by the Shari`a is the *al-ummat al-wasat*, the "just, equitable nation" described by the Qur'an.[19]

---

where specifically noted in brackets, English quotes are taken from the translation by `Umar Farrukh, *On Public and Private Law in Islam* (Beirut: Khayats, 1966), 187-89.

[15] Ibid., 2.

[16] Ibid., 165; cf. p. 12, where Ibn Taymiyya says that those in authority "should make over trust to those worthy of them and...administer justice fairly."

[17] Ibid., 191.

[18] Ibid., 83.

[19] Ibid., 55. Erwin Rosenthal points out in his *Political Thought in Medieval Islam* (Cambridge, 1958) that Henri Laoust translates *umma wasat* as "la nation du juste milieu." "It may be asked," Rosenthal states, "whether this meaning was actually in Ibn Taymiyya's mind. In view of his rigid Hanbalism I am rather inclined to give preference to my second translation, 'the just, equitable nation,' and to take *wasat* in the sense of Aristotle's *mesotes*. The term occurs in the Qur'an (II, 137) in this sense."

Accordingly, Ibn Taymiyya draws a clear distinction between religious and strictly coercive political authority. The example of the Prophet and the Rashidun notwithstanding, leadership of the community is not the sole preserve of the caliphal authorities. He agreed with the prevailing opinion that even unjust rulers are preferable to anarchy (although rulers commanding outright contravention of God's will must not be obeyed).[20] The government's authority is called *wilaya*, a kind of deputyship or management. Ideally, Ibn Taymiyya says, it is a trust (*wakala*), like the responsibility of a shepherd to the flock. He cites a hadith wherein the Prophet is supposed to have said, "All of you are shepherds, and every shepherd is responsible for his flock," and then concludes that the authority of the caliphal government is "a trust, for rulers are trustees of the souls of believers as in a partnership."[21] Referring to the government's work as treasurer for the community, he stresses again: "Treasurers have not the power to apportion the funds as an owner may divide his property; rather they are custodians, representatives, stewards, not owners."[22]

Overall, in fact, Ibn Taymiyya describes the caliphal government as a practical reality, not a sacred or doctrinal issue. He argues against the Shi`i view that the leader of the community is not only essential to the Islamic identity of the community but is infallible.[23] He says that only the leadership of the Prophet was divinely instituted. Even the leadership of the Rashidun was only relatively perfect. They had been close enough to the Prophet to be able to lead the community in a pious way. But since that time political leadership has degenerated into mere kingship, temporal and practical, at best. Furthermore, he agrees with al-Mawardi that executive leadership should be decided by consensus, or at least a preponderance of opinion of an electoral body, and that their opinion should then be offered to the public for ratification. Like any contract, it should be freely accepted by both sides and both have the right to reasonable expectation of benefit. The community has the right to expect peace and social order and the executive has the

---

[20] Ibid., 12; cf. pp. 188-89, where Ibn Taymiyya quotes the maxim, "Sixty years domination by a despotic ruler are better than one single night without a ruler."

[21] Cited by Victor E. Makari, *Ibn Taymiyyah's Ethics: The Social Factor* (Chico, CA: Scholars Press, 1983), 136 from Ibn Taymiyya, *Al-Siyasah al-Shari`iyyah fi'l-Islah al-Ra` i wa'l-Ra`iyyah*, ed. Muhammad al-Mubarak (Beirut: Dar al-Kutub al-`Arabiyyah, 1966), 7.

[22] Ibn Taymiyyah, *al-Siyasah al-Shar`iyyah*, 17.

[23] See Laoust's discussion, op. cit., 282ff.

right to expect obedience so long as he leads in accordance with Islamic. Again, then, the overriding authority is Islamic law, the legislative-judicial branch of government, rather than the executive.

Ibn Taymiyya makes this quite clear when he says that the identifying feature of an Islamic society is not the character of the leader but the people's responsiveness to the Shari`a.[24] For that reason Ibn Taymiyya devotes fully half his book on Islamic government to the duties of the ruled, and a good deal of his other writings to correcting what he believed were deviations that had crept into Islamic practice. Therefore, he says, it is not the sultans – those with executive authority – who bear the legacy of the Prophet's and the Rashidun's righteous leadership; it is the religious scholars. In his treatise on the authority of the founders of the four Sunni schools of law, Ibn Taymiyya reminded readers of the Qur'anic injunction to obey God, the Prophet, and those in authority in the community. But he identified "those in authority among you" as the religious scholars. They are "heirs of the prophets, and [those to] whom God gave the status of stars for guidance in the darkness of land and sea."[25]

In this context Ibn Taymiyya finds the distinction between Shari`a (God's will for human beings) and fiqh (the laws human beings devise) to be essential. He criticized people who confuse the two:

> People who [confuse Shari`a and fiqh] do not understand clearly the distinction in the meanings of the word Shari`a as employed in the Speech of God and His Apostle (on the one hand) and by common people on the other....Indeed, some of them think that Shari`a is the name given to the judge's decisions; many of them even do not make a distinction between a learned judge, an ignorant judge and an unjust judge.  Worse still, people tend to regard any decrees of a ruler as Shari`a, while sometimes undoubtedly the truth (*haqiqa*) is actually contrary to the decree of the ruler.
>
> The Prophet himself said, 'You people bring disputes to me; but it may be that some of you are able to put their case better than others. But I have to decide on evidence that is before me. If I happen to expropriate the right of anyone in favor of his brother let the latter not take it, for in that case I have given him a piece of hell-fire.' Thus, the judge decided on the strength of depositions and evidence that are before him while the party decided against may well have proofs that have not been put forward. In such cases the

---

[24] See, for example, Ibn Taymiyya, *Majmu`at al-Rasa'il al-Kubra*, ed. Muhammad `Ali (Subayh, 1966), 1:312ff.
[25] Ibn Taymiyya, *Raf al-Malam `an al-A'immah al-A`lam*, ed. M. H. al-Faqqi (Cairo: Matba`at al-Sunnah al-Muhammadiyyah, 1958), 9.

Shari`a in reality is just the opposite of the external law, although the decision of the judge has to be enforced.[26]

The weight of Islamic governance having been placed on the jurists, Ibn Taymiyya is careful to guard against claims of infallibility on their part.[27] Furthermore, even a valid judgment is subject to amendment in light of new evidence, so Islamic legislation must remain flexible. For that reason, Ibn Taymiyya is opposed to the practice of *taqlid*, imitation of legal precedents. A devoted follower of Ahmad Ibn Hanbal, Ibn Taymiyya does not deny authoritative judgments – determined on the basis of consensus – by the eponyms of the four schools of Sunni law.[28] But like al-Shafi`i, Ibn Taymiyya says that given the vast extent of the Islamic community, consensus among the legal scholars is no longer feasible. Even if it were, that would not relieve qualified jurists of the responsibility to examine all evidence in every case and all pertinent arguments in their own school and in others, and then determine on the basis of the Qur'an and the Sunna the most suitable judgment. If the jurist determines that there exists a precedent resonant with the spirit of revealed truth, that precedent should be applied regardless of the school of law in which it is found. If he does not find an appropriate precedent, he should not hesitate to judge independently – to exercise ijtihad – in accordance with the principles he has determined most conducive to justice.[29] The direct relationship

---

[26] Fazlur Rahman, *Islam*, 112, quoted from Ibn Taymiyya, *Al-Ihtijaj bi'l-Qadar*, in his *Rasa'il* (Cairo, 1323, 2:96-97).

[27] Contrary to what Coulson said was the ahistoricity of the orthodox position, Ibn Taymiyya, in Fazlur Rahman's words, "seeks to go behind all historic formulations of Islam by all Muslim groups, to the Qur'an itself and to the teaching of the Prophet" (Fazlur Rahman, "Revival and Reform in Islam," in *The Cambridge History of Islam*, ed. P. M. Holt, Ann K. S. Lambton and Bernard Lewis [Cambridge: Cambridge University Press, 1970], 635). Fazlur Rahman criticizes limitations in Ibn Taymiyya's work, including "the fact that rationalism is condemned on principle, and the fact that "the Sunna was taken in a literalist sense" (ibid., 636). Ibn Taymiyya's critique of rationalism, however, was in the context of Greek philosophers who rationalized without regard for revelation. His view on rationality in general, by contrast, was very positive: "[T]raditional authority can never be divorced from reason. But the fact that something is a Shari`a value cannot be validly opposed to something being rational," as Fazlur Rahman quoted in *Islam*, 111 from Ibn Taymiyya's *Muwafaqat Sarih al-Ma`qul li-Sahih al-Manqul* (Cairo, 1321), 1:48.

[28] See his *Raf' al-Muam `an al-Aimmah al-A`lam* (In defense of the learned imams), 3rd ed. (Beirut: Al-Maktab al-Islami, 1970).

[29] See his *Fatwa fi'l-Ijtihad* in the appendix of *Raf' al-Malam `an al-A'immah al-A`lam*.

envisioned here is between the jurist and revelation; no human authority should serve as a filter for the qualified jurist. Only those untrained in Islamic law are allowed (indeed, obliged) to follow the teachings of human authorities.

For Ibn Taymiyya, then, careful scrutiny of the cumulative tradition of Islamic law was essential to the life of the Muslim community. But the fact that an opinion may have been suitable at a given time and place was no guarantee that it would be suitable in another time and place. That is why he rejected taqlid. To convince others of the point, he called upon the witness of the very scholars being imitated: "[T]he imams themselves have demonstrably admonished the people against their imitation and commanded that if they found stronger evidence in the Qur'an or in the Sunnah, they should prefer it to their own."[30] In all cases, it must be the Qur'an which determines a judgment. In particular he cites Malik and al-Shafi`i, as well as the first caliph, Abu Bakr: "Follow me where I obey God; but if I disobey Him, you owe me no obedience." The founder of his own school, Ibn Hanbal, is quoted: "Do not imitate me or Malik or Shafi`i or al-Thawri, but investigate as we have investigated."[31]

Thus, ijtihad for Ibn Taymiyya was not only perennially possible but essential to the practice of Islam, and disagreement among the fuqaha' was not a sign of weakness. It simply reflects the scholars' humanity and the need for flexibility of Islamic law. Here Ibn Taymiyya expands upon the Hanbali notion of *istislah*, which means having regard for social well-being or public interest in rendering legal judgments. The Maliki and Shafi`i schools also use the principle of *istislah*, while the Hanafis use a similar principle, *istihsan*, which means "approval" or juristic prerogative. In either case it is a mechanism whereby strict adherence to established precedent or strict legal reasoning can be bypassed if, under the specific circumstances at hand, the common good would not be served by such a judgment. The well-being of the community, their common interest, as Ibn Taymiyya put it above, is justice, the very purpose of Islamic law, the purpose of public life, and the purpose of the Muslim community. In the commitment to justice lies what Ibn Taymiyya identified as social solidarity (*ta'awun*), not in uniformity of legal judgments. This is what binds the Muslim community into a

[30] Translated by Victor E. Makari in *Ibn Taymiyyah's Ethic: The Social Factor* (Chico, CA: Scholars Press, 1983), 98 from Ibn Taymiyya's *Al-Fatawa al-Kubra* (Cairo: Dar al-Kutub al-Haditha, 1966), 1:484.
[31] See Makari, op. cit., 106-7.

unity throughout history, from its origins with the prophets to the final judgment. It is primarily a moral unity, rather than political unity or even absolute uniformity of practice. Like the judgments of fuqaha, different communities' practices can diverge to a certain extent, as long as the core of moral unity remains.[32] The ideal Muslim community he described is one whose members are mutually supportive in encouraging goodness and denouncing evil, and in issuing the invitation (*da`wa*) to follow the law of God. Participation in issuing this invitation, both in word and in deed, to join the community of God's witnesses on earth – that is, to live Islamic law – is the core of Islamic unity or solidarity. Provided this type of unity exists, differences in practice and judgment are not only acceptable, but inevitable.

Conclusion

What Westerners think of as the three branches of the government are split in classical Islamic theory between those who wield coercive power (the executive branch) and the legislative-judicial branch. The former has authority over matters of defense and is charged with managing the treasury according to the law as well as executing the laws and judgments of the legal scholars. But by far the greatest emphasis is given to the latter branch, particularly in its legislative capacity. For the identity of a community as Islamic or not lies not in the behavior of the leader but in whether or not Islamic law prevails.

This orientation is reflected in the classical designation of the Islamic world as *dar al-Islam*, or "abode of Islam," as opposed to the *dar al -`ahd*, "abode of covenant," *dar al-sulh*, "abode of truce," or *dar al-harb*, the "abode of war." Although these terms do not appear in the Qur'an, dar al-Islam became the most common designation of the Muslim community among the classical legal scholars.[33] Dar al-Islam refers specifically to those territories in which the law of Islam prevails. It does not mean territories whose leaders are Muslim. Dar al-`ahd and dar al-sulh are both regions whose leaders have agreed to pay the Muslim leaders a certain tax and to protect the rights of any Muslims and/or their allies who dwell there, but who otherwise

---

[32] See Henri Laoust's classic discussion in *Essai sur les doctrines sociales et politique de Taki-d-Din b. Taimiya* (Cairo: Institut Francais d'Archaeologie Orientale, 1939), 253ff.

[33] The usage is generally traced to hadith reports. See discussion by A. Abel, "Dar al-Islam," in *Encyclopedia of Islam*, new ed. (Leiden: E. J. Brill, 1963), 2:127.

maintain their autonomy, including their own legal systems. Dar al-harb is a region whose leaders have made no such agreement and where, therefore, Muslims and their allies, unprotected by law, are technically under threat.

In actual practice, most Muslims follow the law of the school prevailing in their region. Shafi`i law, for example, is dominant in Indonesia, while Hanbali law prevails in Saudi Arabia. But theoretically, as Ibn Taymiyya stressed, no one is forced to follow a particular school of thought. Each jurisprudent has not only the right but the responsibility to study as broadly as possible in all the schools before making a judgment on Islamic law, and individuals are technically free to follow the judgments of those they consider wisest and most just. This freedom within Islamic law is, in fact, the focus of contemporary discussions of democracy in Islam. I will leave further development of this topic to Professor Esposito, but I would like to point out here that there is certainly a basis in classical theories of Islamic government to support such a discussion. A claim could even be made for populism in Islamic political theory, since anyone can enter the ranks of the fuqaha' and thus participate in the dominant branch of Islamic government. Indeed, as Wael Hallaq argues, the science of Islamic jurisprudence was developed precisely to set out the procedures whereby anyone with proper training could participate in this branch of the government: "The primary objective of legal theory...was to lay down a coherent system of principles through which a qualified jurist could extract rulings for novel cases. From the third/ninth century onwards this was universally recognized by jurists to be the sacred purpose of *usul al-fiqh* [the roots of Islamic legislation]."[34] Populist or not, however, sacred legislation is considered a communal duty in Islam. That means that although not everyone need assume this responsibility, at least enough people have to undertake it to get the job done. And the job, as articulated by Ibn Taymiyya, is to establish a just society. Therefore, at least in classical Islamic theory, participation in the dominant legislative-judicial branch of government – the one designed to make sure the entire government is functioning according to the law of God – is religious activity.

---

[34] Wael B. Hallaq, "Was the Gate of Ijtihad Closed?" *International Journal of Middle Eastern Studies* 16 (1984): 5.

Glossary

Allah	God
bay`a	"oath of allegiance;" the component of Islamic government whereby the community agrees to abide by the authority of the executive leader chosen by community representatives
caliph	"successor" to Prophet Muhammad's political leadership of the Muslim community; chief executive of the Muslim community in classical Islamic political thought
fiqh	the study of Islamic law; specific codes of Islamic law devised by legal scholars
fuqaha'	Islamic legal scholars
hadith	traditional report of extra-Qur'anic words or deeds of Prophet Muhammad and/or his closest associates, accepted as having varying degrees of reliability
hijra	"emigration" from Mecca to Medina by the Muslim community in 622 C.E.; marks the beginning of the Islamic calendar
islam	"submission" to the will of God
kalam	"disputation;" the branch of Islamic thought that attempts to give rational explanations for revealed truths
nomocracy	government by a codified set of laws
Qur'an	Islamic sacred scripture; the revealed word of God
Rashidun	the first four successors (caliphs) of Prophet Muhammad's political leadership of the Muslim community (Abu Bakr, `Umar, `Uthman, and `Ali, reigning from 632-61 C.E.); considered by Sunni Muslims to have been of exemplary character and therefore "rightly guided"
shahada	the first "pillar" of Islam (essential component of Islamic practice): bearing witness that there is no god but The God (Allah) and Muhammad is the messenger of God
Shari`a	the unchanging will of God for humanity; used generically for the entire body of Islamic law

Shi`i   the smaller of the two major branches of the worldwide Muslim community (12-15 percent of the world's one billion Muslims)

shura   "consultation," a required component of Islamic government

Sunna   the normative example set by Prophet Muhammad as related in extra-Qur'anic traditional literature

Sunni   the largest branch of the worldwide Muslim community (over 85 percent of the world's one billion Muslims)

theocracy government by God/gods or those ruling on the basis of divine authority

theology   the rational study of God

16

True and False Perceptions
of the Islamic State

Nahla A. Al-Arian
University of South Florida

In her well-written paper Professor Sonn presents an introduction to the formation and development of Islamic political thought in the classical period of Islam. The presentation is unique and dynamic as it traverses the crucial developments in Islamic history that contributed to the establishment and evolution of the Islamic state. She argues correctly that the Islamic state is a state of laws and is dominated by legal opinions and authorities. Although unstated in her presentation, the rise of the role of legal scholars (representing different schools of thought) in the development of the state and politics is due to various factors.

First is the notion of exercising a great deal of freedom of thought within the boundaries of Shari`a, which has existed in Islam throughout its history. This process had generated great intellectual and legal ideas, debates, and arguments that resulted in the development of different and unique sciences such as Qur'anic, Hadith, Fiqh and its methodology, as well as the formation of different schools of legal opinions. Secondly, the rift between the rulers and the scholars, at the beginning of the Umayyad era in the second half of the first century A.D., allowed the scholars to develop their political capacity in the "checks-and-balances" role against the coercive power of the ruler or the state. In some instances they represented the loyal legislative power when the state (executive) was perceived as just and popular. In other cases they played the role of the opposition in order to curb the excesses of the state against the rights of the people. Sonn's observations and analogies in that regard are interesting and quite correct. Thirdly, the inference in her list of the duties of the caliph, or the political authority, is that his powers are restricted and his influence limited. This is an extremely important point as it characterizes the essential nature of the Islamic state, namely that of a limited government.

In other words, the perception of the Islamic state as either totalitarian, or theocratic, or both is false. It is neither supported by textual evidence (i.e., Qur'an and Sunna) nor by historical precedent. In fact, the majority of societal functions, such as education, agriculture, economic development, trade, social institutions, *zakat* (almsgiving) and *waqf* (charitable trust), are left to civil society, with very little interference from the state, although the legal scholars (*fuqaha'*) play a great role in establishing the legal framework for such functions. As Professor Sonn pointed out correctly, the gate of *ijtihad* was wide open to anyone to contribute in any field as long as one used appropriate tools, in exercising one's intellectual ijtihad. (This is very similar to the role that legal scholars such as lawyers and judges play in the legislative and executive branches in the secular government.)

Therefore, if one attempts to determine the nature of the Islamic state as compared with modern forms of governments, one will make the following observations. As stated previously, the Islamic state is not a totalitarian regime, which by definition may not have limited influence or powers. This is also evident, as Dr. Sonn also noted, in the fact that different legal schools have survived throughout the vast lands of the Islamic world for centuries along with hundreds of customs, languages, and other local traditions that did not contradict Islamic monotheistic principles. As also implied by Dr. Sonn, the Islamic state is not a theocracy since the inner workings of the state are very much left to human beings to develop and debate. Sonn included in the paper several references to the fact that all founders of the schools of thought expressed to their followers that they had no monopoly over the "truth" or the "correct opinion," but that they merely exercised their best judgment and it was up to the people to follow or exert their own efforts to search for other answers.

Although Professor Sonn implied that the Islamic state could be considered a sort of democratic regime, one would argue this idea with great caution. First, the modern definition of a democratic government is the rule of the people by themselves or through their representatives. In addition, there are other principles and values that are attributed to democratic regimes such as freedoms of expression, religion, and the press. One can easily find bases in Islam for many of these values, both in revelation and practice. The caution, however, is in the role of God in society. In a purely secular democratic system God is removed from public and social policy.

However, in Islam, the purpose of life is not only to establish justice on earth but also to please God and attain Heaven in the hereafter. These objectives are not only for of the individual but also for the society as a whole. Hence, the democratic process in the Islamic state has to be consistent with the Shari`a which, using Sonn's definition, is God's unchanging will for humanity as revealed in the Qur'an and practiced by the Prophet. Moreover, the practical codes of law developed by society (i.e., fiqh) are subject to change, revision, and deletion as long as they do not contradict the supreme law of the state (i.e., the Shar`ia). (For example, in the US the Congress shall pass no law that contradicts the Constitution. However, while there is a process to amend the Constitution, the Shar`ia cannot be amended by human beings).

Once one understands the role of Shar`ia in society, the question of the separation of religion and politics in Islam becomes moot. Dr. Sonn takes exception to this concept by arguing that Islam approves the existence of political as well as religious powers in the state side by side. The problem with this argument is equating politics with political power, and also with the use of the limited definition of religion in the West (i.e., body of beliefs and ethos). The word used in Islam is not religion but *din* (meaning a way of life). It would be unconscionable for the Islamic state to separate din from politics or Islamic principles and laws from public policy or society.

The Islamic state also offers unique rights and freedoms that are not even included in contemporary democratic systems. An example of this is the freedom of minority groups to practice their religious laws. Within the Muslim communities, this notion of pluralism is illustrated in the acceptance of different interpretations and applications of law to the same set of problems. This was also noted by Sonn when she mentioned that different regions of the Islamic world may follow different schools of fiqh. Thus, while the democratic system forces the will of the majority on the minority, the Islamic political system encourages plurality and allows individuals and communities to choose from a set of options as it is considered a religious duty to follow the legal opinion closest to the believer's mind.

Another example illustrating the difference between the Islamic and democratic systems is in the concept of morality. In Islam morality is tied to revelation, while in democracy it is tied to "community standards." Hence, in a democratic system, some communities may legalize prostitution, alcohol, or drugs while others may not. No community in an Islamic state would have the right to legalize an immoral act as defined by revelation.

The dynamism and flexibility of the Islamic legal system and by extension political, economic, and social systems are best illustrated through the development of *Usul al-Fiqh* (methodology of Islamic jurisprudence.) Although Sonn briefly mentions it in her presentation, the importance of this science may have been overlooked. First of all, jurists have deduced from the Shar`ia what is called the "objectives of Shar`ia or *maqasid*," namely: the preservation of religion, life, reason, honor and wealth. Legal opinions must support these objectives. All schools of fiqh agree that the first two sources of legislation are Qur'an and Sunna. However, they differ in the other sources of legislation. The determination of the other sources and their level of importance constitute the main differences among these schools (for example, *qiyas*, "consensus," *istislah, istihsan,* "common interests," etc.). This is what's called *Usul al-Fiqh* or the methodology of legislation. Discussion of these components of Islamic legal theory impacted the development of concepts of public and individual duties. Sonn's reference to the importance of the development of legal thought should be commended, although its relation to the subject of *Usul* was not fully explored.

Moreover, the Islamic legal framework allows for the further development of methodology (*usul*) at any time or place. This dynamism is the reason that Islam transcends time and space; it is flexible, and attuned to the future changes in societies. It is precisely this flexibility which proves that the temporal (adapting to people's changing needs) and the divine (God's unchanging will for mankind) are not in conflict but rather in harmony. Hence, the development of classical political thought and practice should be credited for the continuous evolution of *Usul al-Fiqh* in each of the schools of thought.

Finally, although Sonn's paper explained the political theories of two important legal scholars, it lacked the enumeration of the principles of the Islamic political system. Some of these principles include *shura* (consultation), justice, freedom, equality, the ability to impeach the caliph, and the determination of minority rights and duties. On the issue of impeachment of corrupt and/or unjust rulers, the criterion was the adherence of the ruler to the Shar`ia. The reform of government, it was argued by the majority of scholars, must be peaceful and from within. In other words, it is through a process of evolution and not revolution. The only exception would be if the executive branch defies or challenges the sovereignty of Shar'iah directly. Then it becomes the duty of the scholars and the people to remove the ruler, even by force if necessary. The relationship of the ruler to the ruled was based on a covenant. The ruler is to establish social justice based on the princips of Shar`ia and the practice of *shura* (consultation), and the people are to give their allegiance and obedience in return (*bay`a*). This might explain to a large extent the turmoil that exists today in many Muslim societies. The secular governments in the Muslim world, challenging the role and sovereignty of Shar`ia in society, lose their legitimacy. The contemporary state, furthermore, has grown to the point that it is affecting every aspect and function in society at the expense of the rights and freedoms of individuals and communities. The objectives of the law (*maqasid*) are no longer the basis of societal development. This is considered totally unacceptable by modern Islamic scholars and activists since it defies historical precedents in Islam, even during the most corrupt regimes. In their opinion the modern state has lost its legitimacy not only because of its abandonment of Shar`ia but also because of its unchecked power over its subjects and restriction of their freedom.

In conclusion, the Islamic state is neither totalitarian nor theocratic. Nor is it totally democratic in the modern sense. It is conservative in its insistence on government's limited role in societal functions and policy. It is liberal in the sense that it allows society, including minority groups, a great deal of freedom to organize and express themselves. It embodies many modern democratic principles within the bounds of Shar`ia. It further restricts the powers of the executive and gives legislative and judicial powers to the scholars and the people. It is dynamic and flexible since it can accommodate any modern or future reforms or changes which are not contradictory to the basic principles and objectives of Shar`ia.

17

Islam and the State in Modern Islamic Political Thought

John Esposito
Georgetown University

From the time of the Prophet Muhammad to today, Muslims have grappled with the relationship of Islam to state and society. For more than ten centuries, throughout the caliphate and sultanate periods, to varying degrees and in different ways, Islam provided the basis for political legitimacy and authority and informed the institutions of state and society: its notions of citizenship, law, family, taxation, education, defense and warfare.

Contemporary Muslim politics reveal the ongoing struggle to continue to define or redefine the nature of state and society.[1] While the roots of this process of identity and reaffirmation are often traced back to the example of the Prophet and his community/state in Medina, Islamic political thought has always been the product of sacred texts and contexts, the dynamic interaction of scripture and politics.

The contemporary debate has been more proximately influenced and informed by both socioeconomic and political conditions and the legacies of several waves of Islamic revival and reform. It is in fact the perception of failure that has triggered a reaffirmation and reassertion of Islam in state and society and thus produced new political interpretations and experiments. If Islam was to provide the identity and unity of the state,

---

[1] See, for example, John L. Esposito, *The Islamic Threat: Myth or Reality?* 2nd ed. (New York: Oxford University Press, 1995) or *Islam and Politics* 3rd ed. (Syracuse, NY: Syracuse University Press, 1993), and John O. Voll, *Islam: Continuity and Change in the Modern World,* 2nd ed. (Syracuse, NY: Syracuse University Press, 1995).

so, Islamic revivalists and reformers concluded, the panacea for failed states must be a return to Islam and its "proper or correct" implementation in state and society.

Twentieth-century (Sunni) Islamic political thought can be understood in terms of three periods of development: Islamic modernist, neofundamentalist, and postmodernist. They are not three distinct periods but in fact often overlap.

European Colonialism and the State

Modern Islamic political thought reflects the tensions and conflicts that have accompanied the establishment of modern states and societies in the Muslim world. It must be understood against the background of European imperialism and colonialism. By the nineteenth century, European states (in particular the British, French, and Dutch) had penetrated and increasingly dominated the Muslim world from North Africa to Southeast Asia. In the Islamic world, Western colonial rule precipitated a religious as well as a political crisis. For the first time since the birth of Islam in seventh-century Arabia, political and cultural sovereignty throughout the Muslim world was lost to non-Islamic powers.

Muslim subjugation by Christian Europe confirmed not only the decline of Muslim power but also the apparent loss of divine favor and guidance. The Islamic concept of history views success and power as integral to the Muslims' universal mission to spread the rule of God and as dependent upon their obedience to God's will or law, Shar`ia. Departure from the straight path of Islam meant loss of God's guidance and protection. Despite wars and invasions, from the origins of the Islamic community in the seventh century to the dawn of European colonialism, the Muslim community (*ummah*) found its political expression in Islamic empires and states ruled by caliphs and sultans. European colonial rule, unlike previous wars or invasions, terminated this long and glorious history of Muslim self-rule. Many asked: What had gone wrong in Islam? How could Muslims realize God's will in a state governed by non-Muslims and non-Muslim law? How were Muslims to respond to this challenge to Muslim political identity and rule?

A variety of responses emerged from Muslim reflection on the causes of decline and the solution or path to be followed. Secularists blamed an outmoded tradition. They advocated separation of religion and politics (church and state), and the establishment of modern nation states, modeled on Western political and socioeconomic institutions and practice. Conservative religious leaders attributed decline to divergence from Islam and excessive innovation (*bida*, "deviation from tradition"). Many advocated a total rejection of the West. Muslims, they argued, no longer lived under Islamic rule in an Islamic territory (*dar al-Islam*) and were thus in a land of warfare (*dar al-harb*). Among the possible courses were a holy war (*jihad*, "struggle") against the enemies of God, emigration (*hijra*) to an Islamically ruled land, or withdrawal and noncooperation. Islamic modernists blamed a blind acceptance and unquestioned following of tradition (*taqlid*) of the past; they proclaimed the need for Islamic reform. Islamic reformers stressed the flexibility and adaptability that had characterized the early development of Islamic state and society and pressed for internal reform through a reinterpretation (*ijtihad*) and selective adaptation (Islamization) of Western ideas and institutions. This early internal self-criticism and struggle to define Islam to make it relevant to contemporary society was the first stage in an ongoing process in which successive generations of Muslims have attempted to build twentieth-century religious, political, and social thought. It set the tone and informed the direction of modern Muslim political thought.

Islamic Modernism

Sayyid Jamal ad-din Al-Afghani (1838-97), the father of Muslim nationalism, was a major catalyst of Islamic modernism.[2] Afghani advocated Islamic reform and reemphasized the role of Islam in politics and society when many were ready to either reject or accept modernity wholesale. He traveled throughout the Muslim world to spread his message through an unceasing political activism. Afghani believed that Muslims could repel the West not by rejecting or ignoring the sources of Western strength but rather by reclaiming and reappropriating reason, science, and technology, which were part of Islamic history and civilization. Islam is more than just religion in the Western sense; it is, he contended, the root of civilization, the essence and basis for Muslim survival as individuals and as a community of believers (*ummah*). The strength and survival of the ummah were dependent upon the reassertion of Islamic identity and the reestablishment of Islamic sovereignty and solidarity. Afghani exhorted Muslims to realize that Islam was a dynamic, creative force capable of responding to the

---

[2] For a summary of Afghani's contribution, see Albert Hourani, *Arabic Thought in the Liberal Age* (London: Oxford University Press, 1970), chap. 5; Nikki R. Keddie, *Sayyid Jamal al-Din al Afghani: A Political Biography* (Berkeley: University of California Press, 1972); and idem, ed. and trans., *An Islamic Response to Imperialism: Political and Religious Writings of Sayyid Jamal al-Din Afghani* (Berkeley: University of California Press, 1968).

demands of modernity. For Afghani, Islam was the religion of reason and science. Muslims must reinterpret Islam, making it a relevant force in their lives intellectually and politically. In this way, Islam would serve as the source of Islamic renewal through which colonial rule could be repulsed and independence and the establishment of Muslim nations achieved. Once Islam was revitalized, it would mobilize Muslims, uniting them in providing the means to regain their lost glory and take their rightful place in the modern world. However, Afghani did not resolve the question of the relationship of modern nation-states to the traditional notion of an Islamic ummah, that is, a transnational community of believers. Rather, he appealed to both Muslim nationalism and pan-Islam.

Muhammad Abduh(d. 1905), a prominent religious scholar and protégé of al-Afghani, provided the Islamic rationale for reform.[3] Abduh emphasized the centrality of the ummah. Political unity and social justice were the source of its strength, disunity the cause of weakness. The ummah, he said, rather than any religious authority or theocracy, is the source of the ruler's authority. The ruler (caliph or sultan) is charged with assuring the welfare of the community and the rule of the Shar`ia, Islamic law. As long as he is faithful to God's way, the ummah owes the ruler obedience. However, should he become a despot, the ummah can remove him in the public interest through consultation (*shura*).[4]

Rejecting the unquestioned following (*taqlid*) of tradition or past authority as the reason for Muslim weakness and decline, Abduh advocated a reformulation of Islam. Unless a new path was forged through reinterpretation (*ijtihad*) and reform, Islam and Islamic culture would continue in a state of stagnation and decay. Abduh argued that the process of reinterpretation was consonant with the nature of Islam. He distinguished between Islam's inner core, composed of unchanging truths and values to the needs of a particular age. Thus he stated that although those regulations of Islamic law (Shar`ia) that concerned prayer and worship (*ibadat*) were immutable, the vast majority of Islamic laws were concerned with social relations (*muamalat*), that is, international, penal, commercial, and family laws, and these were open to change. Abduh believed that as historical and social conditions warranted, the core of Islamic principles should be reapplied to new realities and, where necessary, the old layers of tradition discarded. This was important since the crisis of modern Islam was precipitated by Muslim failure to

---

[3] Hourani, *Arabic Thought*, chap. 6; and Muhammad Abduh, *The Theology of Unity*, trans. I. Musaad and Kenneth Cragg (London: George Allen and Unwin, 1966).
[4] Yvonne Y. Haddad and Muhammad Abduh, *Pioneers of Islamic Revival*, ed. Ali Rahnema (London: Zed Books, 1994), 54.

uphold this distinction between the immutable and mutable, the necessary and contingent.

Muhammad Iqbal in India (1875-1938) and Taha Husayn and Ali Abd al-Raziq in Egypt (1886-1966) represent the next stage in modernist reform in which nationalist movements grew and a more secular orientation emerged. They exemplify the dual winds of change, Islamic modernist/Muslim nationalist and secular nationalist.

Iqbal combined a traditional upbringing with an intimate knowledge of the West. He studied in England and Germany where he earned a doctorate (Munich) in philosophy and a law degree (London). Iqbal combined what he thought to be the best of the East and the West, his Islamic heritage with Western philosophy (Hegel, Bergson, Fichte, and Nietzsche), to produce his own synthesis and reinterpretation of Islam.

Like Afghani, Iqbal compared the need for an Islamic reformation to that which was previously undergone by Christianity: "We are today passing through a period similar to that of the Protestant Reformation in Europe and the lesson which the rise and outcome of Luther's movement teaches should not be lost on us."[5]

Though an admirer of the accomplishments of the West, its dynamic spirit, intellectual tradition, and technology, he denounced the excesses of colonialism and imperialism, the exploitation of capitalism, the atheism of Marxism, and the moral bankruptcy of secularism. Iqbal argued that contrary to the Western caricature of Islam as a "religion of holy war," Islam was a religion of peace: "All forms of political and social disturbance are condemned...the ideal of Islam is to secure social peace at any price."[6] Iqbal's goal was to resuscitate the Muslim community so that it could reclaim its political independence and rightful place in history. Iqbal attempted to develop alternative Islamic models for modern Muslim societies. Drawing on Islamic traditions, he sought to "rediscover" Islamic principles and values that would provide the basis for Islamic versions of Western concepts and institutions such as democracy and parliamentary government.

Although Iqbal believed that nationalism was antithetical to the Islamic ideal of a transnational community, pan-Islam, he nevertheless accepted its practical necessity and utility. Muslims must gain independence and rebuild their local and regional communities. Iqbal was an early voice for both independence from Britain and Muslim nationalism in the subcontinent. Originally an Indian nationalist, Iqbal,

[5] Muhammad Iqbal, *The Reconstruction of Religious Thought in Islam* (Lahore: Muhammad Ashraf, 1968), 163.
[6] Muhammad Iqbal, "Islam as a Social and Political Ideal," in S. A. Vahid, ed., *Thoughts and Reflections of Iqbal* (Lahore, 1964), 35.

concerned for the identity and welfare of a Muslim minority in a Hindu-dominated state, turned from the dream of a united India to join the Muslim League and call for a separate Muslim state, governed by Islamic law.

In contrast to Iqbal and his Islamic reformism, Taha Husayn, a former student of Muhammad Abduh, demonstrates the secular European drift of a new generation of Egyptian youths. Although blind from an early age, he was educated at Cairo's two premier institutions of higher learning, al-Azhar University, the famed Islamic center of learning, and the Egyptian (Cairo) University, the new modern national university. This was followed by four years (1915-19) of study in France where he earned a doctorate from the Sorbonne. Husayn became an internationally known writer and educator, and served as Egypt's Minister of Education (1950-52).

Taha Husayn represents that group of Muhammad Abduh's disciples who became leaders in politics and intellectual life but believed that the modern needs of society would best be served by the separation of religion and politics. Like many of his generation, who were not critics of the West but its unabashed admirers, Taha Husayn asserted that secularism had long been part of Egypt's tradition: "From earliest times Muslims have been well aware of the now universally acknowledged principle that a political system and a religion are different things, that a constitution and a state rest, above everything else, on practical foundations."[7] Perhaps no book represents more the cultural crossroads that Muslims faced in the early twentieth century and the Western orientation of many emerging Muslim elites than Husayn's *The Future of Culture of Europe*. It embodies the rationale of those who concluded that future strength was best achieved not by a return to an Islamic past or the path of Islamic modernism but rather by an aggressive pursuit of Western-oriented liberal, secular reform. Although he was careful to speak of a selective borrowing, in fact the enormous attraction and pull of the West as a model for success was obvious both in his discourse and the degree of reliance on Western models of development.

Ali Abd al-Raziq took the Western, liberal, secular tendency to its logical conclusion. A disciple of Abduh, he was educated as a religious scholar at al-Azhar University, a major center of Islamic learning, and became a judge in the Shar`ia court. Abd al-Raziq wrote *Islam and the Principles of Government* in response to the caliphate crisis after World War I. Although the caliphate had ceased to exist with the fall of the Abbasid dynasty (Baghdad) in 1258, it remained a powerful symbol which Ottoman sultans had appropriated. With Allied occupation of

---

[7] Ibid., 74.

Constantinople, many Muslims feared that Christian Europe threatened the future of the Ottoman empire and its caliph. Rashid Rida, Abduh's primary disciple, wrote *The Caliphate*, calling for the restoration of the caliphate. The issue came to a head in 1924 when the newly established Turkish nation abolished the caliphate. Abd al-Raziq's denial that Islam required the fusion of religion and political power, his repudiation of this traditional religio-political doctrine, became a lightning rod for orthodoxy. Ali Abd al-Raziq's position, like liberal secularism, was seen as emulating the West, denying Islam's comprehensive worldview, undermining traditional Islamic beliefs and institutions, contributing to the disunity and weakness of the Islamic community.

He was condemned by a council of al-Azhar religious scholars (*ulama*) and lost his job. The affair epitomized the issue of secularism and the relationship of Islam to the state, an issue that has continued to the present.

Neorevivalism: The Muslim Brotherhood and the Jamaat-i-Islami

Islamic reform and Muslim responses to European colonialism and the West took a significant ideological turn in the 1930s and 1940s with the creation of two modern Islamic organizations, the Muslim Brotherhood of Egypt and the Jamaat-i-Islami (Islamic Society) in the Indian subcontinent. Both embodied a growing ambivalence toward the penetration of Western culture, the threat of secular nationalism, and the continued political presence of Western imperialism.[8]

The development of these Islamic movements occurred within the context of the struggle for national liberation from European colonial rule and the emergence of modern Muslim nation-states. Three paths were followed: Turkey was created as secular state; Saudi Arabia was a self-proclaimed Islamic state; the majority of Muslim states, though retaining some Islamic constitutional provisions, pursued a more secular path, borrowing heavily from the West for political, economic, and social institutions. Their failure to resolve in a coherent, systematic manner the issue of their Islamic identity contributed to growth of Islamic movements and would reassert itself in the 1970s and 1980s with the contemporary resurgence of Islam.

Both the Brotherhood and the Jamaat emphasized Islam's ideological self-sufficiency, were less accommodationist, and far more critical of the West. Whereas Islamic modernism had sought to learn from and emulate the success of the West, the Muslim Brotherhood and the Jamaat emphasized the failure of both the West (capitalism) and the East

---

[8] Richard P. Mitchell, *The Society of the Muslim Brothers* (London: Oxford University Press, 1969), 229.

(Marxism) as models for development in the Muslim world. They denounced the Westernization and secularization of Muslim societies, the divisiveness of nationalism and the excesses of capitalism, as well as the materialism and godlessness of Marxism. Muslims were told to remember that they possessed a third way or alternative to foreign models and systems – Islam. Thus, the true path for Muslims was the creation of an Islamic state, implementation of Islamic law, and the re-Islamization of society.

The significance of the Muslim Brotherhood and the Jamaat-i-Islami extended far beyond their national homelands and in time took on transnational significance. The Brotherhood inspired the establishment of similar organizations in the Sudan, Syria, Jordan, the Gulf, and Africa. The Jamaat developed sister organizations in India, Bangladesh, Afghanistan, Kashmir. The writings of the Brotherhood's Hassan al-Banna and Sayyid Qutb and Mawlana Mawdudi of the Jamaat-i-Islami would in time become widely translated and disseminated throughout much of the Islamic world. Their vision of Islam as an alternative ideology for state and society as well as the example of their organizations and activities provided a model for future generations of Muslims. As such they constituted for many a link between their traditional religious heritage and the realities of modern life.

Hassan al-Banna (1906-49), a school teacher, established the Muslim Brotherhood (Ikhwan al-Muslimin) in Egypt in 1928 and Mawlana Abul Ala Mawdudi (1903-79), a journalist, organized the Jamaat-i-Islami (Islamic Society) in India in 1941.[9] Both movements arose and initially grew in the 1930s and 1940s at a time when their communities were in crisis. Both blamed European imperialism and a Westernized Muslim leadership for much of the problem. Each had in his early years been an anticolonial nationalist who turned to religious revivalism to restore the Muslim community at home and universally. These founders/ideologues of their organizations drew on the example and concerns of both their eighteenth-century Islamic revivalist movements like the Wahhabi of Saudi Arabia and nineteenth/twentieth-century Islamic modernist predecessors for their critique of Muslim society, revivalist/reformist worldview, emphasis on organization, and sociopolitical activism. They did not simply retreat to the past but instead provided Islamic responses, ideological and organizational, to modern society.[10] Hassan al-Banna and Mawdudi sought to produce a new synthesis which began with Islamic sources and either found

---

[9] Richard Mitchell, *The Society of Muslim Brothers* and Charles J. Adams, "Mawdudi and the Islamic State," John L. Esposito, ed. in *Voices...*, chap. 5.
[10] Esposito, *Islam and Politics*, 130-50.

Islamic equivalents or Islamic sources for notions of government accountability, legal change, popular participation, and educational reform.

Though anti-Westernization, they were not antimodernization. Both Hasan al-Banna and Mawlana Mawdudi engaged in modern organization and institution building, provided educational and social welfare services, used modern technology and mass communications to spread their message and to mobilize popular support. Their message itself, though rooted in Islamic revelation and sources, was clearly written for a twentieth-century audience. It addressed the problems of modernity, analyzing the relationship of Islam to nationalism, democracy, capitalism, Marxism, modern banking, education and law, women and work, Zionism, international relations.

At the heart of the message of the Brotherhood and the Jamaat was the conviction that Islam provided a divinely revealed and prescribed third alternative to Western capitalism (secularism and materialism) and Soviet Marxism (socialism and atheism) for modern Muslim societies. Among the primary principles of al-Banna and Mawdudi's ideological worldview were: (1) Islam constitutes a total, all-embracing ideology for individual and corporate life, for state and society; (2) the Qur'an, God's revelation, and the example (Sunna) of the Prophet Muhammad are the foundations of Muslim life; (3) Islamic law (the Shar'ia, the "path" of God), based upon the Qur'an and the Prophet's model behavior, is the sacred blueprint for Muslim life; (4) faithfulness to the Muslim's vocation to reestablish God's sovereignty or rule through implementation of God's law will result in success, power, and wealth of the Islamic community (*ummah*) in this life as well as eternal reward in the next life; (5) thus, the weakness and subservience of Muslim societies must be due to the faithlessness of Muslims who have strayed from God's divinely revealed path and instead followed the secular, materialistic ideologies and values of the West or of the East – capitalism or Marxism; (6) restoration of Muslim pride, power, and rule (the past glory of Islamic empires and civilization) requires a return to Islam, the reimplementation of God's law and guidance for state and society; (7) science and technology must be harnessed and used within an Islamically oriented and guided context in order to avoid the Westernization and secularization of Muslim society.

Mawlana Mawdudi provided a broad treatment of the nature of the ideal political order in Islam, one which influenced Islamic activists from North Africa to Southeast Asia. For this reason, we shall review major aspects of his comprehensive vision.

For Mawdudi, the foundational principle of Islamic state and society is the doctrine of the unity (*tawhid*) and universal sovereignty of God.

"The belief in the Unity and the sovereignty of Allah is the foundation of the social and moral system propounded by the Prophets."[11] As the creator, sustainer, and ruler of the universe is one, so too is God's law which governs all creation. All of reality – all areas of life – comes from God and are subject to his sovereign law, Shar`ia: "The Shariah is a complete scheme of life and an all embracing social order."[12]

Thus, the comprehensiveness of the Islamic way of life is rooted in the unity and totality of God's law revealed in the Qur'an and the example (Sunna) of the Prophet. It is this organic relationship between religion, politics, and society which distinguishes Islam and the Islamic community from the West. Separation of religion from the state for Mawdudi represents the inherent fallacy of Western secularism where the withdrawal of divine guidance has been the basis for its moral decline and its ultimate downfall. Western culture and all who do not follow Islam, God's revealed straight path, exist as did pre-Islamic society in a state of ignorance and darkness.

Mawdudi emphasized that Muslims' vocation must be to live within the limits and according to the precepts of the Shar`ia in its entirety. A Shar`ia-governed community constitutes an Islamic state. While Muslims such as the great Islamic jurists of the law schools may discern and apply God's law, God alone is the supreme lawgiver, the source of all authority and law. Thus, there can be no human lawgiver. However, despite an interdict on human legislation, Mawdudi does acknowledge the role of the state to not only enforce but also create laws in areas not covered by the Shar`ia. The state can do this by virtue of its role as God's agent or vicegerent. For Mawdudi the Qur'anic teaching regarding man's vicegerency (Qur'an 24:55) encompasses both the individual and communal Muslim mission on earth. All Muslims are God's vicegerents or representatives (caliphs). Thus, an Islamic state may quite accurately be called a "caliphate."

The ruler (caliph, imam, amir) is the one whom the community has delegated as their leader. The head of state or amir receives his authority from God and exercises his power on behalf of the people. As with the rightly guided caliphs, he may be elected or selected by the people, directly or indirectly, through their representatives. He is the representative of both God and his fellow Muslim: "answerable to God

---

[11] Abul Ala Mawdudi, "Political Theory of Islam," in *The Islamic Law and Constitution*, 6th ed., ed. by Khurshid Ahmad (Lahore: Islamic Publications, 1977), 130.
[12] Abul Ala Mawdudi, "The Islamic Law," in *Islamic Law* 50.

on the one hand and on the other to his fellow caliphs who have delegated their authority to him."[13]

The ruler oversees the conduct of state: the executive, legislative, and judiciary. His power would include that of both the president and prime minister of a modern state. Yet, because the ruler is bound to observe and enforce God's law, he does not have an absolute power and authority. He is neither monarch nor dictator. According to Mawdudi, the legal qualifications for head of state are that he must be Muslim, male, adult, sane, and a citizen of the Islamic state. More importantly, he should be the best man, that is, the most committed and virtuous Muslim. The idealism of Mawdudi's approach is further reflected in his assertion that this "best man" can neither seek office nor undertake a political campaign. Rather, suitable candidates will be identified by some kind of election or selection committee. The utopianism of Mawdudi's thought is strikingly evident in his assertions that in the time of the early caliphs there was no dissension, only complete harmony: "The Ministers and the Head of State were all along working in complete cooperation and harmony and the question of anybody resigning in protest never arose at all."[14]

Mawdudi's Islamic idealism also gave rise to an "Islamic totalitarianism." Given the comprehensive nature of the Islamic state's divinely revealed law, "no one can regard any field of his affairs as personal or private."[15] Is this not totalitarianism? Mawdudi answered with a qualified yes. The totalitarianism of an Islamic state is a good form of totalitarianism since it requires and enforces God's precepts. Unfortunately, Mawdudi did not indicate how Muslims can safeguard against rulers who falsely use the banner of Islam to legitimate their rule, impose their will, and stifle dissent.

The Islamic state was viewed by Mawdudi as the "very antithesis of secular Western democracy."[16] Western democracy is based upon popular sovereignty, with the people or nation enjoying absolute powers of legislation and thus able to make laws which are even contrary to religion and morality. For this reason, "Islam has no trace of Western democracy...[it] repudiates the philosophy of popular sovereignty and rears its polity on the foundations of the sovereignty of God and the vicegerency (Khilafah) of man" (160).

Mawdudi concluded that the Islamic system might best be called a theo-democracy. He used this term to distinguish the Islamic state as the

---

[13] Adams, "Mawdudi and the Islamic State," in *Islamic Law* 116.
[14] Abul Ala Mawdudi, "First Principles of the Islamic State," in *Islamic Law*, 23.
[15] Ibid.
[16] Mawdudi, "Political Theory of Islam," 159; subsequent citations noted in text.

"kingdom of God" from the Western meaning of theocracy which also implies rule by a religious class or clergy. Here Mawdudi rejected any notion of ulama governance of the state. Furthermore, as a theo-democracy, while affirming the political role of all Muslims, the state was protected from what Muwdudi called the "tyranny of the masses" permitted by Western democracy. Since Islamic democracy must function within the limits of God, no law that is contrary to the Shar`ia may be passed even though it may enjoy mass support. Mawdudi was skeptical about the ability of most people to transcend their narrow self-interest: "The great mass of the common people are incapable of perceiving their own true interests"(134). He cites the repeal of the Prohibition Act in America as an example. Despite alcohol's proven danger to physical and mental health, those who voted for Prohibition subsequently revolted against it and so, Mawdudi asserted, the law was finally repealed by the very people who had voted for it (137). Mawdudi believed that this problem could not occur in an Islamic state which is governed by religious norms, not societal whims. Popular vicegerency in an Islamic state is reflected especially in the doctrine of mutual consultation (*shura*). Since all sane adult Muslims, male and female, are vicegerents (agents of God), it is they who delegate their authority to the ruler (caliph, imam, amir) and whose opinion must also be sought in the conduct of state. This may be done, directly or indirectly, through an elected representative body or assembly. Thus, the head of an Islamic state is not free to do as he likes. According to Mawdudi the consultative assembly or parliament should consist of adult, Muslim males who are good Muslims and sufficiently Islamically trained to interpret and apply the Shar`ia as well as to draft laws which are not contrary to the Qur'an and Sunna of the Prophet. The functions of the parliament are fourfold: (1) to enact legislation which embodies the explicit directives of God and Muhammad as well as regulations which will assure their proper enforcement; (2) where differing interpretations of the Qur'an and Sunna exist, to decide which interpretation is to be enacted; (3) when no explicit directives exist, to deduce rules from the Qur'an and Sunna or where previously enacted laws are found in the legal manuals, to adopt one of them (4) finally, where "even basic guidance is not available," to formulate laws provided such legislation is not contrary to the letter and spirit of the Shar`ia.[17]

Given the ideological nature of the state and the functions of the parliament in an Islamic state, Mawdudi believed the vast majority of its members should be Muslim. While non-Muslims may elect their own representatives, this should be done through a system of separate

---

[17] Mawdudi, "First Principles of the Islamic State," 214.

electorates so that non-Muslims would be excluded from the selection of Muslim representatives. Mawdudi suggested another possible alternative for both non-Muslims and Muslim women, who were not eligible for election. Each might have their own consultative assembly; each could then advise the ruler and the parliament on those issues which affected their lives and welfare. Mawdudi's notion of citizenship in an Islamic state and the rights of non-Muslims followed rigorously from early Islamic practice and classical Islamic political theory. There are two categories of citizenship in a modern Islamic state: Muslim and non-Muslim. Non-Muslims are "protected people" (*dhimmi*). In return for payment of the poll tax, they enjoy protection and have certain rights and duties. They may worship but not proselytize. In religious matters they are governed by their religious leaders. However, in all other areas of life, Islamic law prevails since it is the "Law which commands the approval of the majority alone [which] has the right to become the Law of the Land."[18]

Since an Islamic state is an ideological state, only those who accept that ideology should run the state. Therefore, non-Muslims would be barred both from key administrative positions as well as policy-making posts. Moreover, they should not serve in a standing army since, as believers, they could not be expected to defend Islam. For Mawdudi herein lies the difference between a national state and an Islamic state. For the former, citizenship is based upon belonging to a nation, race, ethnic group. For the latter, citizenship is determined by ideology (belief or nonbelief). Therefore, citizenship is not equal and the same for all. Rather, citizens are classified as Muslim or non-Muslim and, as a result, differ in their rights and duties. Preservation of an Islamic state may necessitate and even require a holy war. Mawdudi believed that jihad is an obligation for the faithful Muslim citizen. Mawdudi began with the broad definition of jihad as the duty of all Muslims to strive or struggle to actualize God's will. "Those who believe fight in the cause of God, and those who disbelieve fight in the cause of force" (Qur'an 4:76). He viewed two kinds of warfare as permissible: defensive jihad and corrective jihad. These become necessary when Islamic belief and practice are threatened by an external enemy, by disruptive internal forces, or by non-Muslim rulers in a non-Islamic state. While many modern Muslims prefer to simply emphasize the meaning of jihad as an internal struggle to lead a virtuous Muslim life, Mawdudi did not shrink from affirming the continuing division of the world into Islamic and non-Islamic territory and the right, indeed duty, of a good Muslim to wage war when Islam and the Islamic way of life were threatened.

---

[18] Mawdudi, "The Islamic Law," 66.

Radical Islam: Sayyid Qutb

Just as the ideological worldviews of Hassan al-Banna and Mawlana Mawdudi were shaped by their faith and social context, so too the ideology of Islamic revivalism in Egypt became more militant and combative in the late 1950s and 1960s as a result of the Muslim Brotherhood's confrontation with the Egyptian state. One man stands out as the architect of radical Islam, Sayyid Qutb. By the 1960s, Sayyid Qutb, increasingly radicalized by Nasser's suppression of the Brotherhood, transformed the ideological beliefs of Hassan al-Banna and Mawlana Mawdudi into a rejectionist revolutionary call to arms. Like Hasan al-Banna, Sayyid Qutb would come to be remembered as the martyr of the Islamic revival.

Sayyid Qutb (1906-66) studied at the Dar al-Ulum, a modern college established to train teachers in modern subjects. It was here that he became familiar with Western literature and like many young intellectuals of the time, he grew up to be an admirer of the West.

During the 1950s Qutb emerged as a major voice of the Muslim Brotherhood and its most influential ideologue. His commitment, intelligence, militancy, and literary style made him especially effective within the context of a growing confrontation between a repressive regime and the Brotherhood. Government harassment of the Brotherhood and Qutb's imprisonment and torture in 1954 for alleged involvement in an attempt to assassinate Nasser only increased his radicalization and confrontational worldview. During ten years of imprisonment in the equivalent of a concentration camp, he wrote prolifically, completing *In the Shade of the Quran,* a Qur'anic commentary, as well as his most influential Islamic ideological tract, *Signposts* or *Milestones (Maalim fil Tariq).* His thought now reflected a new revolutionary vision born of his extended imprisonment and torture. He carried the ideas of Hasan al-Banna and especially Mawlana Mawdudi to their literalist, radical conclusions.

For Qutb, Islamic movements existed in a world of repressive, anti-Islamic governments and societies. Society was divided into two camps, the party of God and the party of Satan, those committed to the rule of God and those opposed. There was no middle ground. Strongly influenced by Mawdudi, Qutb emphasized the development of a vanguard, a group *(jamaa)* of true Muslims within the broader corrupted and faithless society. The Islamic movement *(haraka)* was a righteous minority adrift in a sea of ignorance and unbelief *(jahiliyya).* He dismissed Muslim governments and societies as un-Islamic *(jahili);* in effect, atheist or pagan states and societies. Thus, the classical historical designation of pre-Islamic Arabia as a society of ignorance *(jahiliyya)* was transformed to condemn the state of modern societies as un-Islamic or anti-Islamic. For Qutb, the cause was the displacement of Islam's God-centered universe by a human-centered world.

Qutb maintained that the creation of an Islamic system of government was a divine commandment, and therefore not just an alternative but an imperative.[19] Given the political realities of authoritarian, un-Islamic regimes, Qutb concluded that jihad, rather than futile attempts to bring about change from within the existing repressive Muslim political systems, was the only way to implement a new Islamic order. Jihad as armed struggle in the defense of Islam against injustice became the prescribed path for all true believers in the current crisis. Islam stood on the brink of disaster, threatened by repressive anti-Islamic governments and the neocolonialism of the West and the East. Those Muslims who refused to participate or waivered were to be counted among the enemies of God. Qutb's formulation became the starting point for many radical groups.[20] The two options, evolution – a process which emphasizes revolutionary change from below – vs. revolution – violent overthrow of established (un-Islamic) systems of government – have remained the twin paths or options of contemporary Islamic movements.

For Qutb, as for al-Banna and Mawdudi, the West is a historic and pervasive enemy of Islam and Muslim societies, both a political and a religio-cultural threat. Its clear and present danger comes not only from its political, military, and economic power but also from its hold on Muslim elites who govern and guide by alien standards and values which threaten the identity and soul of their societies. However, Qutb went beyond his predecessors when he declared Muslim elites and governments atheists against whom all true believers should wage holy war.

In 1965 the Muslim Brotherhood was massively and ruthlessly suppressed by the government, blamed for an attempt on Nasser's life. Qutb and several other leaders were arrested and executed.

Postmodern or Contemporary Islam and the State

Political events in the Muslim world have (in a dramatic way) drawn attention to the political and social implications of Islam. The

---

[19] Yvonne Y. Haddad, "Sayyid Qutb: Ideologue of Islamic Revival," 77 ff.

[20] Gilles Kepel, *Muslim Extremism in Egypt: The Prophet and the Pharoah,* Emmanuel Sivan, *Radical Islam: Medieval Theology and Modern Politics* (New Haven: Yale University Press, 1985), and Johannes Jansen, *The Neglected Duty: The Creed of Sadat's Assassins and Islamic Resurgence in the Middle East* (New York: Macmillan, 1986).

contemporary resurgence of Islam in Muslim politics has challenged the accepted norms of political development and the predictions of many analysts. Religion has reemerged across the Muslim world as a major political force. Islamic ideology, symbols, slogans, and actors have become prominent fixtures. Governments and opposition groups have appealed to Islam for legitimacy and to mobilize popular support. New Islamic republics have been declared in Iran and Sudan; Islamic laws, dress, taxes, and punishment have been called for and/or introduced in many other Muslim countries. Thus Islamic politics, economics, law, and education are hotly contested issues.

Amidst the diversity of Islamic revivalism there are common sociopolitical concerns and themes rooted in a general consensus that Muslims have failed to produce a viably authentic synthesis that is both modern and true to their own history and values. Although there are distinctive differences among Islamic revivalists, as shall be seen below, because they share both a common Islamic heritage and a confrontation with the West, common themes in Islamic sociopolitical thought may be identified as (1) the failure of the West; the inappropriateness of its transplanted, imported models of political, social, and economic development; and the need to throw off Western political and cultural domination that is characterized by secularism, materialism, and spiritual bankruptcy; (2) the need to "return to Islam" to restore a lost identity and moral character; (3) an emphasis on the unity and totality of Islam rooted in the doctrine of *tawhid* (unity of God); that is, religion is integral to politics and society; and Islam encompasses faith and government (*din wa dawla*); and (4) a call for the reintroduction of Shar`ia law as the sine qua non for establishing a more Islamic state and society.

In recent years, many Islamic movements have moved toward a populist, participatory, pluralistic political stance, championing democratization, human rights, and economic reform. While many were critical of "democracy" in the past, they claim that this was a response to the secularism of the modern state as well as the autocratic nature and policies of Muslim regimes. To varying degrees, Islamic movements have emphasized change not through force and violence (many have come to view political violence as counterproductive) but through the political and social transformation of society. They speak of the need to prepare people for an Islamic order rather than to impose it. They seek recognition of political rights and participation in the electoral process.

Islam and Democracy

The democratization movement in the Muslim world and the participation (and successes) of Islamic movements in electoral politics in recent years raise the question of the compatibility of Islam and democracy.[21]

Some Muslims have spoken out against Western-style democracy and a parliamentary system of government. Their negative reaction has often been part of the general rejection of European colonial influence, a defense of Islam against further dependence on the West rather than a wholesale rejection of democracy. In recent decades, many Muslims have accepted the notion of democracy but differed as to its precise meaning. The Islamization of democracy has been cast within the framework of the unity and sovereignty of God (*tawhid*) and the role of Muslims as the vicegerent (khilafa, caliph) or agent of God on earth. Thus, the traditional concept of religio-political leadership has been transformed to affirm and legitimate popular participation in the selection and removal of rulers, political responsibility and equality. Within this framework, a modern reinterpretation of traditional Islamic concepts of political deliberation or consultation (*shura*), community consensus (*ijma*), and personal interpretation (*ijtihad*) or reinterpretation of Islam has occurred to support notions of parliamentary democracy, representative elections, as well as social and religious reform.

While radical revolutionaries reject any form of parliamentary democracy as Westernizing and un-Islamic, many Islamic activists have "Islamized" (asserted an Islamic rationale for) parliamentary democracy and appealed to democracy in their opposition to incumbent regimes. Islamic organizations such as the Muslim Brotherhoods in Egypt, the Sudan, and Jordan, the Jamaat-i-Islami in Pakistan, Kashmir, India, and Bangladesh, as well as Algeria's Islamic Salvation Front, Tunisia's Renaissance party, Kuwait's Jamiyyat al-Islah (Reform Society), Malaysia's ABIM and PAS, among others, have advocated the principle of democratic elections and, where permitted, participated in parliamentary elections.

There are differences between Western notions of democracy and Islamic traditions. Increased emphasis on political liberalization, electoral politics, and democratization does not necessarily imply uncritical acceptance of Western forms of democracy. In recent years, it has become more common to argue that Islam possesses or can generate its own distinctive forms of democracy or participatory forms of government. In contrast to Western democracy's unfettered popular sovereignty, Islamic democracy is a limited form of popular sovereignty, restricted or directed by God's law. Thus, both divine and popular

---

[21] For an analysis of this issue, see John L. Esposito and John O. Voll, *Islam and Democracy* (New York: Oxford University Press, 1996) and Esposito and James P. Piscatori, "Democratization and Islam," *The Middle East Journal*, 427-40.

sovereignty are affirmed in a delicate balance capable of producing multiple forms and configurations.

Democracy has become an integral part of modern Islamic political thought and practice. It has become accepted in many Muslim countries as a litmus test by which both the openness of governments and the relevance of Islamic groups are certified. It is a powerful symbol of legitimacy, legitimizing and delegitimizing precisely because it is seen to be a universal good. However, questions as to the specific nature and degree of popular participation remain unanswered. The extent to which practice will follow this evolution in thought and what particular form democratization might take in diverse Muslim political cultures remain difficult to predict. In the new Muslim world order, Muslim political traditions and institutions, like social conditions and class structures, continue to evolve and are critical to the future of democracy in the Middle East.

A major issue facing Islamic movements is their ability, if in power, to tolerate diversity. Pluralism, the status of minorities in Muslim majority areas, and freedom of speech remain serious issues. The record of Islamic experiments in Pakistan, Iran, and the Sudan raises serious questions about the rights of women and minorities under Islamically oriented governments. The extent to which the growth of Islamic revivalism has been accompanied in some countries by attempts to restrict women's rights, to separate women and men in public, to enforce veiling, and to restrict women's public roles in society strikes fear in some segments of Muslim society and challenges the credibility of those who call for Islamization of state and society. The record of discrimination against the Bahai in Iran and the Ahmadi in Pakistan as "deviant" groups (heretical offshoots of Islam), against Christians in Sudan and Arab Jews in some countries as well as increased communal sectarian conflict between Muslims and Christians in Egypt and Nigeria pose similar questions of religious pluralism and tolerance.

Despite democratic tendencies in the Muslim world, multiple and conflicting attitudes toward democracy continue to exist and leave the future in question. Only time will tell whether the espousal of democracy by many contemporary Islamic movements and their participation in the electoral process are simply a means to power or a truly embraced and internalized end/goal, a transformation of tradition which is the product of a process of religious reinterpretation informed by both faith and experience.

The reassertion of Islam in politics and society and the growing chorus of voices calling for greater political participation pose new questions of leadership and orientation: Whose Islam? and What Islam? If governments and societies are to become more Islamically oriented, who is to oversee this process: unelected rulers, kings, military, the traditional religious leadership (the ulama), parliaments?

Similarly, attempts to Islamize society raise the question of What Islam? Is the process to be one of restoration, wholesale reimplementation of classical Islamic law, an interpretation and application of Islam developed in the early Islamic centuries? Or is to be a reformation, a reformulation of Islam and the development of new models or a new ideal for state and society based upon a reinterpretation of scripture and past practice? And with this question a subsidiary concern arises, who are qualified to perform this task of reinterpretation? Is it to be the traditional religious elite, the ulama, or a new class of experts which combines those trained in traditional religious sciences as well as those who possess expertise in the modern disciplines (science, economics, law) that have a direct bearing on modern problems and concerns?

Today, we are witnessing a new historical transformation. Having fought their wars of national liberation and independence, many Muslim countries and societies today face a second struggle over issues of identity (personal and national). Countries in the Muslim world, as in the former Soviet Union, Eastern Europe, and other parts of the world, are undergoing a process of political and social change, prevented in the past by colonialism and more recently by authoritarian governments. At times the process has pitted governments and secular elites against more Islamic populist movements. In light of the Qur'an, the example of the Prophet Muhammad, and a tradition of jurisprudence and political theory, Muslims today are debating and experimenting with a wide range of options as they seek to define or redefine the relationship and role of Islam to the state. It is a long, drawn-out *process*, accompanied by differences, debate, and battle among contending voices and factions with competing visions and interests.

Part V

CONTEMPORARY USA

18

Religion and Politics: Finding Normative Factors in Current Discussions

Walter Capps
University of California at Santa Barbara

The intention in this paper, in keeping with the central theme of this conference, is to identify normative elements in the current discussion concerning the relationship between religion and politics. By normative elements, reference is being made to constant, valid structural factors, which often assume formal status, around which thoughts, sentiments, and attitudes coalesce or are systematically organized. In both religion and politics such normative elements assume both constitutive and regulative functions. That is, they can appear in the form of substance or content (as in religious and/or political convictions and assertions) and/or as factors that shape and direct inquiry and representation about substance and content. To approach the subject this way is to recognize and extend Immanuel Kant's insight: a priori synthetic factors are also present in "creedal" affirmation (whether of religious or political modalities). Thus, recognition of this fundamental interdependence is necessary to understanding relationships between these two spheres of avowal and activity.

Our focus is on the contemporary era, that is, on one or two matters of controversy that exhibit both religious and political dimensionality. Much of the controversy I will be referencing is drawn from contemporary American social, cultural, political, and religious life, which provides a rich but complex setting for the

259

testing of ideas and theses. But I shall also be lifting out a "case study" of post-Marxist character from Eastern Europe, and I shall be doing this in order to have at least two points of reference in advancing my thesis. After dealing with conceptual and definitional matters, I shall offer the beginnings of a phenomenological portrayal of the relationships between religion and politics, a sketch that will reinforce the observation that religion and politics are more alike than unlike, and often come bound together in specific cultural settings.

My inquiry is rooted in leads offered in Professor Jacob Neusner's thorough and provocative background paper, the one in which he offers an abbreviated description of how religion speaks through politics, and, therefore, how religious systems function within the social (and, I presume, political) order. A religious system encompasses three main components, Neusner suggests: "a worldview, a way of life, and an account of the character of the social entity that realizes the way of life and explains that way of life through the specified worldview." It is an abbreviated description since it uses fewer words to get at the oft-cited description proposed by Clifford Geertz in his essay "Religion as Cultural System," in *Anthropological Approaches to the Study of Religion* (1966), edited by Michael Banton. According to Geertz, religion is:

> (1) a system of symbols which acts to (2) establish powerful,
> pervasive, and long-lasting moods and motivations in men by
> (3) formulating conceptions of a general order of existence and
> (4) clothing these conceptions with such an aura of factuality that
> (5) the moods and motivations seem uniquely realistic.

Using these component-based definitional descriptions as a starting point, I wish to point the discussion beyond the ways in which religious systems acquire political entailment, and to employ culture, rather than religion or religious system, as the prevailing context. Then, within a cultural frame, I'd like to identify the various components that have place or influence there, and explore the relationships between these components. My suggestion is that this cultural situation deserves greater in-depth investigation than it has received to date, because the components that relate to each other are more numerous than is usually acknowledged, and, thus, their interdependencies are also more complex. In fact, to understand the ways in which religion and politics actually intersect, inquiry must consult methodology as supple as Aristotle's causal analyses in order to come to terms with the dynamic and complex interaction involved. But it is impossible to proceed any longer in this theoretical and abstract manner. It is time to turn to an example which we will employ to tease out the rudiments of the crucial relationship on which this inquiry is focused.

Religion and Politics in the Prague Revolution

The example I cite draws upon the so-called velvet revolution that occurred in Prague, in what is now the Czech Republic, in 1989. In the social and cultural change that the revolution signified, religion came to speak through politics in rather profound ways. But more than religious system was involved. In addition there was ideology, there was critique of ideology, there was deliberate recollection of previous times in which ideology was challenged in the name of transformed religion, and there was a way in which the new era in Czech life exhibited a representational quality, that is, by providing mythic substance to the new or revised collective identity of the Czech people. Of course, we don't have the time or space here to detail many of the relevant background factors. As it happens, I have the privilege of conducting a graduate seminar at Santa Barbara on this subject, and two of my students, Shawn Landress and John Nemec, each with a special interest in this subject, are engaged in detailed historical and philosophical background investigation. As it also happens, I wrote at some length on this subject in a paper prepared for the World Institute of Phenomenological Research in Guadalajara last summer. The more I probe the more fascination I find with this chapter of contemporary European intellectual history. For the driving questions have been elevated by the late Ernest Gellner, Prague-born Cambridge philosopher, who, at the time of his death, was the director of the Center for the Study of Nationalism at the new Central European University in Prague, and whose most recent book carries the title *Conditions of Liberty: Civil Society and Its Rivals* (1994). My thinking on these matters has also been influenced by Dinko Tomasic and Stjepan G. Mestrovic, each of whom has written extensively on the subject of relationships between ideology and the structure of Eastern European societies. Behind much of such analysis lies the contrast between *Gemeinschaft* and *Gesellschaft* as proposed by the nineteenth-century theorist Friedrich Tonnies. But in this paper I shall follow Gellner's analysis, noting beforehand that the matters he investigated remain unsettled, and are clearly open to additional analysis and interpretation.

Gellner's subject is the relationship between culture and politics, which relationship must always be approached in dynamic rather than static terms. Focused on developments in Eastern Europe in the late 1980s and early 1990s, Gellner is naturally curious about the breakdown of Marxist ideas and society, to which he attaches a more comprehensive theory about the subsequent rise of nationalisms and fundamentalisms. In Gellner's terms, Marxism was done in not because it eliminated the transcendent from religion, but because it "over-sacralized the immanent." As he explains it, "Spinoza had taught that the world was one indivisible unity suffused by the divine, which pervaded it symmetrically. Hegel had added historical movement to this vision, and Marxism was born of this fusion of ideas" (40). Paradoxically, this so-called atheistic orientation to reality had too much sacredness. As Gellner explains:

> Pantheism may be a possible state of mind for an unusual, God-intoxicated man such as Spinoza, but it is caviare for the general: the commonality of men require a spiritually stratified world, in which there is not only the sacred but also the profane. Everything may be sacred, but some things must be much more sacred than others....By sacralizing all aspects of social life, notably work and the economic sphere, Marxism deprived men of a profane bolthole into which to escape during periods of lukewarmness and diminished zeal. (40)

In addition, Marxist soteriology was lacking in precision. As Gellner analyzes it, Marxism offers total salvation, but to humankind as a totality, and not to individuals.

> It has virtually nothing to say to an individual in personal anguish or in some kind of life crisis, except perhaps, at most, to advise him to rejoice in the eventual beatitude of all humanity, and to encourage him to help in the struggle and gird his loins for it....Marxism has nothing to say to personal tragedy and bereavement. (39-40)

Take the city of Prague during the Marxist period, and pay careful attention to the way in which the critique of Marxism assumed political, social, cultural, religious (or should we say "collective spiritual") form. For when instruments of criticism were sought, the Czech (or Prague) political theoreticians found them in revisiting and reconstituting their intellectual and religious legacies. Prague, we recall, is the place where John Huss, benefiting from Bohemian exposure to John Wyclif's ideas, employed commentaries on the *Sentences* of Peter Lombard to call the Czech citizenry back to the teachings of the New Testament and the life of poverty that he believed was characteristic of the original followers of Jesus Christ. We can't recount the entire story here. Suffice it to recall that Huss was imprisoned, that he was tried for heresy, that he appealed to his conscience, and that he was condemned and burned, meeting his death with great courage on July 6, 1415. These, in brief, are the headlines. But in more comprehensive and extensive cultural terms, Huss's courage combined with Huss's martyrdom became the signal event in the acquisition or achievement of Czech national identity.

The historical pattern and precedent was revisited during modern and contemporary Czech resistance to social, political, cultural, and religious repression under Soviet domination. Remarkably, there was a supreme act of martyrdom, likened in collective memory to that of John Huss, in which the citizens of the Czech Republic found identity as well as solidarity. On January 19, 1969, Jan Palach burned himself to death in front of the statue of St. Vaclav in Wenceslaus Square. Palach's dramatic act was a suicidal protest against the repressions of Soviet occupation. A few months later, Vaclav Havel, then a poet and playwright, appealed to Alexander Dubcek, then president, to democratize the society, promising that such an act of defiance "would place before us an ethical mirror as powerful as that of Jan Palach's recent deed." Dubcek, under pressure from the Communists, took no action. But the revolution that was called for was already in process. Havel said that Palach's self-immolation marked the inauguration of a period in which "human existence itself is at stake."

Other figures entered the scene. The influence of Tomas Masaryck, president of the first Czechoslovak Republic from 1919-38, was drawn upon. Masaryck recognized that Czech national consciousness had been grounded and shaped by the Hussite movement; thus, through Masaryck's testimony, Huss gained fresh place in contemporary Czech consciousness. The influence of Jan Patocka is strong too. Patocka is the philosopher who taught Vaclav Havel, who then founded the now famous Charter 77, the statement of resistance to Soviet occupation and Communist ideology. But prior to Patocka there was a Moravian, Edmund Husserl, the founder of philosophical phenomenology, in which Patocka was steeped, and to whose theory Vaclav Havel turned when attempting to update Hussite principles regarding the indispensable qualities of "inner strength." And when Havel sought the ideas and terminology to counter repressive Marxist thinking, he found all that he needed in Husserl's conception of *Lebenswelt*, or life world. For Havel, the resort to *Lebenswelt* fosters the conditions of "living in truth." The alternative to top-down theoretical deduction (as in Marxist presumptions) is attention to the "flow of life" that evidences deep contrasts between the artificiality of ideology and the fundamentality of ideas. In 1989, it was this view – this sense of how life should be lived – that was brought to prominence by the artists, philosophers, educators, musicians, writers, and others who led the successful revolution. Writing about it subsequently, Havel observed:

> I think the end of communism is a serious warning to all mankind. It is a signal that the era of arrogant, absolutive reason is drawing to a close and that it is high time to draw conclusions from that fact.

Then, pointing to the fundamental contrast in the two ways of life that were competing against each other, Havel added:

> Communism was not defeated by military force, but by life, by the human spirit, by conscience, by the resistance of Being and man to manipulation. It was defeated by a revolt of color, authenticity, history in all of its variety, and human individuality against imprisonment within a uniform ideology.

In another place, he describes the same transaction in these terms:

> Communism...was an attempt, on the basis of a few propositions masquerading as the only scientific truth, to organize all of life according to a single model, and to subject it to central planning and control regardless of whether or not that was what life wanted.

Does the transposition qualify as religion or as politics? Do shifts in collective consciousness, as in adoption of worldviews, register as political occurrences or as changes in belief and attitude? When the questions are posed this way, it is difficult to know how first to classify whatever the subject is that deals with ways of life, worldview, the instrumentation by which they are brought to realization, and the interpretive mechanisms through which they are explained.

The Prague Revolution as Working Paradigm

What do we learn about the relationship between religion and politics by studying the velvet revolution of Prague in 1989? First, it is impossible to talk about relationships between religion and politics apart from some precise *Sitz im Leben*, that is, a framework in which they are situated. And, in my judgment, the comprehensive framework is neither religion nor politics, but culture (which must always combine the social characters of the people with what Erik Erikson called "the conditions and accidents of historical time"). Religion and politics come together – sometimes in friendly ways and sometimes in hostile ways, sometimes as partners and sometimes as enemies, sometimes in compatibility and sometimes in controversy – in the composition of culture. Religion and politics are party to the formation, extension, critique, and sometimes dissolution of culture.

But there is more. The creation of culture, a perpetually dynamic process, seems to move from instances and periods of integration to instances and periods of decomposition to instances and periods of reconstitution and recomposition. (One can make such an assertion without "buying into" any dialectic of greater specification or precision.) And the specific form or modality that both religion and politics assume depends very significantly upon the stage in that ongoing dynamic process at which they are called upon to do their respective duty. What I am proposing is that both the Neusner abbreviated definition of the ingredients of a religious system and the earlier definition of religion offered by Clifford Geertz must, like Ezekiel's altar, be placed on wheels. That is, they must be equipped to handle the ebb and flow of cultural change, for the functions that are assigned to religion and politics, together with the relationships they have to each other, are heavily determined by the roles they are assigned in the perpetual composition-decomposition-recomposition process through which culture finds expression and collective identity is both known and enunciated. In cultural terms, ideologies are never fixed and set once and for all, but are always susceptible to criticism, and eventually succumb to postideological identities based on a return to a shared sense of what is fundamentally and uniquely important. This may involve replacing ideology with *Lebenswelt,* or it may be an invocation of the time of origin (for example, directly associating Jan Palach's death with the martyrdom of John Huss), or it may be a call to "live in the truth" (employing Vaclav Havel's now famous injunction) as distinct from dependency upon ideological illusions. But at every stage in this ongoing process, the mythic element asserts itself. In the case before us, the prevailing myth begins with Huss, extrapolates the meaning of his death, moves to Palach, extrapolates the meaning of his death in correspondence with the death of Huss, then to Charter 77 (which owns clear parallels to the "creedal" documents that were issued in conjunction with Huss's death), then to the loss of life and spirit that resulted therefrom together with the numerous extended imprisonments (including that of Havel himself), and then, finally, to the glorious suspension of ideological repression through the successes of the velvet revolution of 1989.

Everything that Professor Neusner said about religious systems is eminently accurate. And I know that he would have no objection to my insisting that the relationships between all of the necessary components – worldview, way of life, and social entity that realizes and explains/interprets this way of life – are always dynamic, are always in process, and thus can never be described or defined in any static way. The same holds for Geertz's definition: the system of symbols, which establishes motives, and is undergirded conceptually and ontologically, is always in process of attestation, criticism, reformation, and reformulation. It is also extremely important to notice that the normative factor, no matter what stage of the composition/decomposition cycle is being considered, is that which most significantly establishes and secures collective identity. The silent revolution occurred in Prague in 1989, when the rudiments of the fundamental fifteenth-century Czech orientational event were repristinated to create the foundation for a late nineteenth-century, post-Marxist, revised collective identity. Moreover, when this identity became secure, its normative factors were enunciable in political and religious terms that were compatible with each other. When identity is not sure – as it was not sure in Czechoslovakia during the Marxist period – such confusion shows up in intense or ever-smoldering conflicts both in and between religion and politics.

At this point we must observe that there is always potential conflict between religion and politics because of jurisdictional matters: their respective spheres of operation contain shared boundaries and overlapping interests. But when collective identity is sure – may I add, under a strong sense of a common good – then jurisdictional matters yield more smoothly to agreement or concord in the form of workable, uncontested arrangements. The "case study" offered by the Prague revolution of 1989 teaches us that the ingredients of cultural memory provide the clue as to how religion and politics are to be harmonized. Such harmonization occurs in close correspondence to the reestablishment (which is also the re-creation) of the basis of collective identity.

The Current Abortion Controversy in the United States

With this analysis of the Czech revolution behind us, I'd like now to turn briefly to the current situation in the United States. As everyone knows there is a crisis in this nation concerning the relationship between religion and politics, and, at the same time, nearly everyone agrees that, for perhaps nearly a decade now, we have been experiencing what is most frequently referred to as "cultural war."

The first observation would be that when religion and politics are in severe crisis and the culture itself – or, more precisely, the cultures themselves – shows signs of profound conflict, these are signs that the pieces have come apart, and that previous compositions have been dissolved. Such times are not periods of cultural integration. Indeed, they are just the opposite, and we can discuss or debate the extent to which disintegration has occurred. In my own view, the disintegration has become so extensive that we've nearly reached its logical limit. We are experiencing a period of such severe *atomization* that we can be sure of no other normative order than that which individuals are able to acquire for themselves and defend successfully against competing interests. We are counseled to "practice random kindness and senseless acts of beauty," as if it has already been conceded that virtue is random, as violence has become random, and image and affectation have replaced reason. Order is no longer dependable or predictable, meaning that there is little or no confidence in institutions, including government, and little or no confidence that traditional forms of social order, such as the family, can make it in a world like this. There is little, if any, public trust. We experiencing diminishing respect for our public schools. We no longer expect much good to come from the workings of political parties. We do not associate political activity with virtues to be emulated. So we experience doom and gloom, anger, despondency, lack of hope. As the philosophies of Lucretius, Democritus, and Epicurus illustrate, atomism is a highly pessimistic orientation to reality. The atomization of life occurs as response to the fear or suspicion that what controls us is both irresponsible and irresponsive, indifferent to us, indifferent to our fate.

It is time, of course (as soon as someone can determine the route), for recomposition. But the recompositional task is not easy because it involves bringing all of the necessary elements, ingredients, and components back into effective alignment. In my judgment, we are experiencing the instinct in this direction in the cause of the Christian Coalition. But the effort is doomed to failure by virtue of the misguided expectation that we can recapture what we had before. In formal, a priori terms, this judgment is correct. That is, the crisis will cease once the ingredients of cultural composition are made party to a constructive venture. But the wish to have it together – to have dependable order, and religion and politics in effective alignment – is not accomplished by an effort to reestablish some previous era, as if we could return to the 1950s, or to the conditions of social and cultural life that pertained prior to the advent of the counterculture. In this regard, there is no turning back. There can be no substantive reversal of cultural change. Yes, items previously born can be transported into the present, but previous cultural dynamics cannot be made to substitute for current cultural conditions. If reformulation is to occur, it can only be enunciated within the specific terms of current cultural conditionality. Thus, the

crucial intellectual task is to submit selected items from collective
memory to the creative processes by which cultures are composed.

Such analysis demonstrates that the abortion controversy is
symptomatic of the crisis this civilization faces. I approach this
topic with fear and trepidation, for I have not yet been party to a
discussion of abortion that has ended amicably. And yet, it behooves
us, for background contextual purposes, to recall Matthew Arnold's
observation, namely, that in the midst of the industrial revolution
and immense colonial expansion, the question that most bothered the
citizens of nineteenth-century England was this: Has the Church of
England committed apostasy? Arnold believed this question had been
brought to the forefront by the tremendous influence vested in John
Henry Newman. (Comment: We'll never know; it might have been
the other way around; it might have been John Henry Newman who
gained such attention because of the national preoccupation with the
collective religious question.) We are employing Arnold's insight for
a very specific reason. It does happen, from time to time, that a
certain question or issue dominates public discussion, and in
twentieth-century America, this question seems to be about the moral
status of the act of abortion. The question is about the morality of
abortion because the line is being drawn precisely there, that is, in
public discussion, concerning whether we believe ourselves to be a
sacred or a secular society.

The consequences are immense. If we have become a secular
society, then large segments of the population – we think specifically
of millions of citizens who continue to worship in traditional ways –
cannot feel at home here, for their birthrights, the bases on which
they understand themselves to relate to the world, have been sold to
alien forces. But if we dare to call ourselves a sacred society, and,
specifically, under the terminology that is being employed in the
abortion controversy, then large segments of the population recognize
or fear that their civil rights and personal freedoms have become
subject to the same kinds of dogmatic tyranny that are responsible for
the most tragic periods of human history. The abortion controversy,
in other words, is carrying extraordinarily heavy moral weight. It
has become the focal point of a serious debate (to employ Professor
Neusner's definitional words once again) about the character and,
thus, the integrity of "our way of life" and the way we, collectively,
view the world.

The moral status of abortion is a tremendously complex issue.
And it does no good to try to appeal to some perceived national
consensus, such as, well, the nation agrees on this subject: the majority
of people believe in choice, and the majority of people wish to reduce

the number of abortions. Even Senator Bill Bradley's comment, that abortion should be legal, safe, and rare is not thoroughly or systematically satisfying. The reason that these responses do not suffice is that the conditions of a sacred orientation to reality cannot be established on a percentage basis. Values that are perceived to be normative values cannot be assigned relative status. And, from the other side, if choice is qualified in any way, it isn't choice. If options are limited, if decisions are constrained, if the ability to choose is made conditional, personal freedom has been abrogated. So the two sides are on a collision course. To return to the terminology we have been employing from the beginning, the controversy is really a matter of contested way of life, and, with this, contested worldview. As has been noted, when there is contested way of life, together with contested worldview, there is also controversy – and, in this instance, competition – over the criteria by which authorized collective identity is determined and claimed.

Everyone recognizes that there is no simple solution. But there may be some helpful clarification if formal conceptual factors can be identified in this situation as they were identified vis-à-vis the Prague situation that was referenced previously. As in Prague, the clarification will come when there is an advance upon the current formulation, apart from which there can be no overcoming of the present impasse. No, the society will not discover perfect clarity on this question, but perhaps, in time, the society will get beyond it. It is already clear how this will happen, namely, when the test case is disconnected from the question about sacred versus secular society, that is, when the morality of abortion is not looked to serve this diagnostic function. When one thinks about it, it is not altogether clear why capital punishment, for example, could not serve the same purpose, for the morality of capital punishment resembles the morality of abortion in that each involves the willful, deliberate taking of human life within the context of unfortunate circumstances. Each is the consequence of a decision about ending life prematurely. But when we move in this direction, we are entering upon a conversation that eventually also references suicide, euthanasia, and even the kinds of premature cessation of human life that occurs on the field of combat. Within this range of potential test-case issues, it is not altogether apparent why abortion was selected as the litmus test that acquired sine qua non characteristics.

When significant that it was not until right now, in the history of the Western world, that this issue gained such prominence. And there were no particular historical reasons to prompt such an occurrence. Thus, our analysis tends to show that abortion is symptom rather than problem, and that its occurrence is driven by ideology or worldview. It will fade from prominence when contextual factors change, and we'll all wake up, not with clearer understandings, but recognizing that, somehow or other, the issue is now behind us. In this regard, it is significant that the issue does not preoccupy people who are not committed to the equation, namely, that attitudes toward abortion are reflective of convictions regarding whether our prevailing worldview is sacred or secular. We can go further. This equation is conceptual and not only attitudinal when it is hooked up to natural-law theory (as in much Roman Catholic thinking about the matter) or when "abortion" stands in for "evolution" (as in much conservative or fundamentalist Protestant thinking). But in both instances it is the formal conceptual scaffolding – that is, the prescribed way of thinking about these matters – that is most in question. Thus, when searching for normative factors in religion and politics, we must be attentive to prescriptions that become attached to patterns/processes of analyses and reflection.

Phenomenological Portrayals of Religion and Politics

Finally, I'd like to offer a very brief comparative phenomenological portrayal of differences and similarities between religion and politics. My colleague Ninian Smart, who fought with British forces in World War II, has frequently observed that human beings seem more willing to die for their country than for their religion. Of course, one can find eloquent exceptions to this rule. But the insight does disclose how much religion and politics are like one another, particularly with reference to the exercising of human commitments, convictions, and passions.

Were one doing a phenomenological portrayal of politics, one could develop a schematism that would look very much like the phenomenological portrayal of religion. Ideational components, for example, are prominent in both cases, so too the tendency to develop associations and movements based on adherence, in Smart's words, to such "doctrinal" strands. Firmly held convictions are prominent in both cases. Both have a tendency to seek ideological sponsorship. Mythos is also prominent in both frameworks too, as devotees find themselves covered by shared stories and narrative accounts. The workings of charisma are implicit too. And we could proceed further. Both religion and politics have a relationship of dependence upon ethical standards, for example. The politician is sometimes assigned roles and functions similar to those displayed by shamans, or personages with perceived or imputed shamanlike powers, to change the content and terms of prevailing order.

Put all of this together, and one encounters a most arresting conclusion, namely, that Clifford Geertz's oft-cited definition of religion ("...a system of symbols that establishes powerful motivations by projecting conceptions of a general order onto the plane of human experience") applies almost as well to politics. This explains how it happens that the two enterprises often overlap, often share common territory, and are sometimes substituted for each other.

Religion and Politics: A Crucial Open Question

One of my esteemed professors at Yale, Robert Brumbaugh, who taught classical Greek philosophy, liked to remind us of Plato's observation, that "fine things run hard." I suggest that Plato's observation is particularly applicable to the subject of this conference, namely, the relationship between religion and politics. In the United States, we have attempted to clarify this relationship by insisting on separation of church and state. This Jeffersonian principle has functioned effectively to prevent us from establishing a national church, and from ascribing to our president the attributes of the divine right of kings. But there are hosts of thorny issues that the formula leaves untouched. Separation is intent on manifesting differences, leaving largely open the related matter of how separated entities can also be significantly alike. For example, in contemporary discussion, the key and crucial relationship is not between church and state, but between "God" and "country." Here "separation" does not function as convincingly. In addition, it may be possible to honor the technicalities of separation of church and state while striving to "Christianize America" or, from the other side, "Americanize Christianity." And clarity regarding whether or not such ventures are valid, since they certainly are viable, has not attained consensus status. Moreover, much religion happens outside formal church sponsorship, even when "church" is expanded into "synagogue, temple, mosque," or embellished into, say, "religious institutions" (or even into what is referred to as "organized religion"). And none of this begins to touch the status and power of what Robert Bellah (following Rousseau and Alexis de Tocqueville) called "civil religion," as in "American civil religion." Civil religion exhibits the components of both religion and politics. Indeed, civil religion is itself the product of a fusing of religion and politics.

This leads to the next thought, namely, that what we are experiencing in the United States today can be described as a contest between competing "American civil religions." Much political capital is being expended in this arena; so too considerable, sometimes intense, religious fervor. In the heat of the controversy, it is often difficult to distinguish political capital from religious ardor. The two come intertwined.

But we can go further: Is Islam religion or politics? Is Judaism religion or politics? Is Christianity religion or politics? Is Tibetan Buddhism religion or politics? The answer in all such cases is both. Judaism, Christianity, Islam, Tibetan Buddhism, Taoism, Shinto, and the other major traditions within the world are both religion and politics. Israel was and is a political entity. Islam is and was a political entity. America, as Sydney Mead and others have attested, is "a nation with the soul of a church." The contest now occurring in Bosnia, as Stjepan G. Mestrovic has illustrated in his brilliant study *Habits of the Balkan Heart* (1993), is over competing claims to legitimate succession from "communist civil religion," another critical instance in which religion and politics have come together. It should not be surprising, then, that the deities that are reverenced in these traditions stand as objects of worship that are also sometimes called upon to assist political goals: the protection of Mecca, the establishment of the kingdom of God, securing "our" needs and interests over against those of our enemy, among others. And we can go further. The quarrels that these traditions have with each other is as much over matters of politics as it is over matters of belief. Or, it may be more accurate to say that even the quarrels over articles of belief appear largely to be quarrels over matters of politics.

All of this attests that clarification of matters of this kind will not occur in the abstract. Clarification will never come by securing valid definitions or by developing systematic conceptual formulae. Rather, the only clarity that is available comes by concentrating on the ingredients of specific contexts and frameworks, which, in every instance, is a distinctive cultural context. My thesis is that culture is the comprehensive term within which both religion and politics are contained. I would suggest that culture assigns normative qualities and normative status to factors that may have had their origins in political and/or religious sensibility. And these normative factors have their basis and origin in the interplay between established social character and the accidents and circumstances of history. In every instance, an acknowledged mythic tradition is invoked to deal with challenges to collective identity, and resolution of the challenge does not occur until the tradition is revisited, reworked, and reformulated to provide effective and comprehensive accommodation.

Thus, the subject of this extraordinary conference presents large and important challenges to intellectual inquiry. It does so because the challenge to the way we view the world, live our lives, and find the instrumentation to harmonize and legitimize these two essential factors to both religion and politics, is even larger.

19

Religious Pluralism, Toleration, and Liberal Democracy: Past, Present, and Future

Stephen Turner
University of South Florida

The problem of the role of religion in contemporary politics is so deeply bound up with the history of the body of modern political thought that is at the basis of liberal democracy, that some discussion of this history is almost inevitable whenever the issue of religion and politics arises. One view of the history of liberalism, and indeed of the modern state, is that the edicts of toleration issued by the French monarchy during the French wars of religion (and subsequently revoked) were the kernels from which the modern secular state grew. Historians of these events are at pains to insist that the creation of such a state was the farthest thing from the minds of the monarchs and ministers who issued these edicts, and this is certainly true (Holt 1995). They were pragmatic steps designed to bring about peace between the Protestants and the Catholics, or to give the Church time to convert the Protestants back by peaceful means.

Peace in itself, however, was not the aim of the kings and ministers, but a means to an end. The end was to protect the French state from the consequences of religious civil violence. It was believed, probably quite correctly, that a state which failed to suppress extensive civil violence would cease to have authority and lose its power to command in the eyes of its subjects. More generally, it was feared that the state would perish in the violence that sectarian antagonism unleashed. This was not an idle fear, given that foreign armies and private armies with powerful military leaders rapidly emerged in the course of the civil violence that we call the French wars of religion. The leaders of the factions and the army they represented, together with foreign allies, could very well overwhelm the powers of the monarch, as indeed they did in England in Cromwell's time.

For political theory, the situations in which the state is assessing the conditions for its own survival and acting with its remaining powers to assure its survival is politics at its ultimate defining point. Declaring a religiously motivated action to be forbidden on the grounds of state interest is a method of dealing with a certain class of problems. Edicts of toleration, supported, if need be, by force, are a political means to the end of survival. The idea of toleration is a part of the technical machinery of the modern state, and in what follows the technical uses of toleration and a series of similar devices will be the focus of the discussion.

Toleration and Liberalism

The connection between this technical method and liberalism is quite direct. Liberalism and parliamentary democracy rely on and would not be possible without at least the availability of this and other methods of eliminating certain kinds of issues from the realm of politics. Toleration proceeds by criminalizing or forbidding certain classes of religiously motivated action against people with particular beliefs. Other techniques, I will show later, are available to liberalism; criminalization is an infrequent method in modern settled regimes. Nevertheless it is used; and it is the possibility of criminalization and the use of state force to suppress religiously motivated action that is at the root of the more benign techniques that are ordinarily used.[1]

Modern states typically use two other techniques, each of which has a similar effect; that is to say, each removes the topic from the arena of politics and puts it into another category. The two techniques we may call "neutralization" and "establishing." They appear to be opposites, but in political terms they serve similar purposes. The United States employs, with respect to religion, the technique of neutralization. The state attempts to be neutral between religions and more recently between religion and irreligion. The First Amendment is the embodiment of the Constitution's commitment to state neutrality with regard to religion and serves many of the same purposes as the edicts of toleration during the

---

[1] In United States in the nineteenth-century there was a clear instance of the state suppression of the religious practice of bigamy by the Mormons. Criminalization, of course, is not a mere matter of passing laws. It must represent, as it did in this case, a strong or, as I am calling it here, "high-threshold" consensus.

French wars of religion. The state, by refusing to establish any particular religion or to be biased toward any particular religion, assures that certain religious disputes, that is to say disputes between religions, do not get expressed in the arena of politics. In theory, there is no incentive for a religious leader to become involved in the politics of a religiously neutral state for specifically "religious" purposes because the politics of the religiously neutral state are limited to nonreligious matters. One could not, except indirectly, advance the cause of one religion against another through a state which in its constitutional rules forbade the state to act preferentially toward a religion.

Curiously, establishing a religion has, under the right circumstances, similar effects. The establisher of the religion is the state and the state sets the limit on what the religion can do politically. In the city of Uppsala there is a striking bit of symbolism that underscores this relation. The city has a royal castle surrounded by cannons. Below the castle is a major cathedral beside the residence of the bishop. One of the cannons is aimed more or less directly at the bishop's residence. It was explained to me that this was intended as a constant reminder that the church was politically subordinate to the state. The effect of establishing a church, then, is not merely to state a preference of one church over others, but to remove the church as an independent political agent.

The church, acting within its domain, was "established" and free to govern its own affairs. But the domain was set by the establishing power which simply delegated a particular domain of freedom to the church. This delegation has the effect of removing the business of the church from political consideration and thus makes the state religiously neutral except with respect to this act of delegation. Establishment, in effect, then, is an act of self-denial or self-limitation by the state akin to neutrality.

Protecting Liberal Democracy

Parliamentary democracy could not exist without the employment of something like the techniques just described. Parliamentary democracy is government by discussion (cf. Schmitt [1926] 1985, 22-50; Schmitt [1934] 1985, 59). The discussion is of a very special kind: one in which representatives are sent to discuss matters of state on behalf of or for constituencies and are free to act independently of the directly expressed wishes of their constituencies. In short, they are allowed to be persuaded by the discussion they enter into and are compelled, by the mechanism of elections, to justify that which they have been persuaded of to their electors. The idea of rational persuasion is a very fragile one. It does not extend to the activities ordinarily understood as religious. Modern theologians at least have been careful to construct a small domain of thought in which acts of faith have a necessary place. But parliamentary politics, though it may require acts of faith, is organized around the real possibility that its discussions mean something, and that those who are sent to make decisions can be rationally persuaded in the course of those discussions (Schmitt [1926] 1985).

If we look at parliamentary democracy from the inside out, and consider the conditions for the survival of the discussion that is central to parliamentary democracy, it is evident that parliamentary democracy is worse off than the king of France whose concern is to avoid civil violence. The king merely needed to be able to vanquish his rivals and assert a monopoly of legitimate force. The defender of parliamentary democracy must preserve a conversation in which rational persuasion occurs. Anything that threatens the possibility of this conversation continuing threatens parliamentary democracy as a meaningful form of rule. Of course, the shell of parliamentary forms may persist after the conversation stops: this was the situation in Weimar Germany. This bad fate is a constant reminder of the fragility of parliamentarism in its meaningful sense, and of the uselessness of its political guarantees if this meaningful sense is lost. So parliamentary democracy must be ruthless, much more ruthless than a monarch, in limiting the issues which the state decides politically. And the best method for limiting the issues to those for which there is a reasonable hope of rational persuasion is to either declare that the issues are *not* political, but either tolerated or criminal, or to establish some viewpoint or result as nonpolitical but taken for granted or established.

Science, it has often been argued, is very much like an established church (Polanyi 1951; Price 1965). We do not expect legislatures to debate technical questions about science or to make scientific matters part of parliamentary discussion. We agree, in effect, to accept the pronouncements of science, when they are sufficiently clear and univocal, as definitive, and to take them for granted in political discussion. Where they are not sufficiently clear or unequivocal we do not ordinarily make them political, that is to say make them the subject of political deliberation and discussion, but rather wait for them to be settled so that they can be taken for granted, though of course the decision to wait is itself political.

Divisions between the Political and the Nonpolitical

There is a sense in which it is better for a liberal regime if the divisions between categories are believed to be extremely clear-cut and the self-limitations of the state are based on natural or rational facts or considerations that are themselves neutral and therefore nonpolitical. Lucky indeed is the state in which there is a clear consensus on these distinctions. Nevertheless these distinctions, as every writer on the social construction of such things as gender categories knows all too well, vary historically, and the degree of consensus represented by them varies historically. Much feminist discussion, for example, has concerned the public/private distinction and its supposed negative effect on women, who are taken to be oppressed by virtue of the self-limitations of liberal politics which relegate their concerns to the realm of the private, that is to say the realm beyond civic action and public discussion (Nussbaum 1996).

The slogan "the personal is the political" is an affirmation that the line between the public and personal is itself political, and political even in the liberal sense that it is a matter that is open to discussion in the "public realm." Of course, one of the concerns of feminism is not only to make this line a matter of public discussion, but to move matters previously considered private into the "public" realm, making them the proper subject of civic action, or even to abolish the distinction and thereby abolish liberalism and its ideal of a separate limited domain of rational public discussion as a basis of civic action.

The same set of issues arises in connection with religion. One version of the defense of the right to have abortions follows very strictly the lines I have described here. It says that the issue over abortion is fundamentally a religious dispute, and therefore not an appropriate subject of civic action, because to be a subject of civic action would require the state to make a decision that cannot possibly be arrived at through public discussion and persuasion but one which would require the actual conversion and commitment of faith of the two sides in the dispute. Another version of the abortion argument, and the one which is the legal basis of the Roe versus Wade decision, holds that the state intrusion into the medical practice of abortion and the decision to have an abortion is an intrusion into a private realm which ought to be beyond the action of the state. The idea of a private domain is essentially an edict of toleration.

Many opponents of these arguments hold different views about the nature of privacy or the limits of public discussion. In this case much of the battleground, as a result of the Supreme Court decision, has involved the claim of privacy, and it is curious, but not entirely surprising, that the religious Right and the feminist Left disagree on the issues but agree on the principle that there is no natural fact of privacy that limits state action and also on the principle that the limitation of state action to that which is subject to rational public persuasion is a limitation which runs contrary to their own deeply held beliefs. Both, in some forms at least, are thus fundamentally opposed to liberalism as an idea on the grounds that liberalism leads to fundamentally immoral results and that morality is not on the table to be negotiated in the public realm.

Mechanisms for Removing Issues from the Political Domain

I have now run together a quite complex series of ideas which will need some disentangling, but let me simply suggest how they could be disentangled and go on from that to a discussion of the more general problem of the future of liberalism in the face of these kinds of conflicts. The notion of privacy is deeply rooted in Western civilization. The idea that the state cannot forbid one to defend one's life, the right of self-defense, is ordinarily held to be a right that no legitimate legal system ought to abrogate, except under special and well-justified circumstances, such as criminal punishment or military orders, the cases in which we have chosen to sacrifice our human rights for the more limited but more secure benefits of civil rights. Nevertheless, as these exceptions suggest, these rights are not absolute and are not clearly fixed historically. The right of self-defense, notoriously, has shrunken from a right to protect one's belongings against any threat or apparent threat to a much more limited right to protect one's person against imminent destruction (Fletcher 1978).

The limits of the private realm, to put it simply, are decided politically. The other devices of liberalism I have listed here are equally a matter of politics, even though the political decisions we make with respect to these devices are unusual ones. They are not temporary compromises constantly up for renegotiation but compromises that become givens of the political discussion itself, at least for a time. They are taken to be not open for continuous challenge in the course of political discussion. All of them, including such basic decisions as the one to accept the results of scientific opinion on matters deemed scientific (and decisions about what is to be deemed scientific), are political. But they are political in a special sense. They require a much higher threshold of acceptance in order to serve their fundamental discussion-limiting role. It may be, for example, that the flat-earth society has adherents and that a large number of Baptists reject evolution. But we do not therefore treat these as topics for political discussion and take away from scientists the role as neutral arbitrators that we usually grant them.

Let me briefly review the argument to this point. Liberalism requires reasoned persuasion in public discussion and liberal parliamentary democracy does this with representatives who are open to reasoned persuasion. The realm of issues that can be processed through reasoned discussion is limited. Consequently there needs to be a means, or several means, by which reasoned discussion is protected from the effects of, or the need to make decisions about, issues that cannot be made subject to reasoned persuasion. Some issues obviously may remain unsettled and not require a decision. They can be relegated to the "private" realm, and we can agree to disagree about their morality, recognizing that we are unable to agree on civic action with respect to them. Or we can disagree about whether to disagree, but keep this disagreement from affecting the discussion of other issues. The problems arise with issues that must be settled, but cannot be settled through the reasoned persuasion of representatives, and with unsettleable disagreements that cannot be separated from the rest of the discussion.

The devices by which such issues are removed from public discussion operate in different and specific ways. Issues do not come, so to speak, prelabeled in categories like "open to rational resolution" and "not open to rational resolution," or even "religious" and "nonreligious." A considerable portion of the law on these matters in fact assumes, for example, that religion is a natural and unproblematic category, so that the courts can easily determine that what the state is establishing or failing to establish is in fact a religion. As I have suggested, parallel to the case of science, the decision of what constitutes a religion or religious action is a political decision, though it may be made by courts, and, similarly, decisions about what is criminal and what is not are political decisions.

The case of bigamy among Mormons is a case in point; the criminalization of the consumption of alcohol during Prohibition is another. Prohibition involved a constitutional amendment. The admission of Utah to the Union also involved a decision that required more than mere majority rule. These mundane constitutional facts reflect a much more fundamental fact that holds for all of these techniques of flushing unsettleable disputes from the political system or protecting public discussion from these unsettleable disputes, and that is this: the agreements which allow for the use of these techniques require a much higher level of consensus than ordinary political discussions. If we agree that something is a private matter, for example, if we agree to disagree on the morality of something, we agree to remove it from political discussion. But people can refuse to agree to disagree, and insist that the issue remain a matter of political discussion. It takes more than a majority vote to deal with this kind of refusal to disagree. The use of the authority of science, for example, in expert testimony in courtrooms and to settle disputes involving the appropriate regulation of pollution, involves a general consensus as to what science is and requires a general respect for science. As I have suggested, this need not be absolute, but it must be pretty overwhelming in order for us to remove scientific issues from the political realm and treat them as facts to be taken for granted by the state and by political discussion.

Making Formerly "Private" Issues "Public"

Religion has played a prominent and dramatic role in challenging or establishing these "high-threshold" matters of consensus. Issues like abortion arise and have their destructive effects on public discourse primarily because they involve these borderline disputes which the system of rational persuasion and compromise cannot handle and which then need to be removed from public discussion by some "high-threshold" means. In itself, abortion is the sort of issue that might be left unsettled for a long period, and the question of its publicness or privacy might be discussed for a long time. However, abortion and many of the other unsettled issues do not ordinarily exist on their own and separate from other questions. They are connected to and often come to represent cultural stands or religious understandings of life, and thus raise a special problem for liberal discussion, especially when the viewpoints they are connected to are viewpoints that it has been agreed are not the proper part of public discussion or civic action, such as particular sectarian religious beliefs. If one's opponents on a given issue are characterized as evil, for example, it will become impossible to hold serious discussions with them on other issues.

Religion also has a positive role to play in forming new "high-threshold" consensuses in which formerly private issues become matters for public discourse. But in the case of liberal democracy it has been a somewhat problematic role. The nineteenth-century consensus on what divided public and private with respect to religion was itself rooted in religion, in the saying of Jesus to "render unto Caesar that which is Caesar's," and particularly in Protestant notions about individual conscience and the individual character of a relationship to God, which could be used as the basis for a kind of mutual respect of private life and belief. "Rooted in" does not mean "determined by," for the same religious ideas sometimes allowed for much in the way of intrusion by religious authorities. In the Reformation the idea of reform was meant to entail the reform of society as well as religion, and thinkers like Calvin and John Knox, when they attained power, had no scruples about persecuting those they believed to be sinners.

I suspect that there was a kind of flattening of denominational differences with respect to these issues in the nineteenth century in the United States. The Great Awakening was a moment at which many Americans changed their denominational affiliations to affiliations that they found to be more consistent with their religious feelings. The westward expansion led to the creation of religious communities with members from diverse denominational backgrounds. The shuffling of denominations helped to strengthen the political commonalities of American Protestantism by bringing together in the same churches persons with divergent but not irreconcilable attitudes toward authority and toward such things as public/private distinctions.

To the extent that there are close connections between religious ideas over which there is no consensus and political disputes which because of their connection to these religious ideas are not processable through reasoned persuasion, religious pluralism is a threat to liberal democracy. One need only look at truly sectarian societies, such as Ulster, to see what happens when religious identity defines political loyalty. If the mechanisms for flushing religiously motivated issues out of the public domain cannot work, and cannot work because they require a high-threshold consensus which religious groups or other groups are actively attempting to undermine, then the mechanisms necessary to the preservation of something for liberal democracy to be about will break down and eventually the appearance of public discussion and persuasion becomes sham. Public life becomes instead a domain for expressive politics and stand taking. Political violence, in the form of arson, assassinations, and killings of opponents, not infrequently follow close on the heels of this kind of expressive politics.

But expressive politics sometimes works: the protests against the war in Vietnam made the war into a political issue rather than a test of loyalty. Opposition was not only, so to speak, decriminalized, the opponents carried the day once the war became a political issue. As a political issue, it had to be settled, and it was – in favor of the protesters. The civil rights movement, in its integrationist phase, worked in a similar way: the formerly accepted fact of segregation in the southern states was moved from the margins of politics, from the status of an issue that people had agreed to disagree about, to the status of an issue that could be addressed through civic action. Religious leaders and religious appeals had a prominent role in both movements, of course. In these cases, then, the process of removing issues from the public realm worked in reverse: formerly "private" topics were made into public topics, subjects for civic action, and more importantly, subjects for public discussion and persuasion. In the case of the abortion issue, the process of moving the issue into either a status in which we agree to disagree or meaningful political discussion has not yet worked, but this is the point of the effort: to persuade people that it is, or is not, a proper subject for political discussion and civic action.

Religious Pluralism and the Schoolhouses of Liberalism

We now arrive at a somewhat peculiar set of puzzles, partly raised by the facts, and partly raised by the interpretations placed upon them by several other authors in this volume, such as Capps and Fasching. The first is this: Is religious pluralism compatible with liberal democracy? One answer based on fact is that it is not, and the present experience of Islamic societies, the fact of sectarian violence in Ulster, and the long history of religious warfare in Europe show that it is not. Liberal democracy, this history suggests, requires in practice an established church or its de facto equivalent, and not merely toleration. Nineteenth-century America probably represents, at least in retrospect, the de facto equivalent of an established church. Protestant sects agreed to treat the differences between them as matters of no concern to the state, and agreed on the dividing line between religion and the state. But they also agreed on a great deal about what else was of concern to the state and what was not. Without a *religiously* based consensus of this sort (which may, as it has in the US, become part of the secular understanding of the relation between religion and politics), it is difficult to see how the mechanisms of removing unsettleable disputes from politics could work, and why politics would not inevitably degenerate into sectarian civil war.

The problem arises in part as a result of the theories we use to think through the problem of the character of religiously motivated politics. If religions are incompatible worldviews, as Capps and Fasching seem to suggest, we have no reason to suppose that liberal politics in the sense I have discussed here is possible if it is conducted between persons who hold these incompatible views. By definition, worldviews have premises that are beyond the reach of rational persuasion. Put simply, if we take these accounts of the relation between religion and politics seriously, liberal democracy is incompatible with liberal democracy, unless the religious conceptions in question happen, by happy accident, not to produce the kinds of conflicts that liberal democracies cannot resolve.

Yet liberal democracies have not, for the most part, collapsed into sectarian civil violence. Civil violence motivated by religious conflicts has indeed occurred, and did in the United States in the case of each of the three movements discussed above. But the authors of civil violence were marginalized and treated as criminals. It did not lead to massive sectarian counterviolence, or to a descent into political sectarianism of the sort found in Ulster or the French wars of religion. In what follows I will try to explain why. Part of the explanation is simple. Secularization, in Europe, has relegated the problem to conflicts between the secularized public and religious minorities, whose conduct becomes, by wide consensus, a police problem. The American situation is somewhat different. But to understand this difference it is necessary to locate it in a somewhat broader picture of the social and political implications and relations of religion.

One of the most striking differences between political orders is to be found in the nature of the "political" experiences available to people outside of politics. An influential view of the French Revolution traced the rise of the revolutionary representative bodies to a long tradition of debate within Masonic lodges (Furêt 1981). Whatever the ultimate validity of this interpretation, it fits with a fact that is obvious to anyone who has looked at the development of social and political institutions: practically operating political forms, such as functioning parliamentary democracies, are not isolated or anomalous institutions, but function in much the same way as other bodies in the same society. In American life, for example, there are literally thousands and thousands of voluntary organizations each of which makes decisions and has a structure of elections, representation, compromise between interests, the articulation of common goals, and so on and so forth that parallels directly the structure of the national political system and the various smaller political units. One's "political" experience in the United States is thus not at all limited to voting but is likely to include participation in the PTA, Little League, and so forth.

It will also include, of course, experience in church politics. Indeed, one can hardly underestimate the importance, in the nineteenth century and before, of church polity both as a schoolhouse of democracy and a source of conflicting political habits and attitudes to authority. The former names and some present names of denominations are the names of their form of church polity – the *grex*, the flock, is the political authority for Congregationalism, just as the presbytery and episcopate are for Presbyterianism and Episcopalianism. If one observed the situation at independence, one might have predicted that the various denominations, each with a different relation to authority, and some quite used to exercising state powers, would produce a political collision. For various reasons, notably the revulsion against things English and the willingness of the religious leaders of New England to give up some of their political authority, the collision did not occur (Bryce 1914, 764-66). Religious groups gave up their political powers, and religious tests for office were abolished. In the nineteenth century itself, a kind of homogenization of attitudes toward the public/private sphere emerged. Perhaps this was in large part a consequence of the fact that people with different denominational origins came to worship together and more importantly to participate in the decision-making processes of churches together. In any case, Protestants with different denominational origins were thrown together in various ways, both within church polities and within the public realm. And they were forced to become more cognizant of differences, and, given their own religious ideas, were led to regard the differences as legitimate matters of conscience and thus "private."

Why is this significant? The collision that should have happened did not. The theory of religions as incompatible worldviews with irreconcilable political implications would have predicted that the religious diversity of nineteenth-century America would have collapsed the public realm, the realm of reasoned persuasion of representatives essential to liberal democracy, into sectarian conflict. The public/private distinction would never have developed, because the propriety and application of the distinction is itself subject to religiously rooted disagreement. Yet a functioning consensus on the limits of religion in politics did develop.

This nineteenth-century history suggests a process by which such consensuses do develop. People acting together for common purposes, religious or secular, must come to some sort of accommodation of the fact that they hold beliefs that differ, if they are to work together and live together. They do so by accepting the legitimacy of differences and relegating the differences to the "private" realm. And they protect the public realm and the possibility of reasoned persuasion in the public realm from the consequences of the fact that people have different religious views by doing so. The important fact about this process of the mutual recognition of religious legitimacy is that it is nonpolitical. It is a basis for tolerance in something other than the political need of the state to suppress civil violence.

As I have suggested, this mechanism serves the purposes that liberal democracy requires, of moving unsettleable topics off the political agenda by underwriting agreements to disagree. The problem with this mechanism is that there is no guarantee that it will work. But there are conditions that increase the probability of it working, and conditions that make it less likely to work. [2] Residential and communal segregation, for

---

[2] The curious history of the Catholic Church's response to these necessities in twentieth-century America reflects the recognition of the hierarchy that membership in voluntary organizations would lead to toleration, and large efforts were made to create Catholic alternatives to these organizations, such as the Knights of Columbus as a Catholic alternative to the Masons, or Catholic enclaves within them, such as Catholic Boy Scout Troops. These efforts were helped by residential segregation in large cities. But in the end the efforts were fruitless and the laity accepted the nineteenth-century Protestant consensus on the public/private distinction and indeed on the role of conscience – thus making the American Church and American Catholicism into a source of considerable anxiety to the Vatican.

example, limit the number and kinds of cooperative ventures that teach the lessons of toleration. But serious political purposes relating to the society as a whole require going beyond local religiously segregated communities, and going beyond sectarian limits. Thus we arrive at a paradox: religiously motivated attempts to transform society in a particular image, in the United States at least, compel their adherents to cooperate with and build coalitions with others whose religious views differ. And this holds even when, and perhaps especially when, the particular policy or political aim, whether it is the prohibition of abortion or civil rights, is in the pile of issues that lie outside the domain of ordinary rational persuasion and have been removed, by agreement, from the continuing conversation of liberal democracy. So these movements tend to become schoolhouses of toleration, though quite unintentionally.

The pro-life movement is a case in point. Who would have imagined, fifty years ago, that a coalition would emerge between the Catholic Church and Protestant fundamentalists in which large numbers of the laity and clergy of each group would cooperate on a continuous basis in a common public endeavor? Yet this is precisely what has happened, and as a consequence the lesson of toleration – the mutual acceptance of religious legitimacy – has been learned by both sides. The tactical necessity of cooperation, in short, has had consequences of the same kind as occurred in nineteenth-century Protestantism. This new tolerance does not resolve the issue at hand. But it changes the conditions under which future issues become located in relation to the conversation of liberal democracy, for it assures that some differences on which we have agreed to disagree will remain "private," under the umbrella of religious differences mutually recognized to be legitimate alternatives. And it may also lead to alterations in the scope of what is accepted as public – for example, in rewriting the limitations on public subsidy of "religious" schools.

Into the Next Century

The lessons of political toleration with which I began this discussion were very painfully learned. They can certainly be forgotten. But they are less likely to be forgotten in a society in which the habit of toleration is learned and sustained in the "political" experiences of individuals in such organizations as the PTA and Little League, and even, paradoxically, in such movements as the right-to-life movement. The sheer fact of religious diversity, indeed, provides a kind of assurance that the lesson of toleration will always be there to be learned and relearned. In the private realm little can be accomplished by relying only on the religiously like-minded because the number of truly religiously like-minded in an era of religious pluralism will always be small. Thus in a way pluralism provides a kind of protection against the potential for sectarian political fanaticism of its various elements. But this is true only in societies in which there is a vital sector of intermediate institutions such as the PTA, or social movements, in which these lessons can be learned. In those societies without such institutions, such as those of the Islamic world, or societies in which such institutions are religiously differentiated, such as Northern Ireland, the habits of toleration are not learnable and the more brutal lessons of civil war must be taught instead.

Liberal democracy, as I have suggested, is more fragile than state authority. It requires effective mechanisms of moving issues in and out of the realm of political discussion. Religious motivations have played a large role in this process of moving issues from public to private, and from private to public. But the religious motivations have, so far at least, been altered by the experience of cooperation in such a way that no issue has yet been forced onto the political agenda that ends the possibility of the rational persuasion of representatives. Because of the process of "privatization" and mutual recognition of religious legitimacy between political allies, religious diversity is a kind of protector of liberal democracy, for it assures that no sectarian movement can succeed without shedding much of its sectarian intolerance.

Bibliography

Fletcher, G. P. 1976. *Rethinking Criminal Law*. Boston and Toronto: Little, Brown and Company.

Furêt, François. 1981. *Interpreting the French Revolution*. Cambridge: Cambridge University Press.

Holt, Mack P. 1995. *The French Wars of Religion, 1552-1629*. Cambridge: Cambridge University Press.

Nussbaum, Martha. 1996. *Times Higher Education Supplement*, 2 February, 17-18.

Polanyi, Michael. 1951. *The Logic of Liberty: Reflections and Rejoinders*. Chicago: University of Chicago Press.

Price, Don K. 1965. *The Scientific Estate*. Cambridge: Belknap Press of Harvard University Press.

Schmitt, Carl. [1926] 1985. *The Crisis of Parliamentary Democracy*. Cambridge: MIT Press.

Schmitt, Carl. [1934] 1985. *Political Theology*. Cambridge: MIT Press.

20

Judaism, Christianity, Islam: Religion, Ethics, and Politics in the (Post)modern World

Darrell Fasching
University of South Florida

Normative questions in religion and politics, Walter Capps has argued, are intimately tied to "culture wars." What are these wars about? They are, he suggests, about our individual and collective identities and whether they are to be defined in terms of the sacred or the secular. This picture is complicated by the fact that religion functions differently in periods of cultural crisis and disintegration than it does in periods of cultural stability and integration. Religion and politics are more likely to be in conflict in the former than in the latter. The conflict will have to do with how the crisis of the present moment is perceived and the prescriptions that are offered for establishing a new period of integration. Currently, Walter Capps observes, American society is in a period of maximum disintegration and atomism and the norms for a new period of integration have not yet made their appearance. Hence – culture wars. The crisis, if Harvey Cox is right, is not just American, it is global and so is the response – religious resurgence, everywhere accompanied by culture/religion wars over who shall define public order and public values.

Walter Capps brings to the subject of religion and politics not only excellent academic credentials but also the experience and insights of someone who has run for political office. I find very little to disagree with in his fine paper on normative factors in religion and politics. Therefore, what I would like to do is amplify what he has done by asking three related questions provoked by his paper: (1) Why religious resurgence? (2) Why now? and (3) Why does it take the form of "culture wars"? Finally, I will suggest a possible religious response to the issues raised.

In 1965, when Harvey Cox first published *The Secular City*, it seemed as if the more "modern" the world became, the less religious and more secular it was becoming. It was not uncommon for social scientists to posit that religion was an ancient superstition that was disappearing. Religious communities then seemed preoccupied with what the Second Vatican Council called *aggiornamento* or catching up with the modern world – of modernizing Judaism or Christianity or Islam. Since then, as Cox notes, there has been a profound religious resurgence around the globe. Gilles Kepel, in his book *The Revenge of God: The Resurgence of Islam, Christianity, and Judaism in the Modern World* (University Park: Pennsylvania State University Press, 1994), notes that "around 1975 this whole process went into reverse." Indeed, "the theme was no longer *aggiornamento* but a 'second evangelization of Europe': the aim was no longer to modernize Islam [Christianity or Judaism] but to 'Islamize [or Judaize or Christianize] modernity'" (2).

Why the profound transition? I can offer no definitive answer, but I can suggest what I believe is an important factor. All civilizations began in religion – in sacred ritual and story. We have been unable to find a single civilization that does not trace its beginnings to sacred powers and/or sacred ancestors. Every ancient culture had its cycle of sacred, ritually enacted, cosmic stories, which attempted to make sense out of the mystery of human existence. These were stories that portrayed the world as an enchanted place.

Then in Europe in the seventeenth, eighteenth, and nineteenth centuries, science emerged and replaced the mythic stories of the origin and destiny of the world with secular, rationalistic, nonreligious stories. In the nineteenth and twentieth centuries this way of viewing the world spread to virtually all cultures around the globe. At first, it seemed to many people that science was replacing religion. Social scientists and historians argued that religion itself would disappear and we would live in a totally secular world.

A defining characteristic of the modern world, then, is the assumption that we live not in a sacred world but a secular one – a world that serves as the home not of the gods but of human beings. In this world human beings are no longer guided in their public life by their ancient sacred stories but by scientific and technical reason. Religion plays a role, if at all, only in people's private and personal lives.

The twentieth century is a century of paradox. For the first time in history human beings attempted to create secular societies. Then, in the last quarter of this century a radical reversal occurred – everywhere religions seemed to surge up again, intent on reasserting their influence in both politics and private life. In Iran a modern secular state was transformed almost overnight into a state governed by religion through an Islamic revolution. In Israel, a modern secular state's national policies have been held hostage by its Orthodox minority parties. In America, where separation of church and state is "dogma," the religious Right has campaigned for prayer in the schools and a return to a "Christian America," and militant Christian identity movements have looked for the overthrow of the government to accomplish this.

This transformation seems to have coincided with socio-historical and intellectual movements that have come to be identified as postmodern. *Postmodern,* which of course literally means "after the modern," is an ambiguous term used to name an ambiguous time of transition in history. It is a name for a period that does not yet have a name, for we do not yet know where we are going. It expresses the sense that wherever human history is going in the twenty-first century, it is taking us in directions that will be different from the modern period. For our purposes, the key contrast between premodern, modern, and postmodern can be best understood in terms of the changing relationship between religion and public knowledge.

In the premodern world, the sacred cosmic stories of all religions provided, each for its own culture, the most public and certain knowledge human beings believed they had about reality. In the modern period, then, secular science replaced religion as the most public and certain knowledge that human beings believed they had of their world, and religious stories were reduced to the most uncertain form of all knowledge – to matters of personal belief and opinion. The ideal of the modern period was to separate church and state (or religion from society), relegate religion to the private or personal realm, and declare the public realm secular and free of all religious influence.

The postmodern period has its beginnings in the nineteenth century with the emergence of the social sciences, which began to compare societies through time and across cultures. What these sciences revealed was that although human beings in every premodern culture had thought they existed within a sacred natural order, the comparison of cultures revealed tremendous diversity in the understandings of the "natural order" of society. Consequently, it became apparent that these diverse descriptions of nature and natural order were not mirrors of reality but imaginative human creations. This discovery was more shocking than the discovery that the earth was not the center of the universe. Suddenly, all our worldviews were relativized.

What we discovered is that human beings live not in nature but in language and story, in their imaginative views of what nature is. Up until the modern period human beings thought of society as part of the sacred natural order of things. They had no distinct awareness of society apart from nature. Even with the emergence of the natural sciences in the seventeenth and eighteenth centuries, philosophers were still confident that a secular and scientific understanding of the order of nature would provide a blueprint for the right order of society. But when the social sciences finally were invented, for the first time in history human beings came to realize that they lived not in nature but in culture – a product of language and human creativity. This awareness of the *plurality* of worldviews tended to *relativize* and *privatize* every worldview. That is, it made people aware that their respective views of the world could not automatically be assumed to be objective descriptions.

The impact of pluralism, relativism, and privatization unfolded in two stages that led to what we now call the emergence of a postmodern world. When the social sciences began their study of history and society, they proceeded to demythologize the sacred stories that had been embodied in the traditions of all cultures, suggesting that these stories could no longer be believed to be literally true. Thus, their first impact was to undermine the authority of religion and contribute to the secularization of society. All of this was done in the name of the authority of science, the new form of public and certain knowledge.

Then, in a second stage, beginning in the late nineteenth century but achieving its full impact in the last quarter of the twentieth century, the same techniques of sociological and historical criticism that had been applied to religion were finally applied to science itself, including the social sciences, leading to the conclusion that scientific knowledge is also an imaginative interpretation of the world.

It was at this point that the transition to postmodernity occurred. The modern period resulted in a loss of innocence by calling into question traditional sacred knowledge based on faith in the name of a new secular scientific knowledge based on reason. The postmodern world began with a further loss of innocence which occurred when human beings realized that scientific knowledge was also relative in important ways, that it too was an imaginative interpretation of the world based on faith (in the intelligibility of the world), and that it too was subject to continuous revision.

From a postmodern perspective all knowledge is relative, including religious and scientific knowledge. Postmodernism brings with it a radical cultural and ethical relativism. Some rejoice in this, arguing that it means the end of all absolutisms that people have used to justify violence against each other. Others are afraid that such a total relativism means the end of civilization and the beginning of a new barbarism – that once we relativize the distinction between good and evil, we will plunge into a relativistic nihilism in which any atrocity can be justified.

One of the most dramatic consequences of this relativization of knowledge has been religious resurgence. With the relativizing of scientific knowledge in the postmodern period, suddenly religious knowledge no longer sees itself as suffering from its previous disadvantage. Now both science and religion come to be seen as equal, if only because both are equally relative. Therefore the logic of why scientific secularism should be viewed as providing public and certain knowledge while religious knowledge should be viewed as mere private opinion no longer seems valid. Consequently, with the emergence of postmodernism there has been a deprivatizing of religion. This has meant a resurgence of religion in the public realm – a resurgence whose diverse forms are responses to both the threat and the promise of postmodernism.

These responses have taken one of two obvious forms – either liberationist or traditionalist. That is, they either embrace the relativity of human societies as human creations, which can be changed so that human beings will be treated more justly, or they revolt against the relativity of human societies and insist that modern societies must return to the sacred order they abandoned. Both types of response have at least two things in common: they break with the presupposition of the modern world that religion is to be kept personal and private and they insist that religion should transform the modern world by bringing to it a religious vision of life.

The problem is that they bring opposing visions of how the social and political life of society ought to be ordered. One insists that the problems of the modern world are all the result of having abandoned a sacred way of life in favor of relativism and personal choice. The other insists that the problems of the modern world are the result of having tried to impose on society a sacred way of life that was filled with prejudice, injustice, and oppression toward women and people of color, people of certain social classes, people of the third world, and so forth. Walter Capps is right, the sacred/secular debate defines our political "culture wars." As he explains, that is exactly the way the debate about abortion is framed in our society:

> If we have become a secular society, then large segments of the population...cannot feel at home here, for their birthrights [a "Christian America"]...have been sold to alien forces. But if we dare to call ourselves a sacred society...then large segments of the population recognize or fear that their civil rights and personal freedoms have become subject to the same kinds of dogmatic tyranny that are

responsible for the most tragic periods of human history [e.g., the Inquisition].

However, whether we are speaking of traditionalist or liberationist responses to the sacred/secular dilemma, both are intent on shaping public values and public order. Both reject the relativism of the postmodern world in order to bring about social and political order which conforms with their religious vision. In doing so, however, their strategies are radically different: traditionalists want to return to "paradise lost" whereas liberationists are utopian – they want to move forward to create a world that has never been. Both are committed to shaping public policy and argue that a religious vision must guide our actions, but their religious visions are radically opposite. Traditionalists argue that the sacred world and way of life revealed in their sacred scriptures provide a blueprint of how the whole of society ought to be ordered, a way of life we once lived and now must choose again. Liberationists argue that past ways of life and the scriptural interpretations that legitimated them were really human interpretations – legitimate but finite and flawed interpretations of the will of God. They argue that it is not the past worldview that should be held sacred but a certain core vision, which demands that humans engage in the continuous revision of society in order to more closely approximate the will of God in this world.

Strikingly, both traditionalists and liberationists reject the presuppositions of the modern world that religion is to be kept personal and private. And both also reject the dominance of individualism in society. That is, just as traditionalists have gravitated to communitarian patterns from the past, liberationists have gravitated to socialist and/or ecological-communal visions of interdependence for the future.

The resolution of the war between the sacred and the secular seems insoluble, says Walter Capps, because "the conditions of a sacred orientation to reality cannot be established on a percentage basis." Harvey Cox raised the same issue when he argued that our postmodern situation is not only that of deprivatization but also of deregionalization. These alternatives (liberationism and traditionalism) share a common dilemma – one that Cox notes: How can religious visions shape public life and public policy when any given region of the world is "marbleized"? That is, given the pluralism within societies all around the globe, will not either type of religious vision for political order seem oppressive to all others in that order who do not share its vision?

This was the problem that splintered Europe in the wake of the Protestant Reformation. It led to the formation of the secular state as a neutral framework for the flourishing of religious diversity, albeit at the cost of privatization. It is no accident, then, that the deprivatization of religion occurring in our postmodern world is resulting not only in a resurgence of religion but also in religiously motivated violence.

The question, then, is whether there is any alternative to traditionalism and liberationism that would be possible within the traditions of Judaism, Christianity, and Islam. On what basis might Jews, Christians, and Muslims (and indeed other religious communities and secular communities) work together to create a new postmodern political order that rejects the relativism of postmodernity without embracing its opposite, the totalitarian absolutism of a single uniform social and political order?

A fruitful avenue, I believe, lies in recognizing what Harvey Cox, for one, has argued in the past, namely that biblical religion – whether Jewish, Christian, or Muslim – and secularity are not opposites but mutually compatible. That is, if all three affirm, as they do, that God alone is holy, then all else is desacralized or secularized. As the sociologist Max Weber pointed out, biblical religion desacralized the ancient world so that it was no longer experienced as the sacred place of the gods, often said to be made from the very substance of the gods. And yet neither was the world considered profane. On the contrary, if the world belongs to God, who is wholly other than the world, and who alone is holy, then the world is just the world – a good place sanctified by God, a place where human life might flourish.

The French sociologist Jacques Ellul has argued that we ought to reserve the term *holy* for the radical transcendence of God – the God who is wholly other and has no equals and cannot be imaged. For Ellul, the holy is the opposite of *the sacred* – a term which should be reserved to describe the temptation to treat our particular identities, ways of life, and sociopolitical orders as absolute – as if equal in value to God.

The sacred sacralizes our particular social/ethnic/religious identities such that we are tempted to view God as created in our own image, leading us to conclude that anyone who is not "like us" is profane and less than human – both in our eyes and the eyes of God. A politics shaped by the experience of the sacred is a politics which excludes the stranger. By contrast, in the biblical traditions, allegiance to the one who alone is holy leads in just the opposite direction – namely, to hospitality to the stranger.

All three biblical religions share a strong emphasis on the theme of hospitality to the stranger. The Hebrew Bible mentions the command to welcome the stranger more often than any other command. Moreover, the encounter with the stranger is described as an encounter with God (Gen. 32:23-32), and to welcome the stranger is said to be an act of welcoming God (Gen. 18). The New Testament adds that to welcome the

stranger is to welcome the Messiah (Matt. 25:35). And the Qur'an tells us
that if God had intended for humans to be one, God would have made
us that way (Sura 5:48). The stranger is the analog for God precisely
because the stranger reminds us of the otherness and transcendence of
God – whose thoughts are not our thoughts and whose ways are not our
ways (Is. 55:8-9). The correlate of hospitality, then, is that to reject the
stranger is to reject God. Biblical faith requires diversity.

It is my conviction that the modern notion of human dignity and
human rights has deep roots in the experience of the holy and the
Abrahamic ethic of hospitality. The tradition of hospitality runs directly
counter to the ethnocentric politics of the sacred – the politics of
exclusion. To welcome the stranger who does not share one's religious
and cultural identity is to recognize that human dignity transcends all
religious and cultural identity. Human dignity is what we all have in
common as human beings regardless of race, gender, religion, or
ethnicity.

To welcome the stranger is to acknowledge the humanity of
precisely the one who is not like me and does not share my identity. To
welcome the stranger as if he or she were God is to recognize the dignity
and equality of all human beings. This is clearly possible for the children
of Abraham – Jews, Christians, and Muslims – because all three
traditions insist that humans are created in the image of a God who is
without image. Therefore, none of us can look more like God than any
others of us – we (and all others) are equally children of the God of
Abraham.

In all three traditions it is this consciousness of the oneness and
imageless transcendence of God that leads to the need for the formation
of holy communities that are distinctly separate from the sacred order of
societies that would treat some as less human than others. The holy
community (synagogue, church, and ummah) is the fence we construct
to protect human dignity – beginning with the dignity of the stranger –
from all violation and degradation. Unlike a sacred society, a holy
community has its center outside itself, in the stranger. Thus the holy
community must be that political presence in society which exists to
extend hospitality to the stranger and protect the dignity of the stranger.
Or to put it another way, while the sacred sacralizes the identity of some
at the expense of others in order to create uniformity, a holy community
secularizes and pluralizes, creating unity in diversity.

Such an Abrahamic ethic of hospitality would allow ethics itself to
embody this unity in diversity. Respect for the dignity of others may
require expression through different customs in different cultures and
even in different subcultures. Indeed, this diversity might itself lead not
only to mutual constructive criticism but also to mutual enrichment

without requiring uniformity, so long as we are all oriented to the "north star" of the imagelessness of God in whose image we are created.

An Abrahamic ethic of hospitality to strangers, if it becomes the deepest commitment of Muslims, Christians, and Jews, ought to lead to the third possibility – beyond either the sacred or secular forms of society – that I heard Walter Capps asking for. A political ethic shaped by the experience of the holy would look for ways to find unity in diversity. For if God enters our lives through the stranger, then, to turn our backs on the stranger by demanding a uniform society (whether sacred or secular) is to turn our backs on the God who alone is holy. To do that is to raise one's own religious, cultural, and political identity above that of God – making an idol of one's own image.

But the one who alone is holy cannot be imaged and is no idol. In all three traditions it is this consciousness of the oneness and imageless transcendence of God that leads to the need for communities that are distinctly separate from the sacred order of all societies that would treat some as less human than others. A world where strangers are not welcome is a world without God, whether or not that name is called upon. Two examples should make this clear: (1) the Inquisition and (2) the death camps of the Nazis. The holy community (synagogue, church and ummah) is the fence we construct to protect human dignity – beginning with the dignity of the stranger – from all violation and degradation.

A holy community exists to extend hospitality to God and the stranger – knowing full well that a world without strangers is a world without God. Therein lies a religious vision for a postmodern world – a normative vision that not only accepts but requires what Harvey Cox calls a "marbleized world" of diversity.

Index

South Florida Studies in the History of Judaism

240001	Lectures on Judaism in the Academy and in the Humanities	Neusner
240002	Lectures on Judaism in the History of Religion	Neusner
240003	Self-Fulfilling Prophecy: Exile and Return in the History of Judaism	Neusner
240004	The Canonical History of Ideas: The Place of the So-called Tannaite Midrashim, Mekhilta Attributed to R. Ishmael, Sifra, Sifré to Numbers, and Sifré to Deuteronomy	Neusner
240005	Ancient Judaism: Debates and Disputes, Second Series	Neusner
240006	The Hasmoneans and Their Supporters: From Mattathias to the Death of John Hyrcanus I	Sievers
240007	Approaches to Ancient Judaism: New Series, Volume One	Neusner
240008	Judaism in the Matrix of Christianity	Neusner
240009	Tradition as Selectivity: Scripture, Mishnah, Tosefta, and Midrash in the Talmud of Babylonia	Neusner
240010	The Tosefta: Translated from the Hebrew: Sixth Division Tohorot	Neusner
240011	In the Margins of the Midrash: Sifre Ha'azinu Texts, Commentaries and Reflections	Basser
240012	Language as Taxonomy: The Rules for Using Hebrew and Aramaic in the Babylonia Talmud	Neusner
240013	The Rules of Composition of the Talmud of Babylonia: The Cogency of the Bavli's Composite	Neusner
240014	Understanding the Rabbinic Mind: Essays on the Hermeneutic of Max Kadushin	Ochs
240015	Essays in Jewish Historiography	Rapoport-Albert
240016	The Golden Calf and the Origins of the Jewish Controversy	Bori/Ward
240017	Approaches to Ancient Judaism: New Series, Volume Two	Neusner
240018	The Bavli That Might Have Been: The Tosefta's Theory of Mishnah Commentary Compared With the Bavli's	Neusner
240019	The Formation of Judaism: In Retrospect and Prospect	Neusner
240020	Judaism in Society: The Evidence of the Yerushalmi,Toward the Natural History of a Religion	Neusner
240021	The Enchantments of Judaism: Rites of Transformation from Birth Through Death	Neusner
240022	Åbo Addresses	Neusner
240023	The City of God in Judaism and Other Comparative and Methodological Studies	Neusner
240024	The Bavli's One Voice: Types and Forms of Analytical Discourse and their Fixed Order of Appearance	Neusner
240025	The Dura-Europos Synagogue: A Re-evaluation (1932-1992)	Gutmann
240026	Precedent and Judicial Discretion: The Case of Joseph ibn Lev	Morell
240027	Max Weinreich Geschichte der jiddischen Sprachforschung	Frakes
240028	Israel: Its Life and Culture, Volume I	Pedersen
240029	Israel: Its Life and Culture, Volume II	Pedersen
240030	The Bavli's One Statement: The Metapropositional Program of Babylonian Talmud Tractate Zebahim Chapters One and Five	Neusner

South Florida Academic Commentary Series

243036	The Talmud of Babylonia, An Academic Commentary, Volume XIX, Bavli Tractate Qiddushin	Neusner
243037	The Talmud of Babylonia, A Complete Outline, Part IV, The Division of Holy Things; B: From Tractate Berakot through Tractate Niddah	Neusner
243038	The Talmud of Babylonia, A Complete Outline, Part III, The Division of Damages; B: From Tractate Sanhedrin through Tractate Shebuot	Neusner
243039	The Talmud of Babylonia, A Complete Outline, Part I, Tractate Berakhot and the Division of Appointed Times A: From Tractate Berakhot through Tractate Pesahim	Neusner
243040	The Talmud of Babylonia, A Complete Outline, Part I, Tractate Berakhot and the Division of Appointed Times B: From Tractate Yoma through Tractate Hagigah	Neusner
243041	The Talmud of Babylonia, A Complete Outline, Part II, The Division of Women; A: From Tractate Yebamot through Tractate Ketubot	Neusner
243042	The Talmud of Babylonia, A Complete Outline, Part II, The Division of Women; B: From Tractate Nedarim through Tractate Qiddushin	Neusner
243043	The Talmud of Babylonia, An Academic Commentary, Volume XIII, Bavli Tractate Yebamot, A. Chapters One through Eight	Neusner
243044	The Talmud of Babylonia, An Academic Commentary, XIII, Bavli Tractate Yebamot, B. Chapters Nine through Seventeen	Neusner
243045	The Talmud of the Land of Israel, A Complete Outline of the Second, Third and Fourth Divisions, Part II, The Division of Women, A. Yebamot to Nedarim	Neusner
243046	The Talmud of the Land of Israel, A Complete Outline of the Second, Third and Fourth Divisions, Part II, The Division of Women, B. Nazir to Sotah	Neusner
243047	The Talmud of the Land of Israel, A Complete Outline of the Second, Third and Fourth Divisions, Part I, The Division of Appointed Times, C. Pesahim and Sukkah	Neusner
243048	The Talmud of the Land of Israel, A Complete Outline of the Second, Third and Fourth Divisions, Part I, The Division of Appointed Times, A. Berakhot, Shabbat	Neusner
243049	The Talmud of the Land of Israel, A Complete Outline of the Second, Third and Fourth Divisions, Part I, The Division of Appointed Times, B. Erubin, Yoma and Besah	Neusner
243050	The Talmud of the Land of Israel, A Complete Outline of the Second, Third and Fourth Divisions, Part I, The Division of Appointed Times, D. Taanit, Megillah, Rosh Hashannah, Hagigah and Moed Qatan	Neusner
243051	The Talmud of the Land of Israel, A Complete Outline of the Second, Third and Fourth Divisions, Part III, The Division of Damages, A. Baba Qamma, Baba Mesia, Baba Batra, Horayot and Niddah	Neusner

243068	The Talmud of Babylonia, An Academic Commentary, Volume XXIII, Bavli Tractate Sanhedrin, B. Chapters VIII through XII	Neusner
243069	The Talmud of Babylonia, An Academic Commentary, Volume XIV, Bavli Tractate Ketubot, B. ChaptersVII through XIV	Neusner
243070	The Talmud of Babylonia, An Academic Commentary, Volume IV, Bavli Tractate Pesahim, B. Chapters VIII through XI	Neusner
243071	The Talmud of Babylonia, An Academic Commentary, Volume XXIX, Bavli Tractate Menahot, B. Chapters VII through XIV	Neusner
243072	The Talmud of Babylonia, An Academic Commentary, Volume XXVIII, Bavli Tractate Zebahim B. Chapters VIII through XV	Neusner
243073	The Talmud of Babylonia, An Academic Commentary, Volume XXI, Bavli Tractate Baba Mesia, B. Chapters VIII through XI	Neusner
243074	The Talmud of Babylonia, An Academic Commentary, Volume III, Bavli Tractate Erubin, A. ChaptersVI through XI	Neusner

South Florida-Rochester-Saint Louis Studies on Religion and the Social Order

245001	Faith and Context, Volume 1	Ong
245002	Faith and Context, Volume 2	Ong
245003	Judaism and Civil Religion	Breslauer
245004	The Sociology of Andrew M. Greeley	Greeley
245005	Faith and Context, Volume 3	Ong
245006	The Christ of Michelangelo	Dixon
245007	From Hermeneutics to Ethical Consensus Among Cultures	Bori
245008	Mordecai Kaplan's Thought in a Postmodern Age	Breslauer
245009	No Longer Aliens, No Longer Strangers	Eckardt
245010	Between Tradition and Culture	Ellenson
245011	Religion and the Social Order	Neusner
245012	Christianity and the Stranger	Nichols
245013	The Polish Challenge	Czosnyka
245014	Islam and the Question of Minorities	Sonn
245015	Religion and the Political Order	Neusner

South Florida International Studies in Formative Christianity and Judaism